1 VOCABULARY
Introductions and personal information

1 **1.1** **Read and listen. Dora is at a language school. She's introducing herself to the class.**

Hello. My name's Dora Ivir. I'm 35 years old and I'm from Croatia. I live in the city of Dubrovnik in the south of Croatia. I'm an accountant and I work for a company that makes office furniture. I'm married. My husband, Rudolf, works in a hospital as a radiologist. We've got two children – a son and a daughter. In my free time I play tennis, I do yoga, and I go sailing with my family. I like listening to classical music, too, and I like watching soap operas on TV.

Language note	Location
in the south of Croatia	in the north-west of Spain

2a **Answer the questions about Dora.**

1 What's her full name?
2 How old is she?
3 Where does she live?
4 What does she do?
5 Is she married?
6 What does her husband do?
7 Have they got any children?
8 What does she do in her free time?

b **Work with a partner. Ask and answer about Dora.**

A *What's her full name?*
B *It's Dora Ivir.*

3 **Copy the table and add three more items to each category.**

Countries	*Croatia, ...*
Jobs	*an accountant, a radiologist, ...*
Marital status	*married, ...*
Relationships	*husband, son, daughter, ...*
Activities	play *tennis, ...* do *yoga, ...* go *sailing, ...* listen to *classical music, ...* watch *soap operas, ...* read *...*

4 **Interview a partner. Use the questions in exercise 2 to help you.**

A *What's your full name?*
B *It's ...*

5a **1.2** **Listen. Roberto is introducing himself to the group. Who is Fernanda?**

b **Listen again. Complete the form.**

Name	Roberto _____
Country	_____
City	Recife
Age	_____
Job	_____
Employer	an insurance company
Marital status	_____
Children	_____
Interests	goes _____ , plays _____ , does _____ , likes _____ , _____ , _____ .

c **Tell a partner about Roberto. Use the information on the form.**

6 **Writing** **Write your own introduction. Use Dora's text as a model.**

English in the world
Greetings

In English-speaking countries people generally shake hands when they first meet.

When people know each other, but haven't seen each other for a while:

Men shake hands with other men.
shake hands with a woman or kiss her on the cheek.
Women normally kiss other women.
shake hands with a man or kiss him on the cheek.

People don't usually shake hands with or kiss people that they meet every day.

How do you normally greet people in your country?

✓ Now I can ...
give some basic information about my life.

English for Life

Intermediate

Student's Book

Tom Hutch

OXFORD

UNIVERSITY PRESS

Contents

1 | 2.1 | **Read and listen.**

My name's Alan. I **work** in an office, but I**'m not sitting** at my desk this week. I**'m doing** a Leadership Course for new managers. At the moment we**'re building** a bridge, because we need to cross a river. We're all working hard, but I think it's great. I certainly prefer this to the office. I'm really enjoying it.

*It's nine o'clock in the evening and Alan **doesn't feel** very happy now. He usually **watches** TV in the evening, but he **isn't watching** TV today. He's **putting up** a tent.*

I **don't like** this. It's raining and I feel cold, wet, and hungry. Perhaps I don't want to be a manager after all.

2 **Read the examples. Study the rules on page 103.**

Present simple and present continuous

1 We use the present simple for:

permanent or general states
I **work** in an office.

regular activities
He usually **watches** TV in the evening.

2 We use the present continuous for:

temporary states
I**'m not sitting** at my desk this week.

what is happening now
At the moment we**'re building** a bridge.

3 | 2.2 | **Drill. Listen. Say what Alan isn't doing this week.**

1 He works in an office.
He isn't working in an office this week.

4 **Make sentences. Put the verbs into the correct tense.**

1 He usually works indoors. This week he's …

1 He/usually/work/indoors. This week/ he/work/outdoors.
2 At the moment/I/cook/a meal. I/normally/not cook/anything.
3 He/usually/not walk/a lot. He/walk/ 10 kilometres today.
4 It's 5 a.m./Alan/get up/now. He/ normally/get up/at 7.30.
5 I/usually/wear/a suit. This week/I/ wear/jeans.

Language note
Describing states (stative verbs)

Some verbs describe states, not actions. We don't normally use these verbs in the present continuous, even when we are talking about the present moment:

need, want, think, believe, know, like, prefer, love.

I **don't want** to be a manager.
NOT ~~I'm not wanting …~~

5a **Put the verbs into the correct tense.**

1 **A** I *I'm going* (go) to the shop now. We *need* (need) some bread.
   B Oh, I _____ (think) the shop _____ (close) at four on Sundays.
2 **A** The Director _____ (want) to talk to Katrin, but I _____ (not know) where she is.
   B I _____ (believe) she _____ (have) lunch at the moment. She usually _____ (go) for lunch at 1.30.
3 **A** I _____ (make) a cup of coffee now. _____ (you/want) one?
   B No, thanks, I _____ (not like) coffee. I _____ (prefer) tea.

b | 2.3 | **Listen and check.**

6a | **Your life** | **Make sentences about your life. Use the cues.**

1 usually   4 at the moment
2 want   5 wear/today
3 (not) like ...ing   6 not/this week

b **Talk to a partner. What things have you got in common?**

 Now I can …
talk about regular and temporary activities.

3 SKILLS
Listen and speak

1   **3.1**   **Look at the pictures. Listen. Answer the questions.**

1   Who are the two people? Tick ✓ the names.
   __ Billy   __ Nicola   __ Charlie   __ Sandy

2   Why is the woman phoning?

3   What is the man doing on his computer at the moment?

2   **Listen again. Complete the survey.**

How do people use their computers?

Name: [   ]   Occupation: [   ]

1 Are you using a computer at the moment?   yes ☐   no ☐

2 If yes, what kind of computer are you using?   a desktop ☐   a laptop ☐

3 Do you use a computer for … ?   work ☐   study ☐   leisure ☐

4 How often do you … ?	often	sometimes	never
send emails	☐	☐	☐
visit chatrooms	☐	☐	☐
shop online	☐	☐	☐
book tickets on the Internet	☐	☐	☐
download music, TV programmes, etc.	☐	☐	☐
edit and print photographs	☐	☐	☐
play computer games	☐	☐	☐

3a   **Answer the questions.**

1   Who is the woman doing the survey for?

2   What is the man studying?

3   What things does he buy on the Internet? Why?

4   Why doesn't he book flights online?

5   Is he using the Internet at the moment?

6   What does he do with his photographs? Why?

7   What does he say about playing computer games?

b   **Listen again and check.**

Language note   **Question forms: present simple and present continuous**

Present simple
Do you **buy** things online?
How **does** he **use** his computer?

Present continuous
Are you **using** the Internet now?
What **are** you **doing** at the moment?

4a   **Speaking**   **Work with a partner. Ask and answer about the man.**

A   *Does he use his computer for work, study or leisure?*

B   *He uses it for …*

A   *What kind of computer is he using at the moment?*

B   *He's using …*

A   *Does he always use … ?*

b   **Interview a partner. Use the questions in the survey.**

5   **Your life**   **Answer the questions in the survey. Write sentences about you (or a member of your family).**

I'm (not) using … at the moment.
I normally use …
I use a computer for … and …
I (don't) often …

Pronunciation
The phonemic alphabet

1   **Circle the correct word to match the phonemic transcription. Use the phonemic alphabet on page 124.**

1 /wɜːk/	walk	(work)
2 /juː/	you	your
3 /nəʊ/	know	now
4 /hɑːd/	head	hard
5 /θɪŋk/	think	thank
6 /ðiːz/	this	these
7 /lʊk/	look	like
8 /wɒtʃ/	watch	wash

2   **3.2**   **Listen, check, and repeat.**

Now I can …
talk about how people use computers.

1 ▢ 4.1 **Read and listen.**

Hi. My name's Cindy Gaskell. My husband Ryan and I own this Internet café – The Coffee Shop. I'm British, but Ryan's Irish. We've got two children – Melanie and Russell. Melanie's a student at Manchester University and Russell works in Spain for a holiday company. That's Ryan over there – the man with the beard. He's talking to Jordan Morris. Jordan's Australian and he's a computer engineer. He fixes our computers, but he isn't doing that now. He's waiting for his girlfriend, Lucy Patterson. Actually, Jordan really wants to be an actor. He was in a TV advert last year.

Here's Lucy now with Sarah Chen and Peter Columbo. Lucy's the woman wearing a skirt. She's British and she works for an advertising agency. She's a personal assistant, but she doesn't like her boss, Olive Green. Sarah's a postgraduate student at London University. She's from Singapore. Peter's from the USA. He works for a magazine company. Peter and Sarah are getting married soon.

2a **What are the relationships between the people?**

1 Cindy and Ryan   3 Lucy and Jordan
2 Peter and Sarah   4 Russell and Melanie

b **Work with a partner. Ask and answer about each person. Use these questions.**

What is his/her full name?
Where is he/she from?
What does he/she do?
What else do you know about him/her?

3 ▢ 4.2 **Read and listen to the story. Answer the questions.**

1 What are Lucy and Jordan planning to do?
2 Why didn't they do it last weekend?
3 Why does Jordan look worried?
4 What do you think he should do? Why?

1 *Thursday morning ...*

Ryan Hi, Lucy. How are you?
Lucy Oh, hi, Ryan. I'm OK, but I'm glad it's nearly Friday.
Ryan Are you doing anything at the weekend?
Lucy Yes. Jordan and I are visiting my parents. They moved down to the south coast a couple of months ago. They've got a lovely house by the sea.
Ryan That sounds nice.
Lucy We wanted to go last Saturday, but Jordan was on emergency call, so we're definitely doing it this weekend.

2 *Thursday afternoon ...*

Jordan Morris? Look, we're filming an advert this weekend and one of the actors is ill. Are you available?

4 **Complete the sentences. What tense is used?**

Everyday expressions
Talking about future arrangements

Are you doing _____ at the weekend?
We _____ visiting my parents.

5a **What are you doing at these times?**

1 this evening   3 at the weekend
2 on Friday   4 next week

b **Ask and answer with a partner.**

1 What are you doing this evening?

6 **Work in a group. Practise the story in exercise 3.**

Now I can ...
talk about future arrangements.

5 VOCABULARY
Expressions with *get*

1 **5.1** **Listen and repeat.**

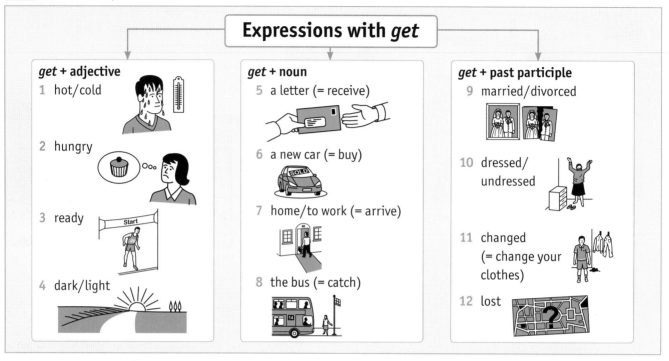

Expressions with *get*

get + adjective
1 hot/cold
2 hungry
3 ready
4 dark/light

get + noun
5 a letter (= receive)
6 a new car (= buy)
7 home/to work (= arrive)
8 the bus (= catch)

get + past participle
9 married/divorced
10 dressed/undressed
11 changed (= change your clothes)
12 lost

2 **5.2** **Drill. Listen. Make the sentences.**

1 I/hungry   *I'm getting hungry.*

> **Language note** *get* + comparative
>
> **We often use *get* with the comparative of an adjective to talk about a changing state:**
> – get better/worse
> – get bigger/smaller
> – get louder/quieter
> – get closer/ further away

3 **Choose an expression with *get* to complete the sentences. Use *getting* + ... or *got* + ...**

1 Can we put the air conditioning on? It's <u>getting hot</u> in here.
2 I went to a wedding on Saturday. My brother _____ .
3 Salim was ill last week, but he's _____ slowly.
4 We went for a walk at the weekend. We didn't have a map and we _____ .
5 Can you put the light on, please? It's _____ .
6 I'm sorry. I can't talk now. I'm _____ to go out.
7 Is lunch ready yet? I'm _____ .
8 Those dark clouds are _____ . I think it's going to rain soon.
9 I missed the bus yesterday, so I _____ late.
10 We didn't come by car. We _____ .

4a **Complete what Berta says about her day. Use these words.**

> home   a cake   light   ready   coffee   emails
> ~~dressed~~   changed   dark   work   hungry   train

I usually get up at 6.15. I have a shower and I get ¹<u>dressed</u> . I don't have breakfast, but I get a cup of ² _____ at the station. I normally get the 7.30 ³ _____ , and I get to ⁴ _____ at 8.45. I always check my emails first. I don't get a lot of ⁵ _____ , fortunately. By 10.30 I start to get ⁶ _____ , so I usually get ⁷ _____ or something from the cafeteria. At ten to five I get ⁸ _____ to leave work, but I get ⁹ _____ quite late, at about 7 p.m. Then I usually get ¹⁰ _____ into my jeans. It's a long day. It's OK, but I don't like it in the winter, because it only gets ¹¹ _____ at about 8 a.m. and then it gets ¹² _____ again before I leave work.

b **5.3** **Listen and check.**

5a **Your life** **Answer the questions.**

1 Did you get the bus this morning?
2 What's a good age to get married?
3 What times of day do you normally get hungry?
4 Do you think the world is getting better or worse?
5 Do you usually get changed after work/school?
6 How many emails do you get in a week?

b **Compare your answers with a partner.**

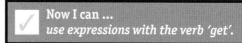
✓ Now I can ...
use expressions with the verb 'get'.

1 `6.1` **Read and listen.**

Cindy You look tired.

Peter Yes, well, I **saw** an advert on Friday for a jazz concert. I really **wanted** to see it.

Cindy Oh, yes? When **was** it?

Peter It **was** on Saturday afternoon. I **tried** to get a ticket on the Internet, but there **weren't** any left.

Cindy Oh, dear. So, what **did** you **do**?

Peter Well, Sarah and I **were** at a party on Friday night. I **didn't go** home after that. I **went** straight to the theatre. I **queued** for six hours.

Cindy Wow! **Did** you **get** a ticket?

Peter Yes, I **did**. I **got** the last one.

Cindy That **was** lucky. **Was** the concert good?

Peter I don't know. I **didn't see** it. I **was** so tired that I **fell** asleep and I **missed** it!

2 **Read the examples. Study the rules on page 104.**

Past simple: *to be*	
I **was/wasn't** tired.	
We **were/weren't** at a party.	
Was the concert good?	Yes, it **was**./No, it **wasn't**.
When **were** they in Paris?	
Past simple: regular and irregular verbs	
regular	He **missed/didn't miss** the concert.
irregular	I **saw/didn't see** the film.
Did you **get** a ticket?	Yes, I **did**./No, I **didn't**.
What **did** he **do**?	

3 `6.2` **Drill. Listen. Say the negative.**

1 We were late.
   We weren't late.
2 I got a ticket.
   I didn't get a ticket.

4a `6.3` **Listen. Where were the people last night? Match the names with the places.**

1 Axel _c_   a at home
2 Corrie and Max __ b at the college
3 Shilpa __   c at the theatre
4 Jack and Davina __ d at a hotel
5 George __   e at the sports centre
6 Leah and Phil __   f at a friend's house

b **Listen again. What did the people do?**

1 Axel saw a play.

c **Write about the people.**

1 Axel was at the theatre. He saw a play.

5 **Work with a partner. Ask and answer about the people in exercise 4.**

A *Was Axel at home last night?*
B *No, he wasn't. He was at the theatre.*
A *Did he see a play?*
B *Yes, he did.*

6a **Your life** **Where did you go and what did you do this week? Talk about these times.**

1 last night
2 on Saturday evening
3 on Sunday afternoon
4 on Wednesday morning

b **Ask and answer with a partner.**

Pronunciation

was/wasn't, were/weren't

1 `6.4` **Listen. Which word do you hear? Write the sentence number.**

was	wasn't	were	weren't
__ , __	__ , __	__ , __	_1_ , __

2 **Listen again and repeat. Are the positive or the negative forms stressed?**

Now I can ...
talk about events in the past.

1 **7.1** **Read and listen. Answer the questions.**
   1 Who are the people in the story?
   2 What did the girl do?
   3 How did the man react … ?
      – in the *A bad start* version of the story
      – in the *Did it have to be a bad start?* version

The 90/10 secret

Did you have a good day yesterday, or was it another day when something went wrong? If you have one bad day after another, you need to learn *the 90/10 secret*.

A bad start

At breakfast yesterday Jack's daughter, Emily, knocked over a glass of milk, and it fell on his trousers. Jack got annoyed. He shouted at his daughter and she started to cry.

'Why did you shout at her?' said his wife. 'Why did you put the glass on the edge of the table?' replied Jack angrily, as he went upstairs to get changed.

Because she was upset, his daughter didn't get ready for school in time and she missed her bus. 'I have to go to work,' said his wife, and she left. Jack had to take Emily to school. As he was in a hurry, he forgot his briefcase. He was forty minutes late for work – and as soon as he got there, he had to go home again to get his briefcase. It was a bad start to the day, and it didn't get any better.

Why did Jack have a bad day? Did the milk, his daughter, or his wife cause it? Let's look at another version of the story.

Did it have to be a bad start?

Again the milk fell on Jack's trousers, but this time he didn't shout. He smiled and said, 'It's OK. Accidents happen. Don't worry.' He went upstairs and got changed. When he came down, Emily said, 'Bye, Daddy,' kissed him and ran out to catch her bus. Jack didn't have to take her to school. He picked up his briefcase, kissed his wife, and they both left for work. He got to work early, and he had a great day.

So, here's *the 90/10 secret.*

Ten per cent of life is what happens to you. You can't control it. The traffic's bad; you lose something; somebody spills coffee on you. That's life. Things happen and you have to deal with them.

Ninety per cent of life, however, is how you react. Jack's bad day started because he reacted badly. Remember that, the next time that something bad happens to you!

2 **Put these events in the correct order for the *bad start* version of the story.**

a _____ Emily missed the bus.
b _____ Jack went home for his briefcase.
c _____ Jack took Emily to school.
d _____ His wife went to work.
e _____ Jack argued with his wife.
f _____ Jack got to work late.
g _1_ Emily spilt her milk.
h _____ Jack got changed.
i _____ Emily cried.
j _____ Jack shouted at Emily.

3a **Read the paragraph which asks *Did it have to be a bad start?* What was different?**

Jack didn't shout at Emily. He smiled and said, 'It's OK.'

b **What is *the 90/10 secret?* Do you think it's useful?**

> **Language note** *have to*
>
> I **have to** go to work.
> = It's necessary.
> He **had to** go home again.
> = It was necessary.
> He **didn't have to** take Emily to school.
> = It wasn't necessary.
> **Did** it **have to** be a bad start?
> = Was it necessary?

4a **Your life** **Tell a partner about an event in your life when you reacted badly.**
What happened?
How did you react?
What were the consequences?

b **Write a new version of your story where you followed *the 90/10 secret.***

> ## English in the world
> ### The weekend
>
> In most countries the weekend is Saturday and Sunday. However, in some countries in the Middle East it is Thursday and Friday (e.g. Saudi Arabia) or Friday and Saturday (e.g. Egypt).
>
> Here are some features of a typical British weekend:
> – Children don't have to go to school on Saturday or Sunday.
> – Saturday is a popular day for shopping. Saturday afternoon is the traditional time for weddings and for football matches.
> – Saturday night is the most popular time to go out to eat, drink, or dance.
> – About 6–7% of people go to church on Sundays. Sunday lunchtime is a traditional time for a family meal.
>
> **What are typical weekend activities in your country?**

> ✓ **Now I can …**
> *compare versions of events.*

1a   `8.1`   **Read and listen. Whose are these things?**

– the mobile phone   – the car

1

Pearl   Whose mobile is this? Is it yours, Gary?

Gary   No, it isn't mine. Maybe it's Aisha's.

Pearl   No, it can't be. Hers is green.

Gary   Wasn't Mick here earlier today?

Pearl   Oh, yes, he was. It must be his, then.

2

Man   Who does that big car belong to?

Woman   I think it belongs to our new neighbours.

Man   It's very big – a lot bigger than ours.

Woman   Yes, but our flat's bigger than theirs.

b   **Practise the conversations with a partner.**

Language note **Possessive pronouns**						
Possessive adjective	my	your	his	her	its	our	their
Possessive pronoun	mine	yours	his	hers	its	ours	theirs

This is my mobile. It's mine. NOT ~~It's the mine.~~

2a   **Complete the expressions.**

Everyday expressions
Possessions

_____ mobile is this?

It's Aisha_____ .

Who _____ this belong to?   (singular)

It belongs _____ me./

It doesn't belong _____ me.

Who do these _____ to?   (plural)

_____ belong to her./

_____ don't belong to her.

b   `8.2`   **Listen, check, and repeat.**

3   `8.3`   **Drill. Listen. Say whose the things are.**

1   This is their car.   2   These are my keys.
   It's theirs.   *They're mine.*

4a   `8.4`   **Listen. Match the things with the names.**

Frank ___   Avril ___   Eduardo ___
Deena ___   Gus ___   Cecilia ___   Eric ___

1   2

3   4

5

b   **Work with a partner. Ask and answer about the things.**

A   *Who do the keys belong to?*

OR

A   *Whose keys are they?*

B   *They belong to …*

5   **Speaking**   **Work in a group. Put some objects on a desk. Ask and answer about the things.**

Whose mobile is this?

Who do these pens belong to?

Ella, is this book yours?

   Now I can …
talk about possessions.

1a 9.1 **Listen and repeat.**

Describing a flat   It's ...

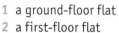
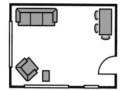
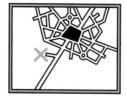

1 a ground-floor flat
2 a first-floor flat

3 spacious

4 convenient for the town centre

5 in a quiet location

6 furnished
7 unfurnished

Facilities   It's got ...

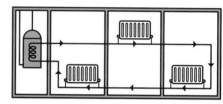

8 a fitted kitchen

9 air conditioning

10 central heating

Getting a flat

11 The landlord lets his flat to a tenant.
12 The tenant rents the flat from him.
13 She pays rent to the landlord.

14 She shares the flat with two flatmates.

15 The accommodation agency finds new tenants for the landlord.

b What other words do you know related to accommodation?

2a Maria is talking about her flat. Complete what she says with these words.

> the rent   central heating   location   a fitted kitchen
> spacious   landlord   ~~first-floor~~   share   rent
> furnished   convenient for   air conditioning   flatmates

I live in a ¹*first-floor* flat. I live with two ²_____ . We don't own the flat. We ³_____ it. Our ⁴_____ lives in the flat above us. The flat's ⁵_____ , so the furniture isn't ours. It's in an old house, but it's got ⁶_____ , and it's very warm. Unfortunately, it hasn't got ⁷_____ , so it can get too hot in the summer. We've got ⁸_____ , with plenty of cupboards, and a new oven and fridge. We've all got our own bedrooms, but we ⁹_____ the other rooms. We share ¹⁰_____ , too, of course. The bedrooms are small, but the living room is quite ¹¹_____ . The flat isn't very ¹²_____ the shops, but it's in a nice ¹³_____ and it isn't noisy.

b 9.2 **Listen and check.**

3a Your life **Work with a partner. Use the words and expressions in exercise 1. Ask each other about the places where you live.**

Do you live in a flat?
How many rooms has it got?
Is it spacious/furnished/convenient for ... ?
Has it got ... ?

b Describe the place where you live. Use the text in exercise 2 as a model.

> **Pronunciation**
> Syllables
> ....
>
> 1 How many syllables are there: 2 or 3?
>
> tenant *2*   location *3*   area __
> furniture __   flatmate __   furnished __
> fitted __   property __   spacious __
>
> 2 9.3 **Listen, check, and repeat.**

> ✓ Now I can ...
> *talk about accommodation.*

1 [10.1] **Read and listen.**

Saturday night ...

Cindy and Ryan are going to ªa party. ᵇThe party's in ᶜa flat on ᵈthe fifth floor of ᵉa block of flats. It's in ᶠan area that they don't know, so it took a long time to find it. Unfortunately, ᵍthe lift is out of order, so now they're walking up ʰthe stairs. Cindy likes parties, but she isn't happy, because she's wearing new shoes. She bought them in ⁱa shop near their café. They were ʲthe most expensive shoes in ᵏthe shop, but they aren't very comfortable.

They're outside ˡthe flat now, but ᵐthe party isn't today. Ryan got ⁿthe date wrong – it's next Saturday. Cindy isn't wearing ᵒthe shoes now, because she's throwing them at Ryan!

2a Read the examples. Study the rules on page 105.

Articles
1 A singular noun normally has an indefinite article (*a/an*) or a definite article (*the*). The party's in a flat.　　NOT ~~Party's in flat.~~
2 The indefinite article: *a/an* **We use the indefinite article for something that is not specific.** They're going to a party. It's in an area that they don't know.
3 The definite article: *the* **We use the definite article for something specific:** **i　when we have mentioned a thing before.** 　　They're going to a party.　The party's in someone's flat. **ii　when there is probably only one.** 　　The lift is out of order. **iii　with ordinal numbers and superlatives.** 　　on the fifth floor　　　the most expensive shoes

b Look at the examples of *a/an* and *the* in the story. Match the uses to the rules above.

3 [10.2] **Drill. Listen. Say when the people bought the things. Use *last week*.**

1　He's wearing a new suit.
　　He bought the suit last week.

4a Choose the correct article, *a* or *the*.

1　**A** Is there *a/the* toilet near here?
　　B Yes, it's on *a/the* second floor next to *an/the* escalator.
2　**A** Would you like to go for *a/the* meal on Thursday?
　　B OK. We can try *a/the* new restaurant that's near *a/the* park.
　　A Yes, that's *an/the* idea. I think that's *a/the* best restaurant in *an/the* area now.
3　**A** That's *a/the* nice shirt and tie.
　　B Thanks. I bought *a/the* shirt at *a/the* shop in *a/the* town centre, but my wife bought *a/the* tie at *a/the* market in Italy.
4　**A** I went to *a/the* play last night. I went with *a/the* friend from work. And we went for *a/the* meal afterwards.
　　B Was *a/the* play good?
　　A Not really. *A/The* main actor wasn't very good, but *a/the* meal afterwards was great.

b [10.3] **Listen and check.**

5 Complete the text with *a/an* or *the*.

Jordan delivered ¹__*a*__ computer to ²_____ office in ³_____ city centre last week. There wasn't ⁴_____ car park there, so he parked his van in the street. ⁵_____ office was on ⁶_____ tenth floor. When Jordan got to ⁷_____ office, he rang ⁸_____ doorbell and ⁹_____ woman opened ¹⁰_____ door. Jordan was very surprised, because ¹¹_____ woman was ¹²_____ old school friend from Australia. She offered him ¹³_____ cup of coffee and they had ¹⁴_____ chat about old times. Then Jordan suddenly remembered ¹⁵_____ van. When he left, he didn't take ¹⁶_____ lift. He ran down ¹⁷_____ stairs, but it was too late. He had ¹⁸_____ parking ticket!

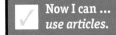 **Now I can ...**
use articles.

1 [11.1] **Listen. George and Ellie are looking at a flat. Do they decide to take the flat? Why? Why not?**

2 **Listen again. What rooms does the flat have?**

3a **Choose the correct descriptions.**
1 There's a good view from the *bedroom/living room*.
2 It's a *first-/third-* floor flat.
3 It's in a *noisy/quiet* location.
4 It's convenient for the *shops/station*.
5 It's in *poor/excellent* condition.
6 It's *furnished/unfurnished*.
7 The *bathroom/kitchen* is dark.
8 The rooms are *small/spacious*.
9 It's *got/hasn't got* central heating.
10 It's in *an expensive/a cheap* area.

b **Listen again and check.**

> **Language note** Accommodation adverts
>
> To Let/Available for rent
> The accommodation consists of three bedrooms, ...
> fully furnished
> in excellent condition
> in a quiet location
> close to local amenities
> a deposit

4a **Use the information from exercises 1–3. Complete the advert for the flat.**

> ## For rent
>
> A ¹_____-floor flat
> The accommodation consists of ²_____ bedrooms,
> ³_____ , a hall, a bathroom and a ⁴_____ kitchen.
> The property is fully ⁵_____ and is in excellent ⁶_____ .
> The rooms are ⁷_____ and there's a nice ⁸_____ from the living room.
> The flat is in a ⁹_____ location and is close to ¹⁰_____ .
> **Please contact Shirley McEwan on 07700 900891 for further details.**

b **What information does the advert give?**
– the landlord's name – a description of the flat
– the floor   – a description of the location
– the rooms   – the address
– the rent   – a contact number

5a **Writing You want to let the place where you live to some tenants. Write an advertisement for it. Use the advert in exercise 4 as a model.**

b **Show your advertisement to a partner. Would he/she take it?**

> ## English in the world
> ### Types of houses
>
> These are typical houses in Britain.
>
>
> a detached house
>
>
> semi-detached houses
>
>
> terraced houses
>
>
> a bungalow
>
> **What are typical houses in your country?**

> ✓ **Now I can ...** *understand accommodation advertisements.*

1 **Look back at Episode 1. What happened?**

2 **12.1 Read and listen to the story. What did Jordan do at the weekend? Why was it a waste of time?**

3 **Are the statements true (T) or false (F)?**
1 Jordan's got a cold.
2 He went to see Lucy's parents on Sunday.
3 Lucy wasn't annoyed.
4 The advert was for dog food.
5 Jordan was a swimmer in the advert.
6 It was wet on Saturday.
7 Sarah and Peter are looking for a house.
8 They cut Jordan's scene because the weather was bad.

4a **Complete the expressions.**

> **Everyday expressions**
> **Showing sympathy**
>
> Bless _____ ! *(only for sneezes)*
> _____ , dear.
> That's _____ shame.
> I _____ imagine.
> What _____ pity.
> Poor _____ !

b **Work with a partner. Use the expressions to respond to these sentences. Try to sound sympathetic.**
1 I lost my mobile yesterday.
2 I've burnt my finger. It's very painful.
3 Atishoo!
4 I've got toothache.
5 I can't go to the party. I'm working this weekend.
6 We missed our flight.
7 Jan failed her driving test.
8 Someone scratched my car. I was really annoyed.

5 **Language check. Underline all the examples of the definite article in the story. Can you say why it is used in each case?**

6 **Work in a group. Practise the story.**

Jordan	Hi, Sarah. *Atishoo*!
Sarah	Bless you! Have you got a cold?
Jordan	Yes, I have. It started at the weekend.
Sarah	Oh, dear. But did you have a good time with Lucy's parents?
Jordan	No. I didn't go.
Sarah	That's a shame. Were you working?
Jordan	No, I wasn't. I got a part in a TV advert at very short notice.
Sarah	Oh, was Lucy annoyed?
Jordan	You bet. She hit the roof when I told her.
Sarah	I can imagine. She was really looking forward to it. What was the advert for?

Jordan	It was for *Doggo* dog food. I was 'a jogger in a park'.
Sarah	How did it go?
Jordan	Really badly! It rained all day on Saturday, so we couldn't do anything.
Sarah	What a pity. But it didn't rain on Sunday. Peter and I went to look at a house.
Jordan	No, but there was a cold wind and I only had shorts and a T-shirt on. I was freezing.
Sarah	Poor you! Is that how you got your cold?
Jordan	Probably. And, after all that, it was a complete waste of time.
Sarah	Really? Why?

The advert was too long, so they cut the scene with the jogger in the park! *Atishoo*!

> **Now I can ...**
> *show sympathy.*

1a 13.1 **Listen and repeat.**

	Noun	Adjective
-ous		
	danger fame humour	dangerous famous humorous
-ful		
	pain success beauty	painful successful beautiful
-ent/-ant		
	intelligence patience importance	intelligent patient important
-y		
	anger luck health	angry lucky healthy

b Check the meanings of any unknown words in a dictionary.

Language note	-y endings

-y is a common adjective ending, but words ending in -ty are often nouns, not adjectives.

Noun	difficulty	safety	security	honesty
Adjective	difficult	safe	secure	honest

2 13.2 **Drill. Listen. Say the adjectives. Use It's very ...**
1 luck
  It's very lucky.

3a Complete the words.
1 You need a lot of *pat_____* in this job.
  You won't have much *suc_____* if you get
  an_____ easily.
2 With her *int_____* and her *bea_____* ,
  she's become one of the most *fam_____*
  people in the country.
3 It's *diff_____* to be *suc_____* without a
  lot of *luc_____* .
4 It was very cold, so the last part of the
  climb was *dan_____* and *pai_____* , but
  we finally reached the *saf_____* of our
  camp.
5 *Hon_____* and a good sense of
  hum_____ are very *imp_____* for a
  hea_____ relationship.
6 We all want *sec_____* and good
  hea_____ , but we need a bit of *dan_____*
  in our lives, too.

b 13.3 **Listen and check.**

4a Your life **Give your ideas. Choose words
from exercise 1 and the Language note.**
1 I admire people who are _____ .
2 The most important things in life are
  _____ and _____ .
3 I would/wouldn't like to be _____ .
4 I think _____ is more important
  than _____ .
5 The ideal partner is _____ and _____ .
6 I think you need _____ if you want to
  be _____ .

b Compare your ideas with a partner.

English in the world
Lucky numbers

In China the number 8 is a lucky number, because it sounds like the Chinese word for 'fortune'. However, people think that the number 4 brings bad luck, because it sounds like the word for 'death'.

In Spain people eat 12 grapes at midnight on New Year's Eve to bring luck in the new year. You should eat all the grapes before the twelfth stroke of the clock.

What things in your country are associated with good luck or bad luck?

Now I can ...
use some nouns and adjectives correctly.

1 **14.1** **Read and listen.**

Lucy and Jordan are going out this evening.

Lucy Hi, Jordan. Peter**'s booked** the restaurant for tonight.

Jordan Great, but I'm going to be a bit late. I**'ve had** an accident in my van. I've hurt my hand a bit, but I'm OK.

Lucy Oh, dear. What happened?

Jordan I **reversed** into a car. It was my fault. I didn't look.

Lucy Oh, dear. Well, we**'ve** all **done** something like that. I **did** the same thing last year. I felt very silly.

Jordan Well, I feel annoyed. I**'ve never had** an accident before.

Lucy Never mind. Anyway, **have** you **called** the police?

No, I **haven't**, but I don't really need to do that. It was a police car that I reversed into!

2 **Read the examples. Study the rules on page 106.**

> **Present perfect**
>
> The present perfect connects the past with the present. We use it:
>
> **1 when we're interested in the present result of an event.**
> Peter**'s booked** the restaurant. (We have a reservation now.)
>
> **2 to talk about experiences up to now (with *ever* and *never*).**
> I**'ve never had** an accident. **Have** you **ever had** an accident?

3a **14.2** **Listen. Jordan has made a list of the things he needs to do now. Which things has he done?**

1 take the van to the garage ✓
2 collect another van
3 phone the insurance company
4 download an insurance form
5 fill in the form
6 write a report about the accident
7 send the report to Head Office
8 see the doctor about his hand

b **Ask and answer about the list.**

A *Has he taken the van to the garage?*   B *Yes, he has.*

4 **Read the examples. Study the rules on page 106.**

> **Present perfect and past simple**
>
> We often use the past simple after the present perfect to give:
>
> **– details about an event.**
> I**'ve had** an accident. I **reversed** into a car.
>
> **– the time or place of an event.**
> We**'ve** all **done** something like that. I **did** the same thing on holiday last year.

5 **14.3** **Drill. Listen. Say when the jobs were done. Use *yesterday*.**

1 We've done the shopping.
   We did it yesterday.

6 **Use the cues. Say what the people have done and give the details.**

1 Cindy and Ryan have been to the cinema. They saw a Spanish film.

1 Cindy and Ryan/go/to the cinema. They/see/a Spanish film.
2 Lucy/do/some shopping. She/buy/ a coat from her favourite shop.
3 Peter and Sarah/look at/some more houses. They/not like/any of them.
4 Ryan/take/the car to the garage. He/leave/half an hour ago.
5 Cindy/book/a holiday in Turkey. She/do/it online.
6 Jordan and Lucy/visit/Lucy's parents. They/go/last Sunday.

7a **Your life** **Have you ever done these things? What happened?**

I've damaged a car. I reversed into our garage door. That was two years ago.

1 damage a car
2 drive a van
3 break a bone
4 phone the emergency services
5 give someone a big surprise
6 get lost

b **Ask and answer with a partner.**

A *Have you ever … ?*

B *Yes, I have …*

A *When/Why/What/Where did you … ?*

 Now I can …
talk about past events and experiences.

1 **15.1** **Read and listen.**

1 What is the man's real name?
2 What do people call him?
3 What does he do?
4 Why does he do it?

Thousands watch Alain in Abu Dhabi.

Spiderman!

Alain Robert likes skyscrapers, but he doesn't just like looking at them, as most people do. He prefers climbing them. Last Friday he was in Abu Dhabi, where he climbed up the Investment Authority Building. It took him just 63 minutes to climb the 35 storeys. He was watched by thousands of people in the car park below.

The French Spiderman, as he is called, has climbed some of the world's highest buildings, including the Empire State Building in New York and the Petronas Towers in Kuala Lumpur. He surprised some workers at the Canary Wharf skyscraper in London, when he knocked on the window and asked for a drink.

Alain has often been in trouble with the police, as he's usually breaking the law when he climbs things. He's been in prison in several countries. When he reached the top of the Golden Gate Bridge in San Francisco, the police were waiting for him and arrested him.

He started climbing after he saw a film about mountaineering when he was a young boy. When he was 12, he came home from school one day and found that he was locked out. So he climbed up the outside of the apartment block and climbed in through a window – on the seventh floor. Later, when he got bored with climbing mountains, he looked for something more dangerous.

He doesn't use any ropes or safety nets, and he doesn't wear a helmet. He just uses his own hands and feet. He's had a few accidents, and he's broken several bones, including his skull. So why does the married father of three do it? 'I'm not really interested in the fame, but I like the danger,' he says. 'I'm a gambler and I gamble with my life. So far I've been lucky, but I know that one day I'll lose.'

2 **Are the statements true (T) or false (F)?**

1 He climbed the building in Abu Dhabi in less than an hour.
2 Alain is from France.
3 The police arrested him in San Francisco.
4 He started climbing when he was 18.
5 He lived in an apartment when he was a boy.
6 He always uses a safety net.
7 He's never fallen while climbing.
8 He isn't married.

3a Make a list of the things he has climbed.

b What is he climbing in the picture?

4 Find words or expressions in the text to match these definitions.

1 a very tall building
2 mountain climbing
3 something that protects your head
4 the bones in your head
5 a floor of a building
6 doing something that you shouldn't do
7 something to catch you if you fall
8 not able to enter

5a Make ten questions to ask Alain. Use these cues.

What did you … ?   When did you … ?
How long did … ?   Do you … ?
What have you … ?   Are you … ?
Have you ever … ?   Why do you … ?

b Speaking Work with a partner. Make an interview with Alain. Use the questions in exercise 5a.

Pronunciation
Final consonants

1 **15.2** **Listen. What happens to the -ed before a consonant?**

1 He climbed mountains.
2 He asked for a drink.
3 He surprised them.
4 He reached the top.

2 Listen again and repeat.

 Now I can …
ask someone about their experiences.

1 `16.1` **Listen and repeat.**

100 **700** **1,000** **3,000,000**

a hundred   seven hundred   a thousand   three million (3m)

6,000,000,000 **1,250** **809** **33%**

six billion (6bn)   one thousand, two hundred and fifty   eight hundred and nine   thirty-three per cent

26.5 **1/4** **1/2** **2/3**

twenty-six point five   a quarter   half/a half   two thirds

2a Choose the correct forms – a or b.

Everyday expressions Saying and writing numbers

We say:

1 (a) two thousand   b two thousands
2 a six hundred twenty   b six hundred and twenty
3 a four thousand and two   b four thousand two
4 a two hundred and twenty million b two hundred twenty million

We write:

5 (one million six hundred and seventy thousand)
  a 1,670,000   b 1.670.000
6 (nineteen point five)
  a 19.5   b 19,5

b Check your answers in exercise 1.

3a Say these numbers.

a 325   d 95%   g $3m   j ¾
b 5,000,000   e 21.7   h €40bn   k 7,036
c 28,000   f 4,932   i 8.2%   l ½

b `16.2` **Listen, check, and repeat.**

Language note *of*

three hundred people   NOT ~~three hundred of people~~
30% **of** families   (thirty percent **of** families)
a third **of** the population   BUT half the population

4a Use the numbers to complete the text about cars.

16,536,075   5%   600 million
¼   4,192   35 million

In 1900, there were very few cars. In that year, the USA produced only [1]_____ cars. However, in 1908 the first mass-produced car appeared – the Ford *Model T*. Between 1908 and 1927, [2]_____ *Model Ts* were made. Today there are over [3]_____ cars in the world and [4]_____ new cars are produced every year. Of all the cars in the world, [5]_____ are in the USA, although the USA has only [6]_____ of the world's population.

⅕   25%   19 billion
1.2   4 billion   7.5

We all love our cars and the world's car companies spend more than [7]$_____ a year on advertising. However, cars come at a high cost. They produce [8]_____ tonnes of carbon dioxide every year. That's [9]_____ of all the CO_2 that is produced. By 2030, this will be over [10]_____ billion tonnes. The United Nations says that [11]_____ million people a year die on the world's roads. That's [12]_____ of all the deaths from accidents.

b `16.3` **Listen and check.**

5a `Your life` **Try to answer these questions.**

1 How many people are there in your workplace or school?
2 What is the population of your country?
3 What is the population of your town?
4 How many drinks do you have a day?
5 How many seconds are there in a day?
6 What percentage of your life do you spend asleep?
7 What percentage of people in your English class are male?
8 How many days are there in a century?

b Compare your answers with a partner.

Now I can ...
understand and use numbers.

17 VOCABULARY
Health and fitness

1a `17.1` **Listen. Write the verbs in the correct places.**

Taking exercise

do   warm   pull   ~~keep~~   injure   lift

1 _keep_ fit

2 _____ up

3 _____ some stretching exercises

4 _____ weights

5 _____ a muscle

6 _____ a joint (your knee/back)

A healthy lifestyle

lose   give up   eat   take   get   cut down on

7 _____ a healthy diet

8 _____ weight/ put on weight

9 _____ sugar/fat

10 _____ vitamins

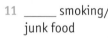

11 _____ smoking/ junk food

12 _____ a good night's sleep

b **Listen again and repeat.**

> **Language note** *go*
>
> go jog**ging**/swim**ming**/cycl**ing**/ski**ing**
> go **for** a walk/a swim/a run
> go **to** the gym/an exercise class/a tennis club

2 `17.2` **Drill. Listen and make questions.**

1 a run
Do you go for a run?

3a `17.3` **Listen to Katrina and Richard. Why does each person take regular exercise?**

1 to lose weight
2 to recover from a heart attack
3 to manage a very stressful job
4 to feel great

b **Listen again. Answer the questions.**

1 What exercise does each person take?
2 Why doesn't Katrina lift weights?
3 How has Richard changed his lifestyle?

4a `Your life` **Answer the questions.**

1 Do you exercise? If so, what do you do? / how often? / why?
2 How do you feel about exercise? (*It's fun / boring …*)
3 What other things do you do to maintain a healthy lifestyle?

b **Discuss your ideas with a partner.**

> **English in the world**
> Giving personal measurements
> ....
>
> In Britain and the USA people use imperial measurements for height and weight.
>
> They give their height in feet and inches.
> 1 foot = 12 inches   1 inch = 2.54 centimetres
>
> I'm five foot six (inches tall).
>
> They give their weight in stones and pounds (UK) or just pounds (US).
> 1 stone = 14 pounds   1 pound = 0.45 kilos
>
> I'm twelve stone four (pounds).
>
> OR
>
> I weigh a hundred and seventy-two pounds.

> **Now I can …**
> *talk about health and fitness.*

1 18.1 **Read and listen.**

Daniel Hi, Lucy. We**'re going to meet** in the pub for lunch today. Do you want to join us?

Lucy No, sorry. Look at all this work. I**'m going to be** very busy today, so I**'ll probably get** a sandwich and eat it at my desk.

Daniel I watched a TV programme last night. It said that in the future robots **will do** most of the work in offices.

Lucy Really? That**'ll be** good.

Daniel Yes, but it said that office life **will be** very different, because the robots **won't have** normal human emotions.

Olive Lucy! I need three copies of the finance report by 11 o'clock.

Lucy OK, Olive. I**'ll photocopy** it now … Robots **won't make** any difference in this office, Daniel. I've already got one as a boss!

2 **Read the examples. Study the rules on page 107.**

The future

For plans and decisions, we use:
will for spontaneous decisions
OK, Olive. I**'ll photocopy** it now.

going to for fixed plans
We**'re going to meet** in the pub for lunch.
We use *going to* when we are more certain about our plans.

For predictions, we use:
will for general predictions
In the future robots **will do** most of the work in offices.
going to when it's clear now that something is certain in the future
Look at all this work. I**'m going to be** very busy today.

3a **Complete the conversations. Use *will* and these expressions.**

| order some coffee | take them |
| post it | book a table | ~~photocopy it~~ |

1 **Maria** We need two copies of this report.
   James OK. I*'ll photocopy it* now.
2 **Max** I haven't got time to take this parcel to the post office.
   Katie OK. I _____ for you.
3 **Gail** These boxes need to go to the basement.
   Pedro OK. Mark and I _____ in a minute.
4 **Dev** Shall we stop for a break at 10.30?
   Paula OK. I _____ .
5 **Hans** Shall we go for a meal this evening?
   Alice OK. I _____ now.

b **Practise the conversations with a partner.**

4 Speaking **What are the people in exercise 3 going to do? Ask and answer about them.**
   1 James   4 Dev and Paula
   2 Katie   5 Paula
   3 Pedro and Mark 6 Hans and Alice
   A *What is James going to do?*
   B *He's going to photocopy a report.*

5 **Choose the correct future form.**
   1 In the future people *will/are going to* live on the Moon.
   2 Look at the sky. It *will/'s going to* rain.
   3 A I can't find my mobile.
     B OK. I *'ll/'m going to* help you look for it.
   4 A Will you be at home this weekend?
     B Yes. We *'ll/'re going to* paint the kitchen.
   5 Ken's filling in a form. He*'ll/'s going to* join the gym.
   6 Most people in the future *will/are going to* live for 100 years.

6a Your life **Write sentences about something that:**
   1 you'll probably do at the weekend
   2 you're going to do this evening
   3 you aren't going to do today
   4 you think will happen in the future.

b **Compare your answers with a partner.**

18

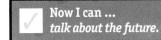
Now I can …
talk about the future.

1 **19.1** **Listen. A man is giving some advice for coping with modern life. Tick ✓ the problems he talks about.**

1 standing up all day
2 sitting down for a long time
3 eating at your desk
4 lifting heavy things
5 not getting enough sleep at night
6 rushing from one meeting to another

2 **Listen again. What solutions does he suggest? Choose the correct pictures and match them to the problems.**

3 **Choose the correct word.**

1 Your spine is part of your *head/back*.
2 A nap is a *short/long* sleep.
3 If you put on weight, you get *fat/fit*.
4 Your *stomach/brain* digests your food.
5 Your palms are part of your *hands/legs*.
6 If you're in good shape you're *comfortable/healthy*.
7 When you're on the go, you're *busy/asleep*.
8 'To lower' is the opposite of '*to lie/to lift*'.
9 If something is flexible, you can *break/bend* it easily.
10 If you drop something, it *falls/rises*.

Language note **First conditional**

If you **do** this exercise, your back **will be** strong.
When you **open** your eyes, you**'ll feel** fresh.

4a **Listen again. Match the causes with the results.**

1 spend all day at your desk *h*	a feel fresh and relaxed
2 do the back exercise ___	b be healthier
3 rush around at work ___	c put on weight
4 take a power nap ___	d learn breathing exercises
5 eat at your desk ___	e get stressed
6 have lunch in the park ___	f spine become strong
7 follow the advice ___	g digest your food well
8 listen tomorrow ___	h get backache

b **Make conditional sentences. Use the causes and results in exercise 4a.**

If you spend all day at your desk, you'll get backache.

5a **Writing** **Look at these problems of modern life.**

> I've got too much work to do.

> I don't get enough sleep. | I work at a computer all day.

> I find it hard to balance work and family life.

b **Choose a problem from exercise 5a. Write some advice to help people. Answer the questions and follow this pattern.**

What is the problem?
What longer-term problems will it cause? Why?
What things should/shouldn't you do?
How can you help?
A common problem today is that people …
If you … , you will/won't …
You should/shouldn't …
Try this activity/advice: …

Pronunciation
Word stress 1

1 **19.2** **Listen and repeat.**
about   healthy   return   advice   muscle   repeat
stomach   relax   second   asleep

2 **Comple the rule.**
Words with two syllables normally have the stress on the _____ syllable, but words that start with *a-* or *re-* normally have the stress on the _____ syllable.

✓ **Now I can …**
understand and give some advice.

1 **Look back at Episode 2. What happened?**

2 `20.1` **Read and listen to the story. Who is Ryan's best friend?**

3 **Are these statements true (T) or false (F)?**
  1 Peter and Sarah are going to get married in London.
  2 The wedding's going to be in July.
  3 All their family and friends will be there.
  4 Their parents don't know each other well.
  5 After the wedding they're going to the USA first.
  6 They'll be away for a month.
  7 They're going to have a holiday, too.
  8 Ryan is talking about his relationship with Cindy.

4a **Complete the expressions.**

> **Everyday expressions**
> **Talking about relationships**
>
> They will _____ to know each other.
> I hope you'll be _____ together.
> We really _____ each other's company.
> She's my _____ friend.
> You've got a _____ relationship.

b **Use the expressions to respond.**
  A *We're getting married soon.*
  B *I hope you'll be happy together.*
  1 We're getting married soon.
  2 You spend a lot of time with Bill.
  3 Do you know Irena well?
  4 My boyfriend and I don't argue very often.
  5 Tina and Mike are both coming to dinner. They haven't met before.

c **Practise your conversations with a partner.**

5 **Language check. Underline all the examples of future forms in the story.**

6 **Work in a group. Practise the story.**

Ryan	Come on, Bessie. That's it. Good dog!
Peter	Hello, Ryan. How are you?
Ryan	Fine, thanks. Cindy says you've finally decided on your wedding plans.
Sarah	Yes, we have. We're going to get married here in London in September.
Ryan	Are all your family and friends going to come over from Singapore and the States?
Peter	No. Our parents will be there, but that's all. It's too expensive for everyone to come.
Sarah	But at least our parents will get to know each other.
Peter	And anyway, after the wedding we're going to fly to Singapore for a celebration with Sarah's family and friends.
Sarah	Then we're going to have another celebration with Peter's family in the States.

Ryan	Wow. How long will that take?
Peter	Three weeks.
Ryan	A round the world trip and three weddings – you'll be exhausted!
Sarah	Oh, we'll probably take some time out for a holiday, too. So it won't be too bad.
Ryan	Well, I hope you'll be as happy together as we are.
Sarah	That's nice. Thank you, Ryan.
Ryan	We really enjoy each other's company. She's my best friend.
Peter	Yes, you and Cindy have got a great relationship.

I didn't mean me and Cindy. I meant me and my dog, Bessie, here!

> **Now I can ...**
> *talk about a relationship.*

1 21.1 **Listen and repeat.**

1 They're **stuck** in a **traffic jam**.

2 There's been an **accident**.

3 The road is **blocked**.

4 There are **roadworks**.

5 The car has **broken down**.

6 The **traffic lights** aren't working.

7 The tunnel is **flooded**.

8 The train is **delayed**.

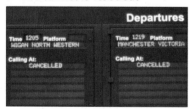

9 All trains are **cancelled**.

10 The bridge is **closed**.

11 There's a **queue** at the **ticket office**.

12 There's a **strike** at the **airport**.

Language note Past participles as adjectives

A lorry is blocking the motorway. The motorway is **blocked**.
The police have closed the airport. The airport is **closed**.

2 21.2 **Drill. Listen. Say the sentence.**

1 Underground/close
The Underground is closed.

3a 21.3 **Listen. Write the problems.**

Problem	Explanation
1 *She can't make her appointment.*	*The train is delayed.*
2	
3	
4	
5	
6	
7	
8	

b Listen again. Write the explanations.

4 Work with a partner. Make conversations.

A *I'm afraid we're going to be late. We're stuck in a traffic jam.*

B *Oh, dear. Why's that?*

A *It's because the traffic lights aren't working.*

B *Oh, OK.*

5 Your life **What forms of transport do you use regularly? What for? Do you often experience delays? Why?**

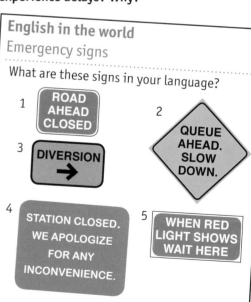

English in the world
Emergency signs

What are these signs in your language?

1 ROAD AHEAD CLOSED

2 QUEUE AHEAD. SLOW DOWN.

3 DIVERSION →

4 STATION CLOSED. WE APOLOGIZE FOR ANY INCONVENIENCE.

5 WHEN RED LIGHT SHOWS WAIT HERE

 Now I can ...
talk about transport problems.

1 | 22.1 | **Read and listen.**

A strange coincidence – but true

One morning, Mrs Willard Lovell was outside her house in Berkeley, California. She wasn't happy, because she**'d locked** herself out by accident. She**'d left** her keys inside the house, and now she couldn't get in. She walked round the house. **Had she left** a window open, perhaps? No, she **hadn't**. Then the postman arrived with a letter. Her brother, Watson, had posted it the previous day. Inside the envelope there was a key to her front door! Watson **had stayed** with Mrs Lovell the week before. She**'d given** him a key, and he **hadn't given it back**. So, he'd posted it to her.

2a **Read the examples. Study the rules on page 107.**

Past perfect
We use the past perfect to look back from one past event to events that happened before that time.
The postman **arrived** with a letter.
(past simple – it happened in the past.)
Her brother **had posted** it the previous day.
(past perfect – it happened a day before.)
Her brother **had stayed** with her the week before.
She**'d given** him a key.
He **given it back**.
Had she **left** a window open?	Yes, she **had**./No, she **hadn't**.

b **How do we make the past perfect?**

3 | 22.2 | **Drill. Listen. Say what Watson had done before the morning when Mrs Lovell locked herself out.**

1 stay with his sister   *He'd stayed with his sister.*

4 **Complete the sentences. Put the verbs in the past perfect.**

1 She couldn't get in because she *'d forgotten* her key. (forget)
2 She didn't have a key, because she _____ her bag. (not take)
3 She was outside, because she _____ something in the garage. (leave)
4 Her husband couldn't help. He _____ on business. (go away)
5 She looked, but she _____ any windows open. (not leave)
6 The neighbours were in, but she _____ them a key. (not give)
7 Luckily, when she left the house, the post _____ . (not arrive)
8 She was so glad that Watson _____ the key home with him. (take)

5a **Put the verbs in brackets into the correct tense.**

John Marsh and his wife own a caravan. Last week two men ¹ *tried* (try) to steal it. They ² _____ (see) the caravan two weeks before and they ³ _____ (decide) to take it. At about four o'clock on Wednesday morning they ⁴ _____ (attach) the caravan to their car and ⁵ _____ (drive) away.

However, they didn't know that John was inside it at the time! He ⁶ _____ (work) very late the day before and he ⁷ _____ (come) home at 1 a.m. He ⁸ _____ (not want) to wake up his wife, so he ⁹ _____ (go) to sleep in the caravan.

The thieves ¹⁰ _____ (get) a big surprise when a police car ¹¹ _____ (stop) them 20 minutes later. When they ¹² _____ (move) the caravan, John ¹³ _____ (wake up) and he ¹⁴ _____ (phone) the police on his mobile.

b | 22.3 | **Listen and check.**

6a | **Your life** | **Think of a strange coincidence or an embarrassing situation that happened to you. Make notes about it.**

What was the situation?
What had happened before that time to create the situation?

b **Work with a partner. Tell him/her your story.**

I was in a café. I'd finished my meal and I stood up to leave. However, when I'd sat down, I'd put my bag under the table. I forgot that I'd put it there. I tripped over it and fell on the floor in front of the waitress. It was very embarrassing.

 Now I can ... *talk about events at different times in the past.*

1 | 23.1 | **Read and listen to Kristof's story. What happened?**

1 He got on the wrong train.   3 He got off at the wrong station.
2 The police arrested his wife.   4 He was in an accident.

The last train

My name's Kristof. Last Tuesday I worked very late, because some important visitors had arrived. When I finally left the office, I hurried to the station and caught the last train home at 11.45. It was warm on the train, so I took off my jacket. I tried to stay awake, but it had been a long day and I soon fell asleep.

When I woke up, we were in a station. I knew that my station was the first stop, so I grabbed my briefcase and ran to the door. I got off just in time and the train moved away. 'That was lucky,' I thought, but then I looked around and I couldn't believe my eyes, because it wasn't my station. The fast train didn't normally stop there, so why had it stopped there that night? And it was the last train! I decided to phone my wife, Selina. Then I realized I hadn't picked up my jacket. My wallet, keys and mobile phone were all still on the train.

I walked out of the station. There were some people in the car park and an ambulance. I spoke to the driver. Apparently, one of the other passengers had become very ill, so the train had stopped there because there was a hospital nearby. The ambulance driver lent me his phone and I phoned Selina. She had already gone to bed. 'Where are you?' she asked.

'I'm at Burton station,' I said. 'I …'

'Just a minute,' she said. 'Whose phone are you using? This isn't your number.'

'It's the ambulance driver's,' I said and I started to explain, but then I realized that she had put the phone down. She thought that I'd had an accident and she was already on her way!

An hour later she arrived. She was happy to see that I hadn't had an accident. However, she wasn't pleased when I explained things, because she had driven very fast to get there and the police had stopped her for speeding – and they had given her a big fine. We drove home together in silence!

2   **Put these pictures in the correct order.**

3   **Answer the questions.**

1 What train did Kristof catch?
2 Why did he get off the train?
3 Why did the train stop there?
4 Whose phone did he use? Why?
5 What did Selina think had happened? Why?
6 Why was she in a bad mood?

> **Language note**   **Sentence linkers**
>
> **We use sentence linkers to connect ideas.**
> Last Tuesday I worked very late, **because** some important visitors had arrived. **When** I finally left the office, I hurried to the station **and** caught the last train home at 11.45. It was warm on the train, **so** I took off my jacket. I tried to stay awake, **but** it had been a long day **and** I soon fell asleep.

4   **Rewrite this part of the story with the correct sentence linkers.**

I woke up. We were in a station. I knew that my station was the first stop. I grabbed my briefcase. I ran to the door. I got off just in time. The train moved away. 'That was lucky,' I thought. Then I looked around. I couldn't believe my eyes. It wasn't my station.

5a | Your life | **Think of a difficult journey that you had in the past. Tell a partner about it.**

b   **Write the story of what happened to you. Try to use some sentence linkers.**

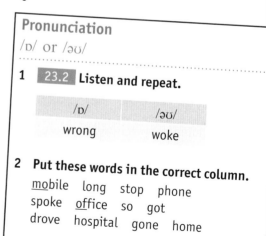

> ## Pronunciation
> /ɒ/ or /əʊ/
>
> **1** | 23.2 | **Listen and repeat.**
>
> | /ɒ/ | /əʊ/ |
> |-----|------|
> | wrong | woke |
>
> **2**   **Put these words in the correct column.**
> <u>mo</u>bile   long   stop   phone
> spoke   <u>o</u>ffice   so   got
> drove   hospital   gone   home
>
> **3** | 23.3 | **Listen, check, and repeat**

> ✓ **Now I can …**
> *understand and tell a story.*

1a **24.1** Read and listen. Choose the correct times to complete the conversation.

| 13.45 | 08.30 | 07.30 | 23.40 | 20.35 | 14.20 |

Customer	I'd like to book a flight to Cyprus, please.
Travel agent	When do you want to travel?
Customer	On 30 November, coming back on 5 December.
Travel agent	OK. Let's have a look. ... Right. Well, there's only one direct flight on Tuesdays. It leaves at ¹_____ and arrives at ²_____ .
Customer	That's very early. Are there any later flights?
Travel agent	No. There aren't many flights in winter, I'm afraid. There's a flight at ³_____ via Amsterdam, arriving at ⁴_____ .
Customer	That's a bit late at night to arrive. Let's try the flight at half past seven.
Travel agent	OK. How many people is it for?
Customer	Two.
Travel agent	And do you want business class or economy class?
Customer	Economy, please.
Travel agent	OK. ... Yes, there are seats available on that flight in economy, but I'm afraid the return flight in December is fully booked.
Customer	Oh, I see. Can you check the other flight, please?
Travel agent	OK. Just a minute.

b Practise the conversation with a partner.

2 Answer the questions.

1 Where does the woman want to travel to?
2 How long does she want to stay?
3 What day of the week is 30 November?
4 Why doesn't she like the direct flight?
5 Why are there only two flights?
6 Why doesn't she like the second flight?
7 Is she travelling on her own?
8 Why doesn't she book the first flight?

3a Complete the expressions.

Everyday expressions	Booking a flight
I'd like to _____ a flight, please.	
Are there _____ later flights?	
The 13.45 flight is _____ Amsterdam.	
Do you want business class or _____ class?	
There are seats _____ on that flight.	
The return flight is _____ booked.	

b Check your answers in the conversation in exercise 1.

Language note	Time prepositions
on + days + dates + parts of a specific day	on Tuesday on 30 November on Friday evening
at + times	at 13.45 at night at the weekend
in + months/seasons + parts of the day + years	in May/winter in the morning in 2009

4 Language check. <u>Underline</u> all the time expressions in the conversation in exercise 1.

5a **24.2** Listen. Complete the table. Does the customer book the flight? Why? Why not?

Destination	
Date out	
Date back	
Departs	
Arrives	
No. of people	
Class	

b Work with a partner. Use the information in the table. Make the conversation. Use exercise 1 as a model.

6 Work with a partner. Put different facts in the table in exercise 5. Make a new conversation.

Now I can ...
book a flight at a travel agent's.

1 [25.1] **Listen and repeat.**

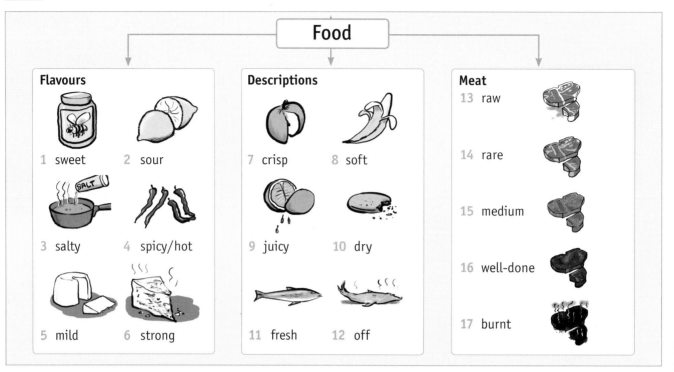

Food

Flavours
1 sweet
2 sour
3 salty
4 spicy/hot
5 mild
6 strong

Descriptions
7 crisp
8 soft
9 juicy
10 dry
11 fresh
12 off

Meat
13 raw
14 rare
15 medium
16 well-done
17 burnt

Language note **Nouns and adjectives**

There's a lot of salt in it. It tastes very salty.

Noun	cream	juice	fat
Adjective	creamy	juicy	fatty

2 [25.2] **Drill. Listen. Say the sentence.**
1 look/spice
It looks very spicy.

3a [25.3] **Listen. Complete the table.**

Kind of food	Description
1 *steak*	*medium-rare*
2	
3	
4	
5	
6	
7	

b **Work with a partner. Use the information in the table. Make the conversations.**
A *How would you like your steak?*
B *Medium rare, please.*

4 **What other food words do you know? Add three more items to each row of the table.**

Ways of cooking	*fry–fried*
Kinds of meat	*beef*
Vegetables	*carrots*
Kinds of fruit	*apples*
Kitchen utensils	*a saucepan*
Other kinds of food	*bread*

5a **Your life** **Answer the questions.**
1 Are any popular kinds of food in your country ... ?
salt spicy sour creamy

2 Do you prefer steak rare or well-done?

3 How do you like your coffee or tea?
strong weak milky sweet

4 Do you normally add any of these things to your food at the table? What kind of food do you add them to?
salt pepper vinegar sugar
cream oil soy sauce chilli

b **Compare your answers with a partner.**

Now I can ...
describe food.

1 **26.1** **Read and listen.**

Sarah is talking to her friends at the university.

Sarah Shall we all go for a meal at The Pizza Experience this evening?

Hamid We went to The Pizza Experience last time, **didn't we**?

Rosa And the time before that. Why don't we go to The Steak House?

Sarah But **Birgit doesn't** eat meat, **does she**?

Rosa No, she doesn't. Well what about The Kingfisher? She eats fish, **doesn't she**?

Hamid Yes, she does, but Arthur doesn't.

Sarah I know. Let's go to that vegetarian restaurant – Carrots.

Rosa Oh, yes. We've had lunch there a couple of times, **haven't we**?

Hamid But **it isn't** open on Tuesdays, **is it**?

Later …

Mmm. **It's** a nice pizza, **isn't it**?

2 **Read the examples. Study the rules on page 108.**

Tag questions 1: *to be*/auxiliary verbs

We use tag questions to check or confirm information:
Birgit doesn't eat meat, **does she**?
We've had lunch there, **haven't we**?

Negative verb + positive tag: **It isn't** open on Tuesdays, **is it**?
Positive verb + negative tag: **It's** a nice pizza, **isn't it**?

3 **26.2** **Drill. Listen. Give the tag question.**

1 It's Tuesday today.
It's Tuesday today, isn't it?

4 **Read the examples. Study the rules on page 108.**

Tag questions 2: present simple/past simple

With present simple and past simple verbs, we use
don't*/*doesn't*/*didn't **in a negative tag:**
She eats fish, **doesn't she**?
We ate there last time, **didn't we**?

5a **Add the correct tag questions.**

1 You like sport, *don't you?*
2 Lucy doesn't like her boss, _____
3 Jordan works at weekends, _____
4 You were here yesterday, _____
5 Sarah and her friends went to The Pizza Experience, _____
6 Cindy and Ryan have got children, _____
7 You aren't an engineer, _____
8 It isn't going to snow tomorrow, _____

b **Work with a partner. Use the sentences from exercise 5a. Make conversations.**

A *You like sport, don't you?*
B *Yes, I do./No, I don't.*

6a **Your life** **Work with a partner. Write eight statements about your partner which you think are true. Use these words.**

1 You were born in this town.

1 be born   5 like/don't like
2 live   6 can/can't
3 married   7 have(n't) been to
4 went   8 have(n't) got

b **Ask and answer with your partner. Are your sentences true?**

A *You were born in this town, weren't you?*
B *Yes, I was./No, I wasn't. I was born in …*

Pronunciation
Intonation in tag questions

1 **26.3** **Listen.**
The meeting is at ten, isn't it? ↗
(You're sure. You just want confirmation.)
The meeting is at ten, isn't it? ↗
(You're not sure. You're checking.)

2 **26.4** **Listen. You will hear each sentence twice. Write S (sure) or N (not sure).**
1 You can't ski, can you? __N__ , ____
2 We're leaving now, aren't we? ____ , ____
3 She isn't twenty-five, is she? ____ , ____
4 You're married, aren't you? ____ , ____

3 **Listen again and repeat. Copy the intonation of the questions.**

 Now I can …
check and confirm information.

1 27.1 **Listen. Which of these dishes do Ramesh and Stefan order? Tick ✓ them.**

> a Chicken Kashmiri b Rice c Lamb Rogan Josh
> d Vegetable Patiya e Naan f Onion Bhaji

You've had Indian food before, haven't you, Stefan?

2a Are the statements true (T) or false (F)?
1 Stefan has had Indian food before.
2 All Indian food is hot and spicy.
3 Ramesh was born in India.
4 Stefan doesn't like spicy food.
5 Stefan is from Hungary.
6 Stefan doesn't like bananas.
7 Ramesh doesn't eat meat.
8 They're going to share the dishes.

b Listen again and check.

3a Listen again. Match the descriptions to the dishes in exercise 1.
___ made from tomatoes and lime juice
___ quite hot
___ cooked with tomatoes and peppers
___ quite sour
___ a kind of bread
___ made with pineapples and bananas
___ quite sweet
___ very tasty
_a_ in a mild and creamy sauce

b Work with a partner. Ask and answer about the kinds of food.
A *What's Chicken Kashmiri?*
B *It's chicken in ...*

Language note
Expressing likes and dislikes

I don't mind ...
I'm (not) very fond of ...
I'm (not) keen on ...
I'm quite happy with ...
I really like ...
I think I'd prefer ...

4a Write a short menu with food from your country.

b Work with a partner. A is a customer, B is a waiter/waitress. Ask and answer about the kinds of food.
A *What's ... ?*
B *It's ... fried/boiled/grilled with ...*
A *Is it spicy/salty/mild ... ?*
B *Yes/No. It's quite ...*
A *What does it come with?*
B *It comes with rice/potatoes/chips and ...*

5 Writing Describe three typical dishes from your country. Use these expressions.
One of my favourite dishes is ...
... is ... cooked in ...
... is made from/with ... and it's a kind of ...
It's quite ... and ...
We normally eat it with ...

One of my favourite dishes is Chicken Kashmiri. It's chicken cooked in a mild and creamy sauce and it's very tasty. The sauce is made with pineapples and bananas, so it's quite sweet. We normally eat it with naan bread or rice.

English in the world
Food labels

Do you have these labels on food in your country? Which things are important to you?

Organic	It was produced without chemicals.
Free range	The animals live outdoors.
Fair trade	The producers get a fair price.
Low fat	It contains very little fat.
Sell by date	The shop can't sell it after this date.
Use by date	You shouldn't use it after this date.

> ✓ **Now I can ...**
> *describe different dishes.*

1 Look back at Episodes 2 and 3. What happened?

2 `28.1` **Read and listen to the story. Where is Jordan? Why is he there?**

3 **Who or what are these?**
1 In The Can
2 Felton Windrush
3 *Doggo*
4 the jogger in the park
5 Red Mason
6 Mrs Roland
7 Violet
8 *Cavendish Park*

4a **Complete the expressions.**

> **Everyday expressions**
> **Recognizing people**
>
> You _____ familiar.
> We haven't _____ before, have we?
> I know your _____ .
> I thought I _____ you.
> I never _____ a face.
> I'm sure I've _____ her before.

b **Use the expressions to complete the conversation. Change the expressions if necessary.**

Dario George, this is Martina.
George Hello, Martina. We _____ , _____ we? You _____ .
Martina Yes, I think we <u>have</u> met actually. I _____ face.
George Yes, I'm _____ before, too. And I never _____ .
Martina I know. It was at the Madrid conference.
George That's right. I _____ you. Anyway, how are you?

5 Language check. <u>Underline</u> all the examples of tag questions in the story.

6 **Work in a group. Practise the story.**

1

Jordan Hi. Sorry to disturb you, but there's nobody at the reception desk. I'm here about …
Felton Ah, come in. I'm Felton Windrush. What's your name?
Jordan It's Jordan Morris.
Felton Mm, you look familiar. We haven't met before, have we?
Jordan No, I don't think so.
Felton But I know your face. … Oh, yes – you were in that advert for *Doggo* dog food, weren't you? We edited it, you know.
Jordan Oh, I see. Yes, I was 'the jogger in the park', but they cut my bit from the final version.
Felton Yes, I thought I recognized you. I never forget a face. Anyway, here you are. Read this.
Jordan I'm sorry. I don't understand.
Felton Come along. You're an actor, aren't you? Read the part of Red Mason.
Jordan OK. 'Who's that woman over there, Mrs Roland? I'm sure I've seen her before. I … Oh, no, it isn't! It can't be … !'

2 *Later …*

Felton Thank you. You read that very well. And you're Australian, aren't you?
Jordan Yes, I am. I'm from Sydney.
Felton That's ideal. Anyway, my secretary Violet will be in touch in the next few days.
Jordan In touch about what?
Felton About the part in our new soap opera, *Cavendish Park*. I'm the producer.
Jordan Oh, right. I didn't know anything about that.
Felton But you came here today for an audition, didn't you?

3

No. Actually I'm here to fix the computer.

> ✓ **Now I can …**
> *talk about recognizing people.*

1 29.1 **Listen and repeat.**

1 an earthquake

2 a volcanic eruption

3 a tsunami

4 a flood

5 a drought

6 a famine

7 an avalanche

8 a hurricane

9 pollution

10 a war

11 a forest fire

12 an explosion

2a Match these words with the disasters. More than one answer may be possible. Use a dictionary to help you.

| the sea rain trees chemicals food |
| snow a bomb wind armies the earth's surface |

the sea   *a tsunami, ...*

b Compare your list with a partner.

Language note
Noun and verb collocations

There has been an explosion/an earthquake/a volcanic eruption/an avalanche in …

There's a flood/a drought/a famine/pollution in …

A tsunami/a hurricane **has hit** …

A forest fire/a war **has broken out** in …

3a 29.2 **Listen to the news items. Match two disasters from exercise 1 with each place.**

East Africa	*6, 10*
the USA	
Central America	
the Philippines	
Australia	
Northern India	

b Listen again and check.

4a Writing **What disasters have been in the news recently? Give some details.**

b Write a short news item about one of the disasters. Follow this pattern.

There has been a … in …
It has damaged/killed/destroyed …
It has also caused …

Pronunciation
Word stress 2

1 Underline **the syllable with the stress.**

1 <u>earth</u>quake	7 explosion
2 vol<u>can</u>ic	8 pollution
3 tsunami	9 forest
4 avalanche	10 disaster
5 famine	11 eruption
6 hurricane	12 chemicals

2 29.3 **Listen, check, and repeat.**

✓ **Now I can …**
talk about disasters.

1 30.1 **Read and listen.**

GLOBAL WARMING

Scientists tell us that the world is getting warmer. How do these people feel about it?

Ivan

I won't mind if the world gets warmer. I live in a cold country. If we **get** better weather, people here **will be** very happy. However, if I **lived** in a hot country, I **would be** very worried.

Amihan

We live on an island. If global warming **continues**, the sea level **will rise** and this island will disappear. We **wouldn't be** on the island now if we **had** more money. My husband and I would move to somewhere safer.

2 Read the examples. Study the rules on page 109.

First and second conditional

We use the first conditional for a real or possible situation and its results.
If global warming continues, the sea level will rise.
present simple   *will* **future**

We use the second conditional for an unlikely or imaginary situation and its results.
If I **lived** in a hot country, I **would** be very worried.
past simple   **conditional form**

The *if* clause can go before or after the main clause.
We **wouldn't be** on the island now if we **had** more money.

3a Put the verbs into the correct tense to make second conditional sentences.

1 If I _was_ (be) younger, I'_d look for_ (look for) another house.
2 We _____ (not stay) here if we _____ (be) worried about floods.
3 They _____ (miss) their home if they _____ (move).
4 If the weather _____ (get) better here, we _____ (not go) abroad.
5 We _____ (not have) a car if we _____ (live) in the city.
6 There _____ (not be) so much pollution if we all _____ (travel) less.
7 If the buses _____ (be) free, more people _____ (use) them.
8 People _____ (not fly) so much if air travel _____ (become) more expensive.

b 30.2 **Listen and check.**

4a Tick ✓ the sentences that are about unlikely or imaginary situations.

1 If sea levels rise, many islands _will disappear_ (disappear).
2 If we _had_ (have) children, we'd be worried about the future. ✓
3 We would save electricity if everyone _____ (switch off) their TV at night.
4 Some parts of Europe _____ (become) deserts if temperatures go up.
5 A lot of scientists will be very surprised if global warming _____ (not happen).
6 If I was the prime minister, I _____ (make) air travel very expensive.
7 There _____ (be) big problems in the future if we don't do something soon.
8 If I lived in a cold country, I _____ (not be) worried about global warming.

b Put the verbs into the correct tense to make first or second conditional sentences.

5a **Your life** **Write suitable endings for these situations.**

1 If I had more money, ...
2 If it rains tomorrow, ...
3 If I was the head of the government, ...
4 If I was younger/older, ...
5 If I get up early tomorrow, ...

b Compare your answers with a partner.

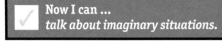

✓ Now I can ...
talk about imaginary situations.

1 `31.1` **Read and listen. Answer the questions.**

1 What is a 'storm chaser'?
2 Where is Tornado Alley?
3 What is the biggest danger for storm chasers?

Storm chaser

If you heard that a tornado was ¹**approaching**, what would you do? Tornadoes can be very dangerous. In 1989, a tornado in Bangladesh killed over 1,300 people. If you were outside, you wouldn't survive. And even if you were ²**indoors**, you wouldn't be completely safe. Tornado winds can be ³**over** 400 km/h and can destroy a building ⁴**in seconds**. The safest place would be in the cellar at the bottom of the house.

One thing that most people wouldn't do is get in their car and drive towards the tornado. But Enrique Gómez would. He's a 'storm chaser'. Tornadoes usually happen together with thunderstorms, so Enrique studies weather forecasts and looks for possible storms. If he finds one, he'll try to get as close as possible to it. He works in Texas and the Midwestern states of the USA, like Kansas and Missouri. This area is called 'Tornado Alley' because there are over 1,200 tornadoes there every year. They usually happen in spring, when cold, dry air from Canada in the north meets warm, wet air from the Gulf of Mexico in the south.

Why does Enrique do it? He's a ⁵**meteorologist**. He wants to learn more about tornadoes and why they happen. 'It's very important now,' he says, 'because of global warming. If temperatures ⁶**rise**, the sea will get warmer and we'll see violent weather, such as hurricanes and tornadoes, more often. This will cause big problems in many areas, for example ⁷**agriculture**, buildings, and transport.'

It's dangerous work. Apart from the high winds, there's usually lightning and heavy rain, which causes floods. However, those aren't the biggest dangers. When Enrique finds his storm, there will be other storm chasers there, too. But most of them aren't scientists. Some are ⁸**photographers**, some work for TV stations, and some are 'tornado tourists' who just want to see a real tornado. 'All these people are chasing the storm in their cars and they're all watching the sky,' says Enrique. So, what's the biggest danger? 'Car accidents!'

2 **Are the statements true (T) or false (F)?**

1 Tornadoes only happen in the USA. _F_
2 You should stay outside in a tornado.
3 When there's a tornado, there's usually a thunderstorm, too.
4 Texas is in Tornado Alley.
5 Most tornadoes happen in winter.
6 Global warming will cause more tornadoes in the future.
7 Enrique is the only storm chaser working in the USA.
8 He's a tornado tourist.

3 **Tick ✓ the problems which the text mentions.**

a thunderstorm ✓	floods	famine
global warming	hurricanes	forest fires
an earthquake	high winds	lightning

4 **Match the numbered words and expressions in the text with these definitions.**

a someone who takes photographs _8_
b get higher ___
c very quickly ___
d coming towards you ___
e farming ___
f someone who studies the weather ___
g inside a building ___
h more than ___

> **Language note** **Giving examples**
>
> He works in the Midwestern states of the USA, **like** Kansas and Missouri.
>
> We'll see violent weather, **such as** hurricanes and tornadoes, more often.
>
> This will cause problems in many areas, **for example** agriculture, buildings, and transport.

5 Speaking **Work with a partner. One person is the interviewer. One is Enrique. Make an interview. Use these questions.**

1 What do you do?
2 Why do you do it?
3 Where do you work?
4 Why do you work there?
5 How do you find tornadoes?
6 Why do other people chase storms?
7 What are the dangers?

> ✓ **Now I can ...**
> *talk about an unusual activity.*

1a `32.1` **Read and listen to the conversation between the receptionist and a guest.**

Guest	Good evening. I've got a reservation in the name of Els.
Receptionist	Yes, here we are. A single room for two nights.
Guest	Yes, that's correct. And I'd like a non-smoking room, please.
Receptionist	All our rooms are non-smoking, sir. Could you fill in your details on the form, please, and sign it at the bottom?
Guest	OK.
Receptionist	And could I take a credit card, please?
Guest	Yes, of course. Here you are.
Receptionist	Thank you. Would you like a newspaper or a wake-up call?
Guest	Yes, I'd like *The Independent*, please, but I won't need a wake-up call. What time is breakfast?
Receptionist	Breakfast is served from 7 to 10.30 in the restaurant.
Guest	Thank you.
Receptionist	So, here's your key, Mr Els. You're in room 58. That's on the fifth floor. Do you need any help with your luggage?
Guest	No, thank you.
Receptionist	OK. The lifts are over there. Enjoy your stay.
Guest	Thank you.

b Copy the hotel form and complete the details for Guest 1.

Hotel guest details	Guest 1	Guest 2	You
Name	*Mr Els*		
Type of room			
No. of nights			
Newspaper			
Wake-up call			
Room no.			

2 Practise the conversation in exercise 1a with a partner.

3 Complete the expressions. Who says each one?

Everyday expressions	Checking into a hotel

I've got a reservation in the _____ of ...
I'd _____ a non-smoking room, please.
Could you fill in your _____ on the form, please.
Could you _____ it at the bottom?
Could I _____ a credit card, please?
Would you _____ a newspaper?
Breakfast is _____ from 7 to 10.30.
Do you need any _____ with your luggage?
Enjoy your _____ .

4a `32.2` **Listen to another hotel conversation and complete the details for Guest 2 on the hotel form.**

b Work with a partner. Make Guest 2's conversation at the hotel. Use the details in the form.

5 Speaking Work with a partner. Complete the details for you on the form. Make a conversation for checking into the hotel.

English in the world
Hotel signs

What are these signs in your language?

1 Emergency exit
2 Please leave all keys at reception
3 Checkout time 11 o'clock
4 Room service available 6 a.m. to 11 p.m.

Now I can ...
check into a hotel.

1a Read the rules and the examples.

Is this luggage yours?

Are these jeans yours?

CUSTOMS

A
These words are uncountable. They have no plural form. They take a singular verb. We use *some/any, this/that*.

1	equipment	4	work	7	litter
2	luggage	5	news	8	accommodation
3	information	6	advice	9	furniture

B
These words are always plural. They have no singular form. They take a plural verb. We use *some/any, these/those*.

10	glasses	13	headphones	16	clothes
11	scissors	14	stairs	17	shorts
12	scales	15	jeans	18	pliers

b 33.1 **Listen and repeat the examples.**

2a Choose the correct words.

1 How much *is/are* the headphones? I like *this/these* ones.
2 *An/Some* advice *is/are* helpful when you buy a computer.
3 We haven't got *a/any* homework today.
4 *This/These* sunglasses *isn't/aren't* mine.
5 I've got *a/some* good news.
6 Do we need all *this/these* equipment?
7 *Is/Are* there *a/any* scales in the bathroom?
8 *That's/Those* are our luggage on the trolley.
9 Have you got *a/any* scissors?
10 *This/These* clothes *look/looks* very expensive.

b 33.2 **Listen and check.**

---

some information
a piece of information
NOT ~~an information~~

some information
two pieces of information
NOT ~~two informations~~

some scissors
a pair of scissors
NOT ~~a scissors~~

some scissors
two pairs of scissors
NOT ~~two scissors~~

3 33.3 **Drill. Listen. Give the plural with the number *three*.**

1 news   *three pieces of news*

4a Writing You are going on a two-week summer holiday. What are you going to take? Make a list. Include details of these things.

– luggage   – equipment
– clothes/toiletries, etc.   – information

b Compare your list with a partner.

English in the world
Warning signs
....
What are these signs in your language?

1
Do not leave luggage unattended

2
Cycling is prohibited

3
It is an offence to drop litter

4
Skateboarding is not allowed

5 It is illegal to park on the yellow lines

Now I can ...
use common uncountable and plural nouns.

34 GRAMMAR
used to/didn't use to

1 | 34.1 | **Read and listen.**

Peter Is that you with the microphone, Ryan?

Ryan Yes, it is.

Peter Did you use to be a singer?

Ryan No, I didn't. That's at one of our karaoke nights. We used to have them every Friday.

Peter What? Here at The Coffee Shop? When was that?

Ryan About ten years ago, I suppose.

Peter Oh, I didn't use to come here in those days. Why don't you have them now?

Ryan When Cindy started singing, everybody used to leave.

2 **Read the examples. Study the rules on page 109.**

> **used to/didn't use to**
>
> **We use *used to* for regular activities and states that were true in the past but are not now.**
>
> We used to have karaoke nights at The Coffee Shop.
> = We had karaoke nights in the past, but we don't have them now.
>
> He used to be a singer.
>
> I didn't use to come here in those days.
>
> | Did you use to have a karaoke night every week? | Yes, we did. No, we didn't. |
> |---|---|
> | What songs did you use to sing? | |

3 | 34.2 | **Drill. Listen. What used to happen?**

1 I don't work in a shop now.
   I used to work in a shop.

4a **Make sentences about Ryan's early life. Use the cues and *used to* or *didn't use to*.**

1 He used to be very fit.
2 He didn't use to have a beard.

1 be very fit ✓
2 have a beard ✗
3 play football ✓
4 live in London ✗
5 work in a factory ✓
6 have short hair ✗
7 ride a motorbike ✓
8 own a café ✗

b **Ask and answer about Ryan.**

A *Did he use to be very fit?*
B *Yes, he did.*

5 **Work with a partner. Ask and answer about when you were ten years old. Use the cues.**

1 Where/live
2 like school
3 have a pet
4 What time/go to bed
5 watch TV a lot
6 Who/play with

A *Where did you use to live?*
B *I used to live …*
A *Did you use to like school?*
B *Yes, I did./No, I didn't.*

6a | Your life | **Make a list of these things.**

– four things that you used to do/have, but don't do/have now
– four things that you didn't use to do/have, but do/have now

b **Compare your answers with a partner.**

> **Pronunciation**
> *used to*
> ....
> | 34.3 | **Listen and repeat. Copy the pronunciation. We normally pronounce *used to/use to* as** /juːstə/.
> 1 We used to live there.
> 2 He didn't use to be a soldier.
> 3 She used to work in France.
> 4 I used to be famous.
> 5 They didn't use to have a dog.

> ✓ **Now I can …**
> *talk about past habits and states.*

1 | 35.1 | **Listen. What did the speaker do for a year?**

2 Listen again. Choose the correct answer.

1 What is the speaker's name?
   a Conrad   b Hermann   c Martin
2 Where did he work?
   a Australia   b Europe   c the USA
3 What day did competitions start?
   a Friday   b Saturday   c Monday
4 What did he do afterwards?
   a He got a job with a TV company.
   b He went to university.
   c He became a sports reporter.
5 How does he describe his year after leaving school?
   a A golden opportunity.
   b A chance of a lifetime.
   c The best year of my life.

3a Answer the questions.

1 Why did Martin use to live near Munich?
2 How did he meet Conrad?
3 How did Conrad spend the three days before the beginning of the bigger tournaments?
4 How did Martin earn money during the year?
5 Why did Conrad give it up at the end of the year?

b Listen again and check.

4 Listen again. Find this information.

1 one reason why Martin took the job
2 two things that he used to do in his job
3 one thing that he didn't enjoy about the job

5a Complete the expressions with these words.

| up   main   time   jumped   away   try |

1 He decided to _____ his luck.
2 I _____ at the chance.
3 I wanted to get _____ from home for a bit.
4 My _____ jobs as an assistant were to ...
5 He decided to give it _____ .
6 It was _____ for me to go to university.

b Listen again and check.

6 | Your life | **Tell a partner about a special time in the past when you did something that you really enjoyed, but don't do now.**

What things did you use to do?
How old were you?
How did you get the chance to do it?
How did you feel about it?
What did you like/dislike most?
How did it end, and what did you do afterwards?

> **Now I can ...**
> *talk about an interesting time in my life.*

1 Look back at Episode 4. What happened?

2 `36.1` Read and listen to the story. Who is fixing the computer?

3 Match the sentence halves 1–8 with a–h.

1 Peter doesn't ___   5 Raj didn't use to ___
2 Melanie has ___   6 Ryan sees ___
3 Lucy remembers ___   7 Jordan has ___
4 Melanie used to ___   8 Ryan thinks ___

a Jordan now and again.
b finished university.
c repair the café's computers.
d Jordan's going to be famous.
e when Melanie was a schoolgirl.
f given up his computer job.
g recognize Melanie.
h work in the café at weekends.

4a Complete the expressions.

> **Everyday expressions**
> **Talking about changes**
>
> She _____ changed a lot.
> I _____ remember when …
> Doesn't time _____ ?
> in _____ days
> That seems a long _____ ago now.
> What's happened _____ that guy … ?
> What's he _____ to these days?

b Use the expressions to complete the conversation.

A What _____ Arthur? I haven't seen him lately.
B Oh, you wouldn't recognize him. He's _____ . He's completely bald.
A Really? I _____ he had long hair.
B Oh yes. He used to play in a rock band in _____ .
A That _____ now.
B Yes, doesn't _____ ?
A Anyway, what's he _____ ?
B He's a bus driver.
A Oh, OK.

5 Language check. <u>Underline</u> all the examples of *used to* in the story.

6 Work in a group. Practise the story.

Peter Who's that young woman talking to Ryan?
Sarah That's Melanie, Ryan and Cindy's daughter. Don't you remember her?
Peter Oh, I didn't recognize her. She's changed a lot. Is she still at Manchester University?
Sarah No, she's finished now.
Lucy I can remember when she was still at school. She used to work in the café at weekends.
Peter Doesn't time fly?
Sarah Did you use to come here in those days, too, Peter?
Peter No, I didn't use to work around here. That seems a long time ago now.

Raj Your computer's working OK now, Ryan. See you again.
Ryan Thanks, Raj. Bye.
Melanie He's nice, isn't he? But what's happened to that Australian guy who used to fix your computers, Dad?
Ryan Do you mean Jordan?
Melanie Yes. I used to enjoy talking to him. Doesn't he come here any more?
Ryan Yes, we see him now and again, but he doesn't repair computers now.
Melanie Oh, what's he up to these days then?
Ryan He's an actor. He's just got a part in a new soap opera, apparently.
Melanie Cool!

Our Jordan's going to be a TV star!

> Now I can …
> *talk about changes.*

1 **37.1** Listen and repeat.

1 a crime / 2 a robbery
3 a victim
4 a criminal
5 a witness

6 The young man is **committing** a crime.
7 He's **robbing** a woman.
8 He's **stealing** her bag.
9 The police will arrest the **robber**.
10 He'll **go to prison** for robbery.

Other crimes

Crime	Criminal	Verb
11 murder	a murderer	to murder somebody
12 burglary	a burglar	to burgle a house
13 vandalism	a vandal	to vandalize something
14 assault	an attacker	to assault somebody
15 blackmail	a blackmailer	to blackmail somebody
16 car theft	a car thief	to steal a car

2 Answer the questions about the picture in exercise 1.

1 What crime is the man committing?
2 What is actually happening?
3 Who is the victim?
4 Are there any witnesses?
5 What will happen to the robber?

Language note *rob* and *steal*	
rob	+ a person or an institution (e.g. a bank)
steal	+ a thing

They **robbed** the man.
NOT ~~They stole the man.~~
They **stole** his wallet.
NOT ~~They robbed his wallet.~~

3 **37.2** Drill. Listen. Say what the robbers did. Use the past of *rob* or *steal*.

1 someone
  They robbed someone.
2 a lot of money
  They stole a lot of money.

4a Complete the news story. Use words from exercise 1.

In July last year, three people ¹ *robbed* the Goldmine jewellery shop. Two men and a woman ² s____e watches and jewellery worth over £80,000. There was a lot of publicity about the ³ c____e, because the ⁴ r____s violently ⁵ a____d the shop's owner, Mr Hall.
Fortunately, several ⁶ w____s saw the ⁷ r____y. The ⁸ p____e soon ⁹ a____d the three people. They went to ¹⁰ p____n for robbery and ¹¹ a____t. The ¹² v____m, Mr Hall, said, 'Those people have ¹³ c____d so many crimes. They are very dangerous ¹⁴ c____s. I thought they were going to ¹⁵ m____r me.'

b **37.3** Listen and check.

5 **Your life** What famous crimes do you know? Describe one to a partner.

What was the crime?
When and where did it happen?
What happened to … ?
– the victim(s)   – the criminal(s)

Now I can …
talk about crimes and criminals.

1 | 38.1 | **Read and listen.**

When Maggie Stone **went out** yesterday, a thief **was watching** her house. After she **had driven away**, he burgled the house. While he was stealing things, he suddenly smelt smoke. Maggie had left the cooker on and a saucepan was burning. The burglar turned off the cooker and threw a wet towel over the saucepan.

When Maggie came home, the burglar was running away. When she went indoors, she found that he had stolen her laptop and some jewellery, but he had also put out the fire in her kitchen. 'I didn't know whether to feel angry or grateful,' she said.

2a **Read the examples. Study the rules on page 110.**

Narrative tenses

We use these tenses to tell a story in the past:
Past perfect   Maggie **had left** the cooker on.
Past continuous   A saucepan **was burning** on the cooker.
Past simple   He **threw** a wet towel over it.

The tenses show us whether something happened at the same time, after, or before another event.
When Maggie **arrived** home, the burglar ...

| 1 **was running** away. | 2 **ran** away. | 3 **had run** away. |

b **Find more examples of narrative tenses in the story.**

3 | 38.2 | **Drill. Listen. Say what the burglar had done before Maggie came home.**

1 break a window   *He'd broken a window.*

4 **What was happening when Maggie arrived? Use the cues and these verbs in the past continuous.**

not burn   come   carry   ~~run away~~   look
1 A burglar was running away.

1 A burglar
2 He/a bag
3 Smoke/from the kitchen window
4 The saucepan
5 Her neighbours/out of their windows

5a **Maggie is telling her story. Put the verbs into the correct tense.**

Yesterday morning I ¹*was cooking* (cook), when the phone ²*rang* (ring). My son ³____ (fall over) at school. While I ⁴____ (collect) my son, someone ⁵____ (break into) our home. When I ⁶____ (arrive) home, a man ⁷____ (run away) from the house. Then I ⁸____ (notice) that smoke ⁹____ (come) from the kitchen window. I suddenly ¹⁰____ (remember) that I ¹¹____ (not turn off) the cooker. I ¹²____ (rush) into the house. The saucepan ¹³____ (be) on fire, but the burglar ¹⁴____ (throw) a wet towel over it. He ¹⁵____ (prevent) a serious fire. Unfortunately, he ¹⁶____ (steal) my laptop and some jewellery, too.

b | 38.3 | **Listen and check.**

6 Speaking **Work with a partner. Make a news interview with Maggie. Use these questions.**

1 What were you doing this morning?
2 Why did you leave the house?
3 What was happening when you returned?
4 What had happened while you were out?

Pronunciation
-ed endings

1 | 38.4 | **Listen. Tick ✓ the verbs which have an extra syllable in the past simple.**

rob	arrest ✓	commit
happen	decide	assault
notice	collect	arrive
want	need	rush

2 **Listen again and repeat.**

✓ Now I can ...
use the correct tenses to tell a story.

1 `39.1` **Read and listen. Who are the people in the picture? What has happened?**

Was it murder?

Magnus Randolph was a rich man. At 2.30 yesterday afternoon he went to his study for a nap. Twenty minutes later he was dead. My name's Jack Lonsdale and I'm a detective. When I arrived at the scene, Randolph was sitting in an armchair. There was a gun on the floor next to his right hand. It was his own gun and his fingerprints were on it. Had he committed suicide? It looked like it, but I decided to ask a few questions.

There were three people at the house yesterday. Randolph's assistant, Belinda Wells; his niece, Caroline Turner; and her husband, Aston. The victim died at exactly 2.51. Belinda and Aston had been for a walk and were just coming back to the house when they heard a gun. The gardener saw them. When they heard the shot, they ran into the house.

They went to the study. Caroline was already there. She hadn't gone for a walk. She had gone to her room to write some emails. Her laptop was still in her room. It showed that she had sent an email at 2.51. It was a very big house, and there wasn't time to work on her laptop in her room, then go down to the study and shoot her uncle. Everyone had an alibi.

However, everyone also had a motive to murder Magnus Randolph. Nobody liked him. Belinda Wells wanted to get a new job, but she couldn't because Randolph was blackmailing her. She had stolen some money a few years before and Randolph had found out. Aston and Caroline Turner owned a small farm, but it was losing money. Caroline had asked her uncle for help, but he had said no. Now that Randolph was dead, Caroline and Aston would get all his money and Belinda could leave! So, was one of them a murderer?

2 **Answer these questions for Belinda, Aston, and Caroline.**
1 What were they doing when Magnus Randolph died?
2 What is their alibi?
3 What did they do when they heard the shot?
4 Why didn't they like the victim?
5 What can they do now that he is dead?

3 **Find words or expressions in the text to match these definitions.**
1 with a lot of money
2 marks that your fingers make
3 to kill yourself
4 the sound of a gun
5 this shows that you didn't commit a crime
6 a reason to do something
7 to get money for keeping a secret

4a **What happened? Discuss these ideas. More than one may be correct.**
1 Magnus committed suicide because he had lost all his money.
2 Aston, Caroline, and Belinda all helped to murder him.
3 Caroline shot him and hoped it would look like suicide.
4 Belinda and Aston killed him before they went for a walk.
5 Magnus shot himself accidentally.

b `39.2` **Listen to the solution of the mystery. Check your ideas.**

5a **Listen again. Which of these does the detective mention? Why?**
– Randolph's hand   – the glass
– the small table   – Caroline's laptop
– the gardener   – the safe
– Aston's fingerprints – the photograph

b **Tell a partner what really happened at Magnus Randolph's house yesterday.**

Belinda Wells went to the study and …

English in the world
Crime fiction

Crime novels (sometimes called **whodunits**) are very popular in English literature. The most famous **fictional detective** is Sherlock Holmes. He appeared with his assistant, Dr Watson, in novels by Sir Arthur Conan Doyle.

Agatha Christie wrote over seventy whodunits and is known as the **Queen of Crime**. Her most famous character was Hercule Poirot, a Belgian detective.

What famous detectives do you know?

 Now I can …
understand and tell a story.

1 | **40.1** | **Read and listen. What's the problem?**

GT Good morning. Granta Taxis. How may I help?

Mrs J Hello. My name's Mrs Johnson. I booked a taxi for ¹_____ this morning, but it's ²_____ now and it hasn't arrived yet.

GT Oh, I'm sorry about that. What address is it?

Mrs J It's ³_____ Tower Street.

GT Just one moment, Mrs Johnson. Uh, I'm sorry, but we've got no record of your booking. When did you make it?

Mrs J ⁴_____ weeks ago.

GT I see, but there's nothing in the computer about it.

Mrs J Well, this is very inconvenient. Can you send a taxi immediately then, please?

GT Let me see. I can get one to you for ⁵_____ .

Mrs J That's no good. I need a taxi now.

GT I'm very sorry, but we haven't got one available at the moment.

Mrs J This is completely unacceptable. I've got a ⁶_____ to catch.

GT I can only apologize, Mrs Johnson, but I'm afraid there's nothing I can do.

Mrs J Well, I shall write and make a formal complaint, and I certainly won't be using your company again. Goodbye.

GT Goodbye, Mrs Johnson.

2a **Listen again. Complete the conversation.**

b **Practise the conversation with a partner.**

3a **Complete the expressions.**

Everyday expressions Making a complaint	
Complaining	**Responding**
This is very _____ .	I'm sorry _____ that.
This is completely _____ .	We've got no _____ of your
I shall write and _____ a	booking.
formal complaint.	I can only _____ .
I certainly _____ be using	I'm afraid there's _____ I can do.
your company again.	

b **Check your answers in the conversation in exercise 1.**

4 **Choose the correct words to complete Mrs Johnson's letter.**

> 68 Tower Street
> Cambridge
> CB5 7YR
>
> The Manager
> Granta Taxis
> Bridge Road
> Cambridge
> CB2 3PH
>
> 17 June
>
> Dear Sir or Madam,

A I am writing to complain about the very poor service that I recently received from your company. I booked a taxi to the ¹*airport/station* at 8.45 on 4 June. However, by 9.15 the taxi hadn't ²*left/arrived*.

B When I phoned your company, the ³*driver/ receptionist* told me that there was no record of my ⁴*taxi/booking* on the computer. I don't understand this, as I had made the booking ⁵*three/five* weeks previously. The receptionist ⁶*apologized/ complained*, but he told me that there was no taxi available ⁷*after/until* 10 o'clock.

C Since I had a plane to ⁸*meet/catch*, my son ⁹*drove/sent* me to the airport, which was very ¹⁰*inconvenient/unacceptable* for him.

D This is ¹¹*completely/very* unacceptable. If I don't receive a written apology, I certainly ¹²*won't/will* be using your taxi service again.

> Yours faithfully,
>
> B Johnson (Mrs)

5 **Speaking** **Work with a partner. You booked one of these things, but when you arrived there was no record of your booking. Make the conversation.**

– a hotel room   – a table in a restaurant

6a **Writing** **Look at the letter. Match these questions to the paragraphs in the letter.**

___ What happened?

___ What were the consequences?

___ What action do you expect now?

___ Why are you writing?

b **Choose one of the situations in exercise 5. Write a letter of complaint about it.**

Now I can ...
make an oral and written complaint.

1 41.1 Listen and repeat.

on

1 put on   2 get on

off

3 take off   4 get off

in

5 fill in   6 put in

out

7 cut out   8 take out

up

9 pick up   10 turn up

down

11 cut down   12 turn down

away

13 run away   14 throw away

back

15 look back   16 give back

2 What is happening in each picture in exercise 1?

1 She's putting on a hat.

3 Read the examples. Study the rules on page 110.

> **Language note** Separable and inseparable phrasal verbs
>
> 1 When a phrasal verb has an object, we can normally put the particle before or after the object.
> Switch off the computer, please.
> Switch the computer off, please.
>
> 2 When the object is a pronoun, the particle **must** go after the object.
> Switch it off, please.
> NOT ~~Switch off it, please.~~
>
> 3 Some phrasal verbs are inseparable.
> look for, look after, look round, get on, get off, get in, get out (of), wait for, listen to
> I got off the train.
> NOT ~~I got the train off.~~

4 41.2 Drill. Listen and give the alternative.

1 Please fill in the form.
Please fill the form in.

5a Tick ✓ the sentences where you can separate the phrasal verb. Rewrite them.

2 It's cold, so you should put a coat on.

1 We looked round a new house today.
2 It's cold, so you should put on a coat. ✓
3 Are you waiting for the bus?
4 Don't forget to switch off your mobile.
5 Are you looking for your keys?
6 Have you thrown away the magazines?
7 You can't cut down that tree!

b 41.3 Listen and check.

6 Your life Ask your partner these questions. Ask follow-up questions to find out more information.

1 Have you ever thrown away something that you needed?
2 When do you switch off your mobile?
3 Where do you take your shoes off?
4 What was the last form that you filled in?
5 Do you ever cut out things from magazines?
6 Do people always give back things that they borrow from you?

> ✓ Now I can ...
> *use some common phrasal verbs.*

1 | 42.1 | **Read and listen.**

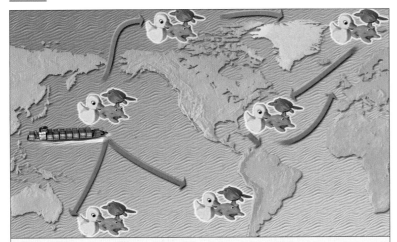

In 1992, a cargo ship **was hit** by a storm in the Pacific Ocean. Twelve of its containers **were thrown** into the sea by the waves. Inside one of the containers there were 29,000 plastic bath toys – yellow ducks, green frogs, and blue turtles. Since then, the toys **have been carried** around the world by ocean currents. They **have been found** in Australia, South America, and even in Europe. The toys **have been studied** by scientists and we've learnt a lot about ocean currents.

However, it is not all good news. Eventually, the toys will break up and the plastic **will be eaten** by fish and birds. Many of these animals will die as a result. Every year, 2,000 to 10,000 containers **are lost** at sea. Consequently, the sea **is polluted** by chemicals. If we are not careful, life in the sea **will be destroyed**. Then, plastic ducks, frogs, and turtles will be the only animals left in the water.

2 **Read the examples. Study the rules on page 110.**

The passive voice
We normally use the passive when we are more interested in the action than the subject.

Active	Chemicals **pollute** the sea.
Passive	The sea **is polluted** by chemicals.

We can make the passive in any tense.	
Past simple	Twelve of its containers **were thrown** into the sea.
Present perfect	The toys **have been studied** by scientists.
Present simple	Every year containers **are lost**.
Future	Life in the sea **will be destroyed**.

When we give the agent, we use *by*.	
Active	Ships lose thousands of containers.
Passive	Thousands of containers are lost **by** ships.

3a **Put the verbs into the present simple passive (paragraph 1) and the past simple passive (paragraph 2).**

Plastic ¹*is used* (use) to make almost anything – toys, tools, shoes, computers. Often these products ²_____ (make) in one part of the world and they ³_____ (transport) to other continents. They ⁴_____ (carry) in containers on very large ships. Sometimes a ship ⁵_____ (hit) by a storm and some of the containers ⁶_____ (lose).

In 1992, thousands of plastic toys ⁷*were thrown* (throw) into the sea when a cargo ship ⁸_____ (hit) by a storm in the Pacific Ocean. Some of the toys ⁹_____ (carry) north to the Arctic. Here, they ¹⁰_____ (trap) in ice. The ice ¹¹_____ (take) into the Atlantic by ocean currents. One plastic duck ¹²_____ (see) on a beach in Scotland. Other toys ¹³_____ (take) south. Several toys ¹⁴_____ (find) in Australia.

b | 42.2 | **Listen and check.**

4 **Look at these environmental issues. Make passive sentences. Use the same tense.**

1 Pollution is produced by traffic.

1 Traffic produces pollution.
2 Cigarettes start some forest fires.
3 Factories have dumped chemicals in rivers.
4 Loggers have cut down rainforests.
5 Oil from the Exxon Valdez killed millions of animals.
6 The world's population will need more food.
7 Shoppers will buy more organic food.

5 **Write five sentences about how the environment in your country is damaged.**

Forests are destroyed by fires.

English in the world
Eco-friendly products

Do you look for labels like these on products?

Contains no artificial colourings.
Made from 100% recycled material.
Fully bio-degradable.
Made with wood from sustainable sources.

| ✓ | Now I can ...
describe a process. |

1a Look at the pictures in exercise 3. What do you think the listening is about?

b 43.1 Listen and choose the correct words.

1 Pierre is from *Indonesia/ Hawaii/Tahiti*.
2 He's a *pearl diver/farmer/ jewellery maker*.
3 His pearls are sent to *Europe/Japan/the USA*.

2 Listen again. Are the statements true (T) or false (F)?

1 Most pearls are found by divers.
2 It takes five years for oysters to make a pearl.
3 Oysters are killed to get the pearls out of them.
4 Pink pearls aren't produced by Pierre's farm.
5 All pearls are round.
6 More than one pearl is produced by an oyster in its life.

3a Put the pictures in the correct order.

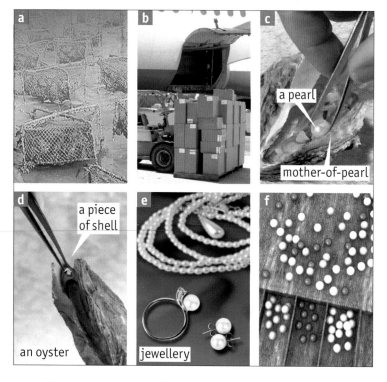

a
b
c a pearl
mother-of-pearl
d a piece of shell
an oyster
e jewellery
f

b Describe the process. Use these verbs in the passive.

send take out put sort make into keep

1 A small piece of shell is put in the oyster.

Language note
Questions in the passive

Statement
The pearls **are sorted** by Pierre.

Yes/No question
Are the pearls **sorted** by Pierre?

Answer
Yes, they are./No, they aren't.
NOT ~~Yes, he does./No, he doesn't.~~

Statement
They **are made** into jewellery.
***Wh-* question**
Where **are** they **made** into jewellery?

4a Answer the questions.

1 Why are the oysters turned regularly?
2 What colours of pearl are mentioned?
3 How are different coloured pearls made?
4 What are the most expensive pearls?
5 What kinds of jewellery are mentioned?
6 What happens to the oysters when they aren't needed any more?

b Listen again and check.

5a Choose something that is produced in your workplace/town/district. Write about it.

What is produced?
Where is it produced?
How is it produced?
What materials are used?

b Work with a partner. Ask about the product that your partner has chosen.

Pronunciation
/ɔː/ or /ɔɪ/

1 Put the words in the correct column.

/ɔː/	/ɔɪ/
sort	oyster

sort oyster form toy destroy
noise worn normally coin morning
storm boy

2 43.2 Listen, check, and repeat.

✓ Now I can ...
ask about a process.

1 Look back at Episodes 4 and 5. What happened?

2 44.1 Read and listen to the story. How does Lucy feel? Why?

3 Write the correct names.

1 _____ is putting out some tables and chairs.
2 _____ doesn't feel very happy.
3 _____ is working long hours.
4 _____ are making plans for getting married.
5 _____ told Ryan about the wedding plans.
6 _____ is going to study in the USA.
7 _____ has gone to work in France.
8 _____ wants to talk to Lucy.

4a Complete the expressions.

> **Everyday expressions**
> **Reporting information**
>
> It s_____ms (that) …
> App_____ly, …
> Cindy t_____s me (that) …
> I h_____r (that) …
> I u_____d (that) …

b Use the expressions to report this information.

1 It seems that Daniel really likes his new job.

1 Daniel really likes his new job.
2 Lucy's bored with her life.
3 Sarah's nearly finished her degree.
4 Peter's parents are coming to the wedding.
5 The Managing Director wants to see Lucy.
6 Ryan wants to get a new car.
7 Melanie's going to study at Harvard.
8 They used to have karaoke at The Coffee Shop.

5 Language check. <u>Underline</u> all the examples of the passive in the story.

6 Work in a group. Practise the story.

Ryan Hello, Lucy. You look down in the dumps.
Lucy Oh, hi, Ryan. Yes. I feel really fed up at the moment.
Ryan Things can't be that bad. What's the problem?
Lucy Well, it's just that everyone's life is changing except mine.
Ryan It seems that Jordan's very busy with his new acting job.
Lucy Yes. Apparently, it's all going well. But it isn't just him. Peter and Sarah are busy with their wedding plans, too.
Ryan Yes, Cindy tells me that the restaurant's been booked and the invitations will be sent out soon.

Lucy And I hear that Melanie's been accepted by a university in the States.
Ryan Yes. She's very happy about it.
Lucy And my friend Daniel at work was transferred last week.
Ryan Oh yes, I understand he's gone to your Paris office.
Lucy Yes, but I'm still in the same old job with the same old boss.
Ryan Oh, dear. You are feeling sorry for yourself, aren't you?
Lucy Yes, I am. Everyone else is moving on and I've been left behind.
Ryan Cheer up! I'm sure there's something interesting round the corner for you, too.

3 *The next day …*

Lucy, the Managing Director wants to see you in his office this afternoon.

> ✓ Now I can …
> *report information.*

1a `45.1` **Read and listen.**

What's your friend like?

1 She always does the right thing. She's a *sensible* person.
2 He always finishes his work on time. He's very *reliable*.
3 She doesn't mind waiting for things. She's very *patient*.
4 He's won a lot of prizes, but he doesn't talk about them much. He's very *modest*.
5 She found some money and she took it to the police station. She's an *honest* person.
6 Everything on his desk is always in the right place. He's very *tidy*.
7 She always looks happy. She's a *cheerful* person.
8 He always asks for things nicely. He's very *polite*.
9 She's always ready to help if you've got a problem. She's very *kind*.
10 He loves meeting people. He's a *sociable* person.
11 She doesn't worry about things. She's very *easy-going*.
12 He wants to be the Director. He's an *ambitious* person.
13 She's good at understanding people's feelings. She's very *sensitive*.
14 He always defends his friends. He's very *loyal*.

b `45.2` **Listen and repeat the bold words.**

2 **What other words for describing personality do you know?**

shy, generous …

Language note *What is/does he like?*

What **is** he **like**?   = What is his personality?
He's very sociable.

What **does** he **like**? = What things does he enjoy?
He likes football.

3a **Find the opposites of the words in exercise 1 in the box below. Use a dictionary.**

1 sensible – silly

unreliable   tense   impolite   unambitious insensitive   untidy   dishonest   miserable impatient   unsociable   disloyal   big-headed ~~silly~~   unkind

b `45.3` **Listen and check.**

c **Which of the words make opposites with these prefixes?**

un- im- dis- in-

reliable – unreliable, …

4 **Use the adjectives from exercises 1–3. Describe these people.**

1 yourself   3 your parents
2 a friend or colleague   4 your boss

5a `45.4` **Listen. Who are these people in Fatima's life? Match them with the relationships.**

Josh   Mrs Bell   Richard   Maxine

– her boss   – her flatmate
– her favourite teacher   – her new colleague

Name	Relationship	Description
1 Josh	*her new colleague*	*unsociable, …*
2 Mrs Bell		
3 Richard		
4 Maxine		

b **Listen again. How does Fatima describe each person? There are three adjectives for each person.**

6a **Your life** **Describe a good or bad boss, friend, or wife/husband. Write three adjectives for each kind of person.**

– a boss – a friend – a wife/husband

b **Compare your answers with a partner.**

I think a good boss is …

✓ **Now I can …**
describe someone's personality.

1 `46.1` **Read and listen.**

Cindy and Ryan have joined a walking group. They're going on their first walk today …

Ryan Why are we taking that umbrella?

Cindy It **might** rain later.

Ryan It won't rain. It's a beautiful day.

Cindy It **might not** be fine all day. And we **should** take jumpers and coats, too. It might be cold in the evening.

Ryan You **shouldn't** be so pessimistic.

Stop complaining, Ryan. The weather **might** change later.

2 **Read the examples. Study the rules on page 111.**

> ### *might / might not*
> **We use *might / might not* to express possibility.**
> It **might** / **might not** rain. = It's possible that it will/won't rain.
> **Compare this to:**
> It will/won't rain. = It's definite that it will/won't rain.

3 `46.2` **Drill. Listen. Say what might/will happen.**

1 Will she be late? Yes, possibly.
  She might be late.

4a **Make sentences about the things people worry about on holiday. Use the cues and these verbs.**

| be | not arrive | burgle | lose | ~~miss~~ | not like |

1 We might miss the plane.

1 We/the plane
2 Someone/our house
3 We/the hotel
4 There/an earthquake
5 We/our passports
6 Our luggage

b **Think of four more things (good or bad) that might/might not happen on holiday.**

5a **Read the examples. Study the rules on page 111.**

> ### Giving advice
> **We often use *should / shouldn't* with *might / might not* to give advice.**
> You **should** take your coat. It **might** be cold later.
> You **shouldn't** worry. The bad things **might not** happen.

b **Give some advice. Use the cues.**

1 You shouldn't put your mobile on the table. Somebody might steal it.

1 put your mobile on the table
2 drive when you're tired
3 wear something light-coloured at night
4 always put your seatbelt on in a car
5 leave things on the stairs
6 play a personal stereo very loud

6a **Your life** **Write sentences about these things.**

1 I might watch …

1 something that you might watch on TV this evening
2 something that you shouldn't do, but often do
3 a friend or colleague that you might not see this week
4 a job that you should do at the weekend

b **Compare your sentences with a partner.**

> ### English in the world
> Taboos
> ....
> Here are some things that you shouldn't do in certain countries. You might offend people.
> In Japan you shouldn't blow your nose in public. It's very rude.
> In Thailand it's impolite to show the soles of your feet.
> In Egypt you shouldn't eat with your left hand. This hand is unclean.
> In Britain it's impolite to jump a queue.
>
> **What taboos are there in your country?**

 Now I can …
express possibility and give advice.

1a `47.1` **Read and listen.**

How do people see you?

1 When do you feel best?
a in the morning
b in the afternoon or early evening
c late at night

2 Do you usually walk ... ?
a slowly, often with your head down
b quickly
c moderately, with your head up

3 When you talk to people, do you ... ?
a put your hands together
b fold your arms
c play with your ear or touch your chin

4 When something amuses you, do you ... ?
a smile
b laugh quietly
c laugh loudly

5 When you go to a party, do you ... ?
a enter quietly and look for a friend
b enter and talk to the nearest person
c enter noisily, so that everyone sees you

6 Which colours do you like best?
a white, brown or grey
b yellow, green or blue
c red, orange or black

7 Do you normally go to sleep ... ?
a on your side
b on your stomach
c on your back

8 What are your dreams like?
a Do you usually have pleasant dreams?
b Do you often dream that you are looking for something?
c Do you normally forget your dreams?

b Work with a partner. Ask and answer the questions.

Language note Adjectives and adverbs

You're a **quiet** person. You do things **quietly**.

Adjective	quiet	noisy	sensible		good	fast	hard
Adverb	quietly	noisily	sensibly	BUT	well	fast	hard

---

2 `47.2` **Listen. Write the scores. Then calculate your total.**

3 `47.3` **Read and listen to the results. What does your score mean? Do you agree?**

What does your score mean?

21–24: People think that you are brave, strong, and exciting. You're very ambitious, but people also think that you're a bit big-headed and can be insensitive. You know a lot of people, but you don't have close friends.

17–20: People think that you are an interesting and friendly person. You are good at most things, but you're modest, too. You're kind and helpful. You're sociable and easy-going, so you make friends easily, but you forget them easily, too.

13–16: People think that you're sensible, careful, and intelligent. You're very honest. You don't make friends easily, but you're very loyal to the friends that you have. You're a sensitive person, so people find it easy to talk to you about their problems.

8–12: People think that you're shy and serious. You're very tidy and you worry a lot. You always try to do things correctly. You're usually quiet and you're happy when you're on your own. People like you, however, because you work hard and you're very reliable.

4a Writing **Think of someone that you know well (a friend or a member of your family). Describe his/her personality.**

1 Answer questions 1–6 in the quiz for him/her.
2 Think of some personality adjectives to describe his/her:
– positive aspects
– negative aspects
3 What do you think is the most important aspect of his/her personality?

b Write about the person. Use your ideas from exercise 4a. Follow this pattern.

I think ... feels best in ...
He/She usually walks ...
I think he/she is a ... and ... person.
However, he/she can be ... and he/she is sometimes quite ...
Most of all, I think that he/she ...

Now I can ...
complete a personality quiz.

1a `48.1` **Read and listen.**

Les	Do you like this painting?
Dan	Yes, I do.
Fay	So do I.
Les	Oh, I don't.

Amy	Have you ever been to New Zealand?
Tim	No, I haven't.
Amy	Neither have I.
Meg	Oh, I have.

b Which people in the conversations ... ?

– like the painting   – have been to New Zealand

2 Work in a group of three. Practise the conversations.

3a Read the examples. Study the rules on page 111.

Everyday expressions	Comparing experiences	
Positive statement	**Same**	**Different**
I was away last week.	So was I.	(Oh,) I wasn't.
I can play the piano.	So can I.	(Oh,) I can't.
I like rock music.	So do I.	(Oh,) I don't.
Negative statement	**Same**	**Different**
I'm not going to work today.	Neither am I.	(Oh,) I am.
I haven't got any money.	Neither have I.	(Oh,) I have.
I didn't like the film.	Neither did I.	(Oh,) I did.
We can say *neither* or *nor*:	Nor am I. = Neither am I.	

b How do you compare experiences in your language?

4 `48.2` **Drill. Listen and say that your experience is the same. Use *so* or *neither*.**

1 I like my job.
   So do I.

5 Work with a partner. Make conversations. Use these cues.

A *Do you like sunbathing?*
B *Yes, I do. I love it.*
A *So do I.*
OR
A *Do you like sunbathing?*
B *No, I don't.*
A *(Oh,) I do. I think it's great.*

1 Do you like ... ?
2 Can you ... ?
3 Have you got ... ?
4 Did you ... yesterday?
5 Are you going to ... ?
6 Are you ... ?
7 Would you like to ... ?
8 Have you ever ... ?

6a `Your life` **Complete the sentences with information about yourself.**

1 I don't drink milk.

1 I don't drink ...	6 I've got ...
2 I can't ...	7 I've never ...
3 I'm ... this evening.	8 I wouldn't ...
4 I ... yesterday.	9 I usually ...
5 I eat a lot of ...	10 I didn't go ...

b Work with a partner. Use your sentences in exercise 6a. Say and respond.

A *I don't drink milk.*
B *Nor do I.* OR *(Oh,) I do.*

Pronunciation			
Strong and weak forms			

1 `48.3` **Read and listen.**

weak form		strong form	
1 So can I.	/kən/	2 Oh, I can.	/kæn/
3 So have I.	/həv/	4 Oh, I have.	/hæv/
5 So am I.	/əm/	6 Oh, I am.	/æm/
7 So are we.	/ə/	8 Oh, we are.	/ɑ:/
9 So was I.	/wəz/	10 Oh, I was.	/wɒz/
11 So were we.	/wə/	12 Oh, we were.	/wɜ:/

2 Listen again and repeat.

Now I can ...
compare experiences.

1 49.1 **Listen and repeat.**

6 The bride and groom are getting married.
7 They're having the wedding at a registry office.
8 The wedding guests are throwing confetti.

9 The bride is carrying a bouquet.
10 She's wearing a wedding ring.

11 They've had the reception.
12 They're going on their honeymoon.

2 49.2 **Listen. Adam is talking about a wedding. Write down two things that he says about these things:**

– places   – clothes   – people
It was at a church, …

Language note	Family relationships

the bride's parents
→ the groom's parents-in-law

the groom's wife from his first marriage
→ the groom's ex-wife

the groom's daughter from his first marriage
→ the bride's stepdaughter

3 Olivia and Nick have just got married. Complete the sentences with the correct relationships.

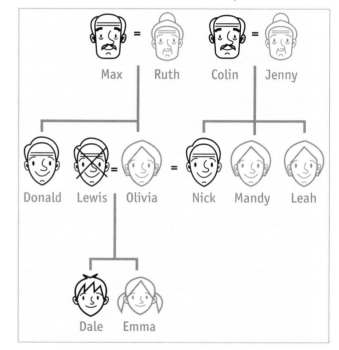

1 Dale is Nick's _stepson_ .
2 Lewis is Olivia's _____ .
3 Mandy and Leah are Olivia's _____ .
4 Nick is Donald's _____ .
5 Olivia is Colin's _____ .
6 Nick is Dale and Emma's _____ .
7 Olivia is Lewis's _____ .
8 Dale and Emma are Nick's _____ .
9 Colin and Jenny are Olivia's _____ .
10 Ruth is Nick's _____ .

4 Your life **Are weddings in your country similar to the one in the pictures? Think of a wedding that you have been to. Tell a partner about it.**

Now I can … *talk about weddings and family relationships.*

50 GRAMMAR
Direct and indirect objects

1 50.1 **Read and listen.**

Lucy likes to give **presents to all her friends** at Christmas. Last year she gave **Cindy and Ryan a glass vase**. They didn't really like it, however, so Cindy gave **it to her mother** for her birthday. Cindy's mother has only got a small flat and she didn't have room for it. Jordan helped her with her computer, so she gave **the vase to him** to say thank you.

It's Valentine's Day, and Jordan is taking Lucy out to dinner. However, he's forgotten to buy her a present, so he's going to give **her the glass vase**. He's sure she'll be pleased!

2 **Read the examples. Study the rules on page 111.**

Direct and indirect objects			
	verb	**direct object**	*to* **+ indirect object**
Lucy	gives	presents	to her friends.
Cindy	gave	it	to her mother.

3 **Make sentences in the past.**

1 Peter sent a birthday card to his father.

1 Peter/send/a birthday card/his father
2 I/write/a letter/the manager
3 My sister/post/a present/me
4 I/email/some photos/her
5 Jordan/give/the vase/Lucy
6 Cindy/lend/her mobile/her son
7 You/give/the wrong address/us
8 We/write/postcards/our friends

4a **Read the examples. Study the rules on page 111.**

Direct and indirect objects: word order			
	verb	**direct object**	*to* **+ indirect object**
Lucy	gives	presents	to her friends.
		to **indirect object**	**direct object**
Lucy	gives	her friends	presents.

b **Change your sentences in exercise 3.**

1 Peter sent his father a birthday card.

5 50.2 **Drill. Listen. Change the sentences.**

1 Did you give a book to Sarah?
Did you give Sarah a book?

6a Your life **Answer the questions. Give examples.**

1 I usually give my mother some flowers for her birthday.

1 Who do you normally give presents to?
2 Do you ever lend people things?
3 Have you ever written a letter to a newspaper?
4 Who do you email photographs to?
5 Who normally sends you a birthday card?
6 What was the last thing that you posted? Who to?

b **Compare your answers with a partner.**

English in the world
Giving gifts

Most countries have different gift-giving traditions. For example, when people meet on business in Indonesia they normally give each other a small gift. You should always give and receive the gift with both hands. When you receive a gift, you shouldn't open it immediately. It means that you are greedy.

Are there any traditions about giving gifts in your country?

Now I can ...
talk about giving things to people.

1   Look at the pictures. What are the things?

a red envelope with money _2_   thirteen coins ___
cows ___   bread, salt and vodka ___
a garland of flowers ___   a plant with a pink ribbon ___

2a 51.1 Listen. Write the names of the countries that you hear in the first column of the table.

| Poland | Sudan | Russia | Syria | Mexico |
| South Africa | Vietnam | Uruguay | China | |

Country	The gift	Who gives it?	Who receives it?
1 Mexico	13 coins	the groom	the bride
2			
3			
4			
5			
6			

b Listen again. What is each gift? Who gives and receives it? Complete the table.

3a What does each gift mean? Match these reasons with the gifts in exercise 1.

a We have respect for you and hope our children will be happy. ___
b Welcome to the family. ___
c This unites our two families. ___
d I promise to support you. ___
e You'll have good times and bad times and we hope you'll be happy. ___
f Thank you for letting her go. ___

b Listen again and check.

4   Work with a partner. Look at the table in exercise 2a. Discuss these questions.

1 Do you have similar traditions in your country?
2 What other wedding traditions do you have?
3 Who normally pays for a wedding in your country?
4 Who is normally invited to a wedding?
5 How do people give gifts to the couple?
6 What sort of things do people normally give as wedding gifts?

5   Writing Describe some wedding traditions from your country. Answer the questions and follow this pattern.

What people are involved?
What do they do?
Why? What does the tradition mean?
It's traditional (for the bride/groom/ parents/guests) to ...
This symbolizes ...
It means that ... People ... to bring the couple good luck/children/happiness.

Pronunciation
Consonant clusters

51.2 **Listen and repeat.**
Try to pronounce the consonants clearly.

bridesmaids   children   countries
something   bridegroom   respect
parents   birthday   stepdaughter
presents   welcome   invited

✓ Now I can ...
describe and explain wedding traditions.

1 Look back at Episodes 5 and 6. What happened?

2 **52.1** Read and listen to the story.

3 Are the statements true (T) or false (F)?
1 Lucy is going to see the Managing Director next week.
2 Olive told her what the MD wants.
3 His personal assistant is leaving.
4 Lucy's appointment is at half past one.
5 She's going to get a certificate.
6 There isn't a prize.
7 Peter and Sarah are getting married on 6 September.

4a Complete the expressions.

> **Everyday expressions**
> **Discussing possibilities**
>
> What do you t_____ he wants?
> I've got no i_____ .
> P_____ps./Ma_____e. / Po_____ly.
> It's more l_____ly that ...
> I h_____ you're right/wrong.
> ... w_____er he wants, ...

b Use the expressions. Complete the conversation. Change the expressions if necessary.
A Look. The police are stopping the cars.
B What *do you think they want?*
A I've _____ .
B P_____ they're looking for criminals.
A P_____ . I think it's _____ they're checking driving licences.
B M_____ .
A But I hope _____ , because I've left my licence at home.
B Oh, dear.
A Well, _____ , we'll know in a minute.

5 Language check. <u>Underline</u> all the examples of direct and indirect objects in the story.

6 Work in a group. Practise the story.

Marco What do you think the Managing Director wants?
Lucy I've got no idea, Marco. Olive didn't tell me.
Marco Perhaps his PA is quitting and he's going to offer the job to you.
Lucy No, they always advertise for posts. It's more likely that he's going to give me the sack.
Marco They can't fire you, Lucy. They wouldn't find anyone else to work with Olive.
Lucy I hope you're right. Anyway, whatever he wants, I'll find out at 2.30 this afternoon.

Later ...

Sarah Employee of the Month? Congratulations. Were you surprised?
Lucy I was absolutely amazed.
Sarah Well, maybe Olive has got a heart after all.
Lucy Possibly. Anyway, there's a small ceremony at work tomorrow when the MD will present the certificate and the prize to me.
Sarah What's the prize?
Lucy It's a trip for two to Paris.
Sarah Wonderful! I suppose Jordan's going with you.
Lucy Of course. He was delighted when I told him. It's all booked for Saturday 6 September.
Sarah Oh, that's the weekend before our wedding.

Yes. Oh, I feel so much happier now.

> ✓ **Now I can ...**
> *discuss possibilities.*

1 53.1 **Read and listen.**

My name's Jason. I'm an **undergraduate** student at Newcastle University. I'm studying for **a degree** in Law. It's a three-year **course** and I'm in my second year at the moment. In my first year I had a room **on campus**, but I live **off campus** now. I share a house with five other students.

On most days I attend one or two **lectures**. I take **notes**, and then at the end of the lecture the **lecturer** usually gives us a reading list and **an assignment**. A week later we have **a seminar** in a small group. One of the students has to read his or her assignment and we talk about it.

At the end of our third year we'll take our **final examinations**, and if I pass them, I'll **graduate**. I'll get my **degree certificate** at **a graduation ceremony**.

2 **What people, things and events can you name in the pictures?**

3 **Find bold words or expressions in the text to match these definitions.**

1 the lectures and seminars on a subject
   a course
2 the place where the university buildings are
3 the exams at the end of a degree course
4 to finish a degree
5 a student who is studying for a first degree
6 a piece of work that students have to do
7 someone who teaches at a university
8 the time when students get their certificates

> **Language note**
> **Verb + noun collocations**
>
> **study for** a degree in ...
>
> **do** an assignment/a course
>
> **attend** a lecture/a seminar/a university
>
> **take/sit/pass/fail** an exam
>
> **take/make** notes

4 **Read the text again. Answer the questions.**

1 Which university is Jason studying at?
2 What subject is he studying?
3 How many more years will he be at university?
4 Where does he live when he's at university?
5 How many lectures does he normally have?

5 Your life **Compare Jason's life as a student to life as a student in your country. What differences are there?**

> **English in the world**
> Oxford and Cambridge
> ....
>
> The two most famous universities in Britain are Oxford and Cambridge.
>
> Oxford University started at the end of the 11th century and is the oldest in Britain. Many famous people have studied there, including famous authors, such as J.R.R.Tolkien, Lewis Carroll and Oscar Wilde, as well as 25 of Britain's prime ministers.
>
> Cambridge University was created in 1209 by some professors and students from Oxford. Cambridge has produced more Nobel Prize winners than any other university in the world.

> **Now I can ...**
> *talk about life as a student.*

1 `54.1` **Read and listen.**

Sarah Hello, Lucy. **Have** you **been waiting** long?

Lucy No, I **haven't**. Where's Peter?

Sarah He'll be here in a minute. ... Oh, here he is now.

Lucy What's he **been doing**?

Sarah He**'s been looking** for somewhere to park. It's very busy tonight.

Peter Hi, Lucy. Sorry we're late.

Lucy It's OK. I **haven't been waiting** long. Anyway, I**'ve been reading** this book. It's called 'Improve Your Memory'. It's really good.

Peter Oh, right. Well, come on. The show starts in ten minutes. Have you got the tickets?

Lucy The tickets? Oh, no! I've forgotten them. I've left them at home.

Sarah It sounds as if you need that book, Lucy!

2 **Read the examples. Study the rules on page 112.**

Present perfect continuous
We use the present perfect continuous for a recent activity when we want to emphasize the time that it takes.
I**'ve been reading** this book. I **haven't been waiting** long. He**'s been looking for** somewhere to park. He **hasn't been talking** to anyone.

Have you **been waiting** long?	Yes, I **have**. No, I **haven't**.

| What's he **been** doing? | |

3 `54.2` **Drill. Listen. Say what you've been doing.**

1 play volleyball

I've been playing volleyball.

4a `54.3` **Listen. What have the people been doing?**

1 Ian hasn't been swimming. He's been cycling.

1 Ian/swim/cycle
2 Tom and Amy/run/ski
3 Sophie/write letters/send emails
4 Jack/have a shower/clean his teeth
5 Max and Kim/watch a film/play tennis
6 Muriel/cook dinner/take the dog for a walk

b **Ask and answer with a partner.**

A *Has Ian been swimming?*

B *No, he hasn't. He's been cycling.*

5a **Read the examples. Study the rules on page 112.**

Present perfect simple and present perfect continuous
We often use the present perfect continuous for an activity that is still continuing now. We often use the present perfect simple if the activity has finished.
I**'ve been waiting** for ten minutes. (And I'm still waiting now.)
I**'ve waited** for ten minutes. (But I'm leaving now.)

b **Put the verbs into the present perfect simple or the present perfect continuous.**

1 I've read that book. I'm reading his second novel now.

1 I (read) that book. I'm reading his second novel now.
2 Peter (read) *Birdsong*. He's nearly finished it.
3 Lucy (photocopy) for an hour now, and there's still a lot to do.
4 I (photocopy) everything now, so I'm going home.
5 You (repair) that computer all morning. What's wrong with it?
6 Raj (repair) the computer, so it's fine now.
7 Sarah (run) for half an hour now, but she isn't tired.
8 I (run) in both the London and New York marathons.
9 I (play) tennis three times this week.
10 I'm tired. I (play) tennis since 2 o'clock.

6a `Your life` **Answer the questions.**

1 What have you been doing for the last half hour?
2 How long have you been studying English?
3 How long have you been living at your current address?
4 Have you been using a computer today?
5 Has it been raining today?

b **Compare your answers with a partner.**

Now I can ...
talk about continuous recent activities.

1 | 55.1 | **Read and listen.**

1 Who is the letter to?
2 Who is it from?
3 What job is the person applying for?
4 Where does he work at the moment?

153 Martin Street
Portsmouth
PO4 9FG

Personnel Manager
Happy Holidays
Winston House
Cardiff Street
London NW3 6BQ   19 July

Dear Sir or Madam

I would like to apply for the post of Operations Manager with *Happy Holidays*.

As you can see from my CV, I am 32 years old and I have a degree in Business and Management from Manchester University. It was a four-year course, and as part of my studies I had a work placement for nine months with a small telecommunications company in Spain.

After leaving university, my first job was with *A-2-B Travel*. I worked for *A-2-B* for five years. After three years I was promoted to the position of Assistant Manager and I was in charge of a department of six people. For the last three years I have been working for *Flywise Airlines*, where I am responsible for publicity.

In addition to my degree, I have a qualification in Spanish. I have been studying Italian since May, too, but I have not taken any examinations in it yet. I have also done courses in Human Resources and in Marketing.

I have enjoyed my time at *Flywise*, but I now feel the need for a new challenge. I believe I have the qualifications and experience for the position of Operations Manager with your company.

I look forward to hearing from you.

Yours faithfully,

Orson Barnes

Orson Barnes

Language note *for* and *since*

for + a period of time
I've been working here **for** three years.
since + a point of time
I've been studying Italian **since** May.

2a | 55.2 | **The personnel assistant is talking about Orson, but some things are wrong. Listen and** underline **the differences in the letter.**

b Listen again and write down the different facts.

3a Complete the expressions.

1 I would like to apply _____ the post _____ Operations Manager.
2 As part _____ my studies, I had a work placement.
3 I was promoted _____ the position of Assistant Manager.
4 I was _____ charge _____ a department of six people.
5 I'm responsible _____ publicity.
6 I have a qualification _____ Spanish.
7 I've done courses _____ Human Resources and in Marketing.
8 I feel the need _____ a new challenge.

b Check your answers in the letter.

4a Writing What qualifications would the ideal candidate need for this job?

Music FM Radio Station needs
A Manager

b Write a letter to apply for the job. Follow this model. Use the expressions in exercise 3 and Orson's letter to help you.

– reason for writing
– educational qualifications
– work experience
– other qualifications and/or experience
– reasons for applying for the job

Now I can ...
write a letter of application.

1a Match the news with the responses.

News

1 I've got a place at university. _c_
2 Coleen and Mack have split up. __
3 Henry's moving. He's bought a flat. __
4 Tania's expecting a baby. __
5 I've lost my job. __
6 Bill and Jolene are getting married. __
7 Mr Woods died last week. __
8 Elizabeth has had her baby. __
9 I've got an interview for a new job today. __
10 Carlos has had an accident. __

Responses

a I'm sorry to hear that. How long have you been working there?
b That's great news! Did she have a boy or a girl?
c I'm very pleased to hear that. Congratulations.
d That's wonderful news. When's the wedding?
e I didn't know that. I hope it was nothing serious.
f That's very sad. How old was he?
g That's good. He's been looking for a place since last year.
h Great. Well, good luck. I'll keep my fingers crossed for you.
i Really? That's great. When's it due?
j They're getting divorced? Well, I know they've been having problems lately.

b 56.1 **Listen and check.**

2a Complete the expressions with these words.

> sorry dear afraid very good
> news what have hear

Everyday expressions News

Introducing some news
Guess _____ ?
_____ you heard?
I've got some _____ news.
I've got some bad news, I'm _____ .
Responding to good news
That's wonderful _____ .
I'm very pleased to _____ that.
Congratulations.
Responding to bad news
Oh, _____ .
That's _____ sad.
I'm _____ to hear that.

b 56.2 **Listen, check, and repeat.**

3a Speaking Work with a partner. Use your answers to exercise 1 and the expressions in exercise 2. Make the conversations.

A *Guess what? I've got a place at university.*
B *I'm very pleased to hear that.*

b Continue two of the conversations.

4 Your life Make conversations with a partner for these situations.

1 A friend is in hospital.
2 Two of your friends are moving abroad.
3 You've been promoted.
4 You didn't get a place at university.
5 You and your partner are getting married.

Pronunciation
Positive and negative intonation

1 56.3 **Listen.**

I've got some good news.
I've got some bad news.

2 56.4 **Listen and repeat. Is the person happy or unhappy about the news?**

Now I can ...
give and respond to news.

1 **57.1** Listen and repeat.

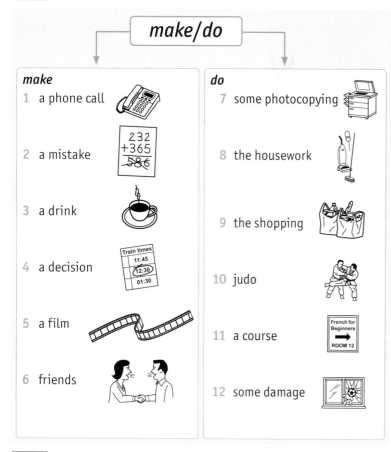

make / do

make
1 a phone call
2 a mistake

232
+365

3 a drink
4 a decision

Train times
11:45
12:30
01:30

5 a film
6 friends

do
7 some photocopying
8 the housework
9 the shopping
10 judo
11 a course

French for
Beginners
ROOM 12

12 some damage

2 **57.2** Drill. Listen. Say what you've made or done.

1 a mistake   2 the shopping
I've made a mistake.   *I've done the shopping.*

Language note *make* and *do*

1 We usually use *make* + a thing:
make a sandwich (= to produce)

2 We usually use *do* + a job/an activity:
do the washing up

3 We use *do* in the general sense of 'activity':
What are you **doing**?/Are you **doing** anything this evening?
I'm not **doing** anything at the weekend.

3a Put these things in the correct column in the table.

a meal   your homework   notes   a plan   karate
a job   the ironing   a noise   money   an assignment
a cake   some exercise   some work   an appointment

make	do
a meal	your homework

b **57.3** Listen and check.

4a Complete what Bella says. Use the correct form of *make* or *do*.

My name's Bella and I work for a film company. I'm an assistant to a director. I ¹_do_ photocopying and ²_____ appointments – and I ³_____ a lot of cups of coffee, too! I don't ⁴_____ a lot of money, but I'm ⁵_____ a job that I really enjoy. I've ⁶_____ some good friends, too.
It isn't all fun. At the moment we're ⁷_____ a film about a hospital and we have to ⁸_____ a lot of the work at night.
I really want to be a film director, so in my free time I'm ⁹_____ a course in film directing. It's quite hard. I had to ¹⁰_____ a big assignment last week.
I'm not ¹¹_____ anything today. I'm going to ¹²_____ a bit of housework this morning and then I'll probably ¹³_____ some exercise later. But first, I'm going to ¹⁴_____ a few phone calls.

b **57.4** Listen and check.

5 **Your life** Complete the questions with *make* or *do*.

1 Do you find it easy to _____ decisions?
2 What housework do you normally _____ ?
3 What mistakes do you sometimes _____ in English?
4 What jobs do you have to _____ today?
5 Have you _____ any new friends in the last year?

Pronunciation
The letter *a*

1 Put the words in the correct column.

/eɪ/	/æ/
make	plan

make   plan   save   married
sandwich   take   same   have
flat   made   sad   male

2 57.5 Listen, check, and repeat.

3 What effect does the *-e* have at the end of a word? Which word breaks the rule?

Now I can ...
talk about activities.

1 58.1 **Read and listen.**

1 *Monday morning ...*

Cindy The coffee machine isn't working. We **can't** make any coffee and we **have to** open in two hours. I **must** phone the engineer.

Ryan You **don't have to** do that. I'll take a look at it.

Cindy You **mustn't** touch it, Ryan – it's dangerous! You **won't be able to** fix it, and we **must** have a coffee machine. Remember the last time it broke down. We **couldn't** make any hot drinks and we **had to** close the café.

Ryan Don't worry. I can fix anything!

2 *Later ...*

I'm sorry, but you**'ll have to** buy a new machine. We haven't got any in stock, I'm afraid, so we**'ll have to** get one from Italy. We**'ll be able to** get it in three days.

2 **Read the examples. Study the rules on page 112.**

can/must (future and past forms)	
1 *Can* has no future form. We use *be able to*.	
Past	We **couldn't** make any hot drinks.
Present	I **can** fix anything.
Future	You **won't be able to** fix it.
2 *Must* has no past or future form. We use *have to*.	
Past	We **had to** close the café.
Present	I **must** phone the engineer.
Future	You**'ll have to** buy a new machine.

3 58.2 **Drill. Listen. Cindy is saying what happened last time. Say what they will have to do this time.**

1 We had to close the café.
  They'll have to close the café again.

4 **The machine is broken and Ryan has hurt his hand. What will the consequences be? Use the cues and *will/won't have to* or *will/won't be able to*.**

1 They won't be able to make hot drinks, so they'll have to close the café.

1 make hot drinks/close the café
2 work in the café all day/go to the cinema
3 get up early/stay in bed
4 Ryan/drive the car/take the bus
5 Cindy/serve customers/do what she wants
6 pay for a new machine/take a holiday this year
7 Ryan/lift heavy things/Cindy/do it

5a **Complete the sentences. Use the past or future forms of *can* and *must*.**

1 My car broke down yesterday, so I ¹*couldn't* drive to work. I ²_____ take the bus. It isn't a serious problem, so I ³_____ buy a new car. The car will be ready today, so I ⁴_____ collect it after work and then I ⁵_____ go by bus again tomorrow.

2 Martin had flu last week, so he ¹_____ go on holiday. He ²_____ stay in bed for the first few days, because he felt very ill. After that he ³_____ get up. He feels OK now, but he isn't happy because he ⁴_____ go back to work on Monday. He ⁵_____ go on holiday again before next year.

b 58.3 **Listen and check.**

6a **Your life** **Write down something that you:**

– had to do yesterday
– didn't have to do yesterday
– won't have to do tomorrow
– won't be able to do tomorrow
– couldn't do when you were a child
– could do when you were two years old

b **Compare your ideas with a partner.**

✓ Now I can ...
talk about abilities and obligations.

1a `59.1` **Listen and repeat.**

1 a comedy

2 a western

3 a cartoon

4 an adventure film

5 a musical

6 a thriller

7 a romance

8 a horror film

9 a science fiction film

b **Write your answers to these questions.**

1 How often do you go to the cinema?
2 Do you watch films on TV and DVDs?
3 What kind of films do you like best?
4 What's your favourite film?
5 What was the last film that you saw?

c **Discuss your answers with a partner. Do you like the same things?**

2a `59.2` **Listen. You will hear somebody talking about the history of the film industry. Tick ✓ the topics that the speaker talks about.**

1 how a film works   5 the first sound film
2 the first films ✓   6 cartoons
3 silent films   7 special effects
4 the first colour film   8 the future of films

b **Match these names with the topics you have ticked in 2a.**

a *Gladiator* _____
b Charlie Chaplin _____
c *The Jazz Singer* _____
d The Lumière brothers *2 the first films*
e *Star Wars* _____

c **Listen again and check.**

3 **Which of these predictions does the speaker make about the future of films?**

1 The film industry will disappear.
2 Directors won't have to use actors.
3 You'll be able to change the ending of a film.
4 People will make their own films with computers.

4 **Listen again. Answer the questions.**

1 When and where were the first films shown?
2 Why did Hollywood become the centre of the film industry?
3 How could film companies make films very quickly?
4 Why did sound make film-making more difficult?
5 Why did the director have to use computer technology in *Gladiator*?

5 **Writing** **Write a review of a film that you have seen recently. Follow this pattern.**

Paragraph 1 – facts about the film
The last film that I saw was …
It starred … and …
It was directed by …
It's a comedy/thriller/horror/ … film
It's about three people/a man/ … who …

Paragraph 2 – your opinion of the film
I really liked/didn't like the film.
It was very interesting/boring/ …
The actors were excellent/ … and the special effects/clothes/ … were amazing/ …
However, the story was very sad/a bit too long/ …

English in the world
Bollywood

India produces more films than any other country, including the USA. People call the Indian film industry 'Bollywood'. The name comes from Bombay (the old name for Mumbai), which is the centre of the industry, and Hollywood. Bollywood makes over 800 films a year. Most are made in Hindi, but more and more are in English, and they are becoming popular internationally. The films are usually musicals and have traditional stories about love, families, heroes, and villains. However, nowadays a lot of the films are about city life in modern India.

What types of film are popular in your country? Who are the biggest directors and stars?

Now I can …
talk and write about films.

1 Look back at Episodes 6 and 7. What happened?

2 [60.1] **Read and listen to the story. Why is Lucy angry?**

3 Answer the questions.

1 What has happened at Wormwood Studio?
2 Where will they have to film now?
3 How long is it available for?
4 Why is that a problem?
5 What did Lucy do today?
6 Why won't Jordan be able to go?
7 Will he be able to be best man?
8 Has he told Peter yet?

4a Complete the expressions.

> ### Everyday expressions
> **Checking and confirming negative news**
>
> **Checking**
> Does that _____ (that) … ?
> _____ you saying (that) … ?
> Don't _____ me (that) …
> **Confirming**
> Yes, un_____ .
> Yes, I'm afraid _____ .
> Yes, it looks _____ it.

b Use the expressions. Make conversations about this information.

1 A Are you saying that you didn't send the email?

B Yes, I'm afraid so.

1 You didn't send the email.
2 We'll have to cancel the meeting.
3 I won't be able to leave on Friday.
4 We'll have to change our flights.
5 You had to pay for everybody.
6 Nick's been fired.
7 You couldn't find the tickets.
8 I'll have to buy a new TV.

5 Language check. <u>Underline</u> all the examples of *have to* and *be able to* in the story.

6 Work in a group. Practise the story.

1 *Felton Windrush is talking to the actors and actresses in his new soap opera.*

Felton I'm sure you've all heard that there's been a fire at Wormwood Studio.
Amber Does that mean that we won't be able to use it?
Felton Yes, unfortunately, Amber. We'll have to use KP Studio instead.
Amber Is that available, Felton?
Felton Yes, it is, but only for six weeks.
Amber Are you saying that we'll have to do two months' filming in six weeks?
Felton Yes, I'm afraid so. We'll have to work every weekend from now on.

2 *At Jordan's flat …*

Lucy I got the tickets for Paris today.
Jordan Oh, er, what date is that again?
Lucy It's 6 September – the weekend before the wedding. Why? What's that?
Jordan It's our new schedule for filming, and …
Lucy Don't tell me you'll have to work that weekend.
Jordan Yes, it looks like it. And the weekend of the wedding, too.
Lucy What?! And does Peter know that his best man won't be able to be there?
Jordan No, not yet. Look. I'm really sorry, but …
Lucy Oh, don't worry, Jordan. I'll just have to find someone else to share the most exciting weekend of my life.

And share the rest of my life, too! That's it! We're finished!

> ✓ Now I can …
> *check and confirm information.*

61 VOCABULARY
Verb + *-ing* or infinitive

1 `61.1` **Read and listen. What's Tony's big decision?**

I **enjoy driving**, but I've **given up going** to work by car. The traffic's terrible and I **can't stand sitting** in traffic jams. I **don't mind going** by train, because I can read. In fact, I've just **finished reading** *War and Peace*. But the trains are usually crowded. I try to **avoid travelling** in the rush hour, but sometimes I **don't fancy getting up** that early. I can't **imagine doing** it for years.

So I've **decided to look** for a new flat. I really **want to find** a place near my office. Then I won't **need to use** any transport. I **hope to have** a look at some flats this week. My sister has **offered to help** me. I don't **expect to find** one straightaway, but when I **manage to find** somewhere, I **plan to sell** my car. I **promised to sell** it to my sister. I think that's why she's helping me!

2a **Read the examples. Study the rules on page 113.**

> ### Verb + *-ing* or + infinitive
>
> **1 Some verbs are followed by the *-ing* form:**
> I enjoy driving.
> NOT ~~I enjoy to drive.~~
>
> **2 Some verbs are followed by the infinitive:**
> I've decided to look for a flat.
> NOT ~~I've decided looking for a new flat.~~

b **Put these verbs in the correct column.**

> ~~decide~~ ~~enjoy~~ want plan imagine can't stand
> promise avoid offer (don't) mind hope fancy
> need give up manage expect finish

+ infinitive	+ *-ing*
decide	*enjoy*

3 `61.2` **Drill. Listen. Make the sentences with *playing tennis* or *to play tennis*.**

1 We've finished
   We've finished playing tennis.

4 **Choose the correct words.**

We've decided [1]*to move/moving* to Australia. We both fancy [2]*to live/living* somewhere warmer. I can't stand [3]*to get up/getting up* on cold, dark winter mornings. We managed [4]*to find/finding* jobs in Australia quite easily and we plan [5]*to go/going* next month. I don't mind [6]*to leave/leaving*, although I can't really imagine [7]*to live/living* anywhere else. We don't really want to [8]*leave/leaving* all our friends here, but we both enjoy [9]*to meet/meeting* people, so we hope [10]*to make/making* new friends quickly. We haven't finished [11]*to pack/packing* all our things yet, but our friends have promised [12]*to help/helping* us.

> **Language note** *like, love,* etc.
>
> These verbs can take either the *-ing* form or the infinitive:
> like, love, hate, prefer, start
> **The meaning is similar:**
> We love *dancing*. OR We love *to dance*.

5a `61.3` **Listen to what Katrina says. Match verbs from the table in exercise 2b to these activities. (Some verbs may be negative.)**

1	*decide*	change her job
2	_____	do something different
3	_____	travel round the world
4	_____	save some money
5	_____	have lunch in restaurants
6	_____	commute by car
7	_____	save a lot of money
8	_____	leave her job

b **Say what Katrina did.**

1 She decided to change her job.

6a `Your life` **Write sentences about your life. Use these expressions and a verb in the correct form.**

1 I've always wanted …
2 I enjoy …
3 I plan … this year.
4 I've promised …
5 I'd like to give up …
6 I need … today.

b **Compare your answers with a partner.**

> **Now I can …**
> *use some common verb patterns correctly.*

1 `62.1` **Read and listen.**

Jonas Paulsen, 47, loves paragliding, but when he went paragliding last week, he didn't expect to be gone for three days! He jumped off a mountain in Norrbotten in Sweden. However, he landed in a forest, and he spent the next three days 30 metres up a tree. '**There were people looking** for me,' he said, 'but the weather was very bad. After three days **I saw a helicopter flying** over the forest. Then **I heard a dog barking**. When I looked down, **there was a man looking** up at me.'

'When I reached the tree,' said Lars Odell, '**I saw him hanging** upside down, like a bat.'

It was Jonas's third paragliding accident. His wife, Laila, said, 'From now on he's going to take up a quiet hobby, like stamp collecting.'

2 **Read the examples. Study the rules on page 113.**

Verb + noun + -*ing*
We use verb + noun + -*ing* to describe a scene:
1 after *There is/are/was/were*: There were people. They were looking for me. **There were people looking** for me.
2 after *see/hear/feel/smell*, etc.: I saw a helicopter. It was flying over the forest. **I saw a helicopter flying** over the forest.

3 `62.2` **Drill. Listen. Combine the sentences to describe the rescue scene.**

1 There was a man. He was climbing the tree.
 There was a man climbing the tree.

4 **Write eight sentences about the picture. Use *There's* or *There are* + -*ing*.**

There's a man selling newspapers.

5 **Look at the man and woman having a cup of coffee. What things can they see and hear happening?**

They can see a man selling newspapers.

6 **Writing** **Imagine one of these four scenes. Write six sentences to describe it. Use these expressions.**

There's/are ... -ing

I can see/hear/feel/smell ... -ing

1 a beach
2 by a lake in a park
3 skiing
4 a market

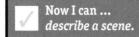

Now I can ...
describe a scene.

1 Look at the picture below. What is each of the animals doing? What do you expect to happen? Why?

2a Read the story. Complete the story with these missing phrases.

 a I think that leopard's forgotten about me.
 b That leopard was delicious.
 c Where's that monkey?
 d I'm in trouble now.
 e That old dog has just tricked the leopard.

b | 63.1 | Listen and check.

THE OLD DOG

a leopard

a dog

a monkey

bones

a tree

One day, in Africa, an old dog wandered into the forest. It was a nice day and the old dog was looking at the flowers and the butterflies. Soon he was a long way from home. When he stopped to have a rest, he saw something moving. There was a young leopard coming towards him. 'Oh, dear,' he thought. [1] '_____'

He looked around and saw some bones on the ground. The old dog sat down and started to chew them. When he heard the leopard approaching, he stopped chewing the bones, stood up, and said, 'Mmm. [2] _____ But it was very small. I could eat another one!' When he heard this, the leopard stopped and walked quietly away.

There was a young monkey sitting in a tree. He saw all this happening. [3] '_____' he thought. 'If I go and tell the leopard, maybe he'll be my friend and he'll stop trying to eat me.'

The old dog saw the monkey following the leopard and he thought, 'What am I going to do now? I'm sure that monkey's going to tell the leopard that I tricked him. He'll be angry when he hears it, but I'm too old to run away.'

Soon, as he expected, the old dog saw the leopard running towards him with the monkey on his back. The old dog sat down and waited for them. When they were close enough to hear, he stood up and said loudly, [4] '_____ I'm hungry and I sent him to bring me another leopard half an hour ago!'

When the dog looked round, he saw the monkey jumping off the leopard's back. He watched the leopard chasing the monkey up into a tree. [5] '_____' he said to himself, and he started walking slowly back home. The moral of the story is: 'A wise, old head can always beat a strong, young body.'

3 Answer the questions.

1 When did the old dog first see the leopard?
2 Why didn't the dog run away when he saw the leopard?
3 Why didn't the leopard attack the dog the first time?
4 Why did the monkey follow the leopard?
5 Why didn't the leopard attack the dog the second time?
6 Why did the leopard chase the monkey?

> **Language note** *stop*
>
> *stop* + **infinitive** has a different meaning from *stop* + *-ing*.
> He stopped **to have** a rest.
> = He stopped because he wanted to have a rest.
> He stopped **chewing** the bones.
> = He was chewing the bones and then he stopped.

4 Speaking Work with a partner. Close your books and re-tell the story. Student A tells the story up to where the monkey decides to follow the leopard. Student B then continues to the end.

> **English in the world**
> Proverbs
>
> These are common English proverbs.
>
>
>
> The early bird catches the worm.
>
> A leopard never changes its spots.
> While the cat's away the mice will play.
> A bird in the hand is worth two in the bush.
> You can't teach an old dog new tricks.
> Don't count your chickens before they're hatched.
>
> **Give some examples of proverbs in your language.**

> **Now I can ...**
> ✓ *understand and re-tell a simple story.*

1a | 64.1 | **Read and listen. Where are the people going to go? When?**

Man	¹Do you fancy going for a meal later?
Woman	No, I don't really ²feel like going out this evening. I'm tired.
Man	OK. How about tomorrow?
Woman	Tomorrow's ³no good for me, I'm afraid. Are you free on Wednesday?
Man	No, I'm sorry. I can't ⁴make Wednesday or Thursday. I'm away. Friday?
Woman	Yes, Friday's ⁵free at the moment. Where shall we go?
Man	⁶How about trying that new Lebanese restaurant near the square?
Woman	Yes, that sounds good.
Man	OK. Great. I'll book a table and text you.

b Practise the conversation with a partner.

2a Replace the underlined items with these words and expressions.

want to go out   Would you like to go   manage
Why don't we try   out   OK

b | 64.2 | **Listen and check your new conversation.**

3 Complete the expressions with *go out, going out*, or *to go out*.

Everyday expressions Suggestions

Suggesting
Would you like/Do you want _____ ?
Shall we /Why don't we _____ ?
Do you fancy /How about _____ ?

Saying no to a suggestion
I don't really want _____ .
I don't feel like _____ .
I can't make/manage that.
That's out/no good for me.

4 | 64.3 | **Drill. Listen. Make suggestions with the correct form of *go for a meal*.**

1 How about
How about going for a meal?

Language note Modifiers

It sounds rude to say *no* directly, so we normally use a modifying expression to make it more polite.
I don't really want to go out.
I'm sorry, but I can't make that.
That's out for me, I'm afraid.

5 | Your life | **Work with a partner. Make new conversations.**

A	B
Suggest going out.	Say no and give a reason. Suggest another time.
Say no and give a reason. Suggest another time.	Accept. Ask where you should go.
Suggest a place.	Agree and offer to make the arrangement.
Agree.	

Pronunciation
Reduced syllables

1 | 64.4 | **Listen and repeat. Underline the words with the stress. Notice how we reduce the syllables that aren't stressed.**

1 Do you <u>want</u> to <u>go</u>
  Do you <u>want</u> to <u>go</u> for a <u>meal</u>?
2 Would you like to go
  Would you like to go to the cinema?
3 Do you fancy going
  Do you fancy going to the park?
4 Why don't we go
  Why don't we go to the café?

2 Listen again and repeat.

 Now I can ...
make and respond to suggestions.

1 What names of sports do you know?

football, tennis, …

2 65.1 Listen and repeat.

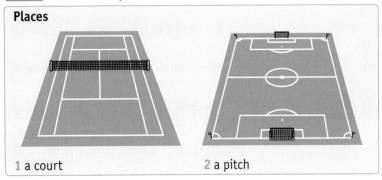

Places

1 a court   2 a pitch

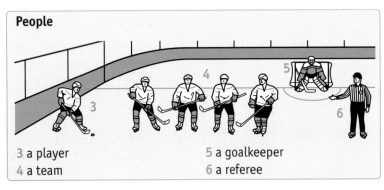

People

3 a player   5 a goalkeeper
4 a team   6 a referee

Equipment

7 a net   8 a goal   9 a bat   10 a racket
                                  11 a ball

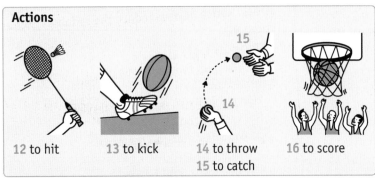

Actions

12 to hit   13 to kick   14 to throw   16 to score
                           15 to catch

Language note *win/lose; beat/lose to*

win/lose + a thing: We won/lost the match.
beat/lose to + a person or team: We beat/lost to Chelsea.

3a 65.2 Listen. Brendan is talking about his favourite sport – five-a-side football. Find this information.

1 How often does he play?
2 Where does he play?
3 Who does he play with?
4 What happened in the last match?

b Listen again. Find this information.

– two differences between five-a-side and normal football
– two things that are the same
– two reasons why Brendan likes the sport

4a Your life Answer the questions.

1 What sports do you like?
2 How often/When/Where do you play it?
3 Who do you play with?
4 How do you play the sport?
5 Have you (or your favourite team) won/lost any matches recently?

b Compare your answers with a partner.

English in the world
Giving scores

> MANCHESTER UNITED......2
> CHELSEA..................0
>
> 45:00 HALF-TIME

Manchester United: two. Chelsea: nil
OR
It was two-nil to Manchester United at half-time.

> BENFICA..................1
> JUVENTUS.................1
>
> 90:00 FULL TIME

Benfica: one. Juventus: one
OR
It's one-all./It's a (one-all) draw.

How do you give scores in your country? Give the scores from some recent matches.

Now I can …
talk about sport.

1 **66.1** **Read and listen.**

Jordan They're the couple **who moved into the flat below me** a few months ago.

Sarah Oh, are they the people **who have the parties**?

Jordan Yes, that's right. The party **they had last month** kept me awake all night.

Sarah You should complain about all the noise **they make**.

Jordan I did. And we reached an agreement **that keeps everyone happy**.

Sarah That's good. So did they agree to keep the noise down?

Jordan No, they agreed to invite me to all the parties **which they have**!

2 **Read the examples. Study the rules on page 113.**

> **Relative clauses**
>
> **Relative clauses show which thing or person we are talking about.**
> They're the couple **who (that)** moved into the flat below me.
> They agreed to invite me to all the parties **which (that)** they have.

3a **Make relative clauses to complete the text. Use these cues and *that*.**

- I won two years ago
- makes sports equipment
- I can't do at all
- I like best   *1*
- have very cold winters
- we want to see
- I beat in the final
- is very close to my flat

I like all kinds of sport, but tennis is the sport ¹*that I like best*. I'm a member of a club ²_____ , so I play several times a week. In this picture I'm holding a cup ³_____ . I was pleased to win it, because the player ⁴_____ was very good. One sport ⁵_____ is ice skating, but I like to watch it on TV. It isn't a big sport here in Spain. It's most popular in countries ⁶_____ .
I like to watch football, too. My husband works for a company ⁷_____ , so he often gets tickets to matches ⁸_____ .

b **66.2** **Listen and check.**

4 **Replace *that* with *who* or *which* in the text in exercise 3a.**

I like all kinds of sport, but tennis is the sport which I like best.

5a **Read the examples. Study the rules on page 113.**

> **Omitting the relative pronoun**
>
> **When the relative pronoun is the object of the relative clause, we can omit it.**
> You should complain about the noise
> (**that**)   they   make.
> **object**   **subject**   **verb**
>
> **We can't do this when the relative pronoun is the subject of the relative clause.**
> Are they the people
> **who**   have   the parties?
> **subject**   **verb**   **object**
> NOT ~~Are they the people have the parties?~~

b **Look at the completed text in exercise 3a. Remove the relative pronoun where possible.**

I like all kinds of sport, but tennis is the sport I like best. I'm a member of a club that's very close to my flat, …

6a **Look at these items. In which ones can you omit the relative pronoun?**

1 a place which you've always wanted to visit
2 someone who you'd like to meet
3 something that annoys you
4 the people who you spend most time with
5 something that's very important to you
6 something that you don't like doing
7 a person who always remembers your birthday
8 a sport that you like to watch on TV

b **Write a sentence for each of the things in exercise 6a.**

A place I've always wanted to visit is … , because …

c **Tell a partner about your ideas.**

> ✓ **Now I can …** *give more information about people and things.*

1 **67.1** Read and listen. Tick ✓ the things that the professor used in his talk.

a a glass of water

b stones ✓

c two cups of coffee

d a box

e golf balls

f sugar

g a glass jar

h sand

i ketchup

Priorities

One day a professor gave his philosophy class an unusual lesson. Without saying anything, he put a glass jar on the desk. Then he took some golf balls and put them in the jar. When he couldn't put any more balls in the jar, he asked, 'Is the jar full?' The students all said, 'Yes.'

The professor didn't say anything, but he took a small bag of stones from under the desk. He put the stones into the jar. The stones fell down between the golf balls. When he couldn't put in any more stones, he said, 'Is the jar full now?' The students all said, 'Yes.'

The professor then took another bag from under the desk. There was some sand in the bag. He carefully poured the sand into the jar. The sand filled all the spaces in the jar. When the sand came to the top, he asked the question again. The students all said that the jar was full.

The professor didn't say anything, but he took two cups of coffee from under the desk. He poured the coffee into the jar. The coffee came up to the top of the jar. The students laughed. This time they all agreed that the jar was full. You couldn't put anything more into it. The students all wondered, 'What is the professor trying to show us?'

2 What do you think the professor was trying to show the philosophy students?

3a Copy the table. Complete the 'Item' column. Write the five items from exercise 1 that the professor used in the correct order.

Item	Meaning	Examples
1		
2		
3		
4		
5		

b **67.2** Listen. What is the meaning of the five items? Complete the 'Meaning' column in the chart with these things.

a things that are really important
b time with your friends
c things that are quite important, but you can replace
d your life
e ordinary everyday things

c Listen again. Complete the 'Examples' column for items 2–4.

4a **Your life** What are your priorities? Add one more example to items 2–4 in the table.

b Compare your list with a partner.

Pronunciation
Voiced and voiceless consonants

1 **67.3** Listen and repeat.

	/g/	/k/		/b/	/p/
1	glass	class	5	buy	pie
2	bag	back	6	cub	cup

	/d/	/t/		/v/	/f/
3	do	two	7	veal	feel
4	sad	sat	8	leave	leaf

2 **67.4** Listen. Which word in each pair do you hear?

Now I can ...
understand a talk and discuss it.

1 Look back at Episodes 7 and 8. What happened?

2 **68.1** Read and listen to the story. Why doesn't Jordan tell Peter his news?

3 Complete the sentences with the correct subject.

1 _____ is going to be Sarah's bridesmaid.
2 _____ offers to alter the dress.
3 _____ says that she's very busy.
4 _____ is in a TV show.
5 _____ phones about some visitors.
6 _____ can't entertain the visitors.
7 _____ are coming to England.
8 _____ are going to meet them.

4a Complete the expressions.

Everyday expressions Talking about priorities and commitments

... if I _____ time.
There are so _____ things I need to do.
I'm already _____ something.
They'll have to do _____ me.
I promised _____ go.
I don't want to _____ her down.
It _____ wait.

b Use the expressions to complete the conversations.

1 **A** Will you be at the meeting on Wednesday afternoon?
  B Yes, if _____ .
2 **A** Do you want to talk about the conference today?
  B No, it _____ . There are _____ today.
3 **A** Are you going to watch your daughter's school play?
  B Yes, I _____ and I don't _____ .
4 **A** The team really needs you. Are you sure you can't make it?
  B Yes, I'm afraid they _____ . I'm _____ on Saturday.

5 Language check. Underline all the examples of relative clauses in the story.

6 Work in a group. Practise the story.

Sarah It looks beautiful, Lucy, but it's too long and it's too big here on the shoulders.
Lucy Yes, you can't have a bridesmaid who looks terrible.
Sarah There's a shop that alters clothes near my place. I'll take it tomorrow, if I have time.
Lucy There's no need. I can alter it myself.
Sarah Really?
Lucy Yes, I quite enjoy sewing. I always put on my headphones and listen to some music while I'm doing it. It's very relaxing.
Sarah Oh, thanks, Lucy. That would be great. There are so many things I need to do at the moment.

Peter So, how's the acting going?
Jordan Fine. I'm playing an Australian guy who works as a computer engineer.
Peter Well, you shouldn't find that too difficult.
Jordan No, but look, there's something I wanted to talk to you about . I ...
RING RING ...
Peter Excuse me, Jordan. That's my secretary. Hi. ... No, I'm already doing something that evening. ... I know, but they'll have to do without me, I'm afraid. ... OK. Bye.
Jordan Problems?
Peter Yes, there are some visitors who need entertaining, but I'm going to the airport to meet Sarah's parents.
Jordan Couldn't she go on her own?
Peter Yes, but I promised to go with her and I don't want to let her down. It's all about priorities.
Jordan Yes, I see.
Peter Anyway, what was this thing you wanted to talk to me about?

Oh, it's nothing important. It can wait.

Now I can ...
talk about priorities and commitments.

1 | 69.1 | **Read and listen.**

I've been doing the same job for seven years. It's a good job, but I'm **getting bored with** it. Actually, my boss is leaving soon, so I could **apply for** her job, but I'**m tired of** going to the same office every day and I'**m** not **afraid of** a new challenge.

Anyway, I was off work a few weeks ago because I **was suffering from** flu and I had a lot of time to **think about** it. When I was better, I started to **look at** job adverts in the newspapers, but all the jobs **were similar to** the one I've got now.

I **talked to** my wife and she said, 'What do you really want to do?' I said, 'Well, I'd really like to be a sculptor.' I've always **been interested in** art, and I'**m good at** painting. Last year I **took part in** a summer school on sculpture and I really enjoyed it.

I thought that my wife would **be worried about** money. We've got two young children and we've just moved house. But she **agreed with** me. 'If you **wait for** the perfect time, you'll never do it,' she said. So last week I decided to leave my job. This time next year life will certainly **be** very **different from** now.

2 | 69.2 | **Listen and repeat the expressions from the text.**

3 **Find two expressions in the text for each of these prepositions.**

| in   with   for   to   about   at   from   of |

in: be interested in …, take part in …

Language note **Preposition + noun/gerund**

After a preposition we use a noun or a gerund (-ing form).
We're interested in **art**.   (noun)
We're interested in **visiting** art galleries.   (gerund)
NOT ~~We're interested in visit art galleries.~~

4 | 69.3 | **Drill. Listen. Say the sentence. Use the past simple.**

1 be tired/travelling
   I was tired of travelling.

5a **Complete the sentences with the correct prepositions.**

1 I wanted to talk _to_ Umberto today, but he's suffering _____ a bad cold.
2 I'm not interested _____ clothes, so I soon get bored _____ shopping.
3 I'm tired _____ taking part _____ competitions and losing!
4 Our new flat is very different _____ our old flat. Actually, it's similar _____ yours.
5 I've looked _____ your email again, and I'm afraid I don't agree _____ you.
6 She's very good _____ her job, but she's thinking _____ leaving.
7 I'm worried _____ going on holiday. I'm afraid _____ flying.
8 Steve has applied _____ a new job. He's waiting _____ an interview.

b | 69.4 | **Listen and check.**

6a | Your life | **Choose eight of the bold expressions in exercise 1. Write sentences about your life.**

b **Discuss your sentences with a partner.**
   A *I'm taking part in a marathon this weekend.*
   B *Really? Where is it going to be?*

Pronunciation
Reduced stress

1 | 69.5 | **Listen. What happens to the prepositions?**
   1 I'm afraid **of** spiders.
   2 She suffers **from** hay fever.
   3 We're waiting **for** John.
   4 He's good **at** sport.
   5 Can I talk **to** you?

2 **Listen again and repeat.**

Now I can … *use some common expressions with prepositions.*

1 ⬛ 70.1 **Read and listen.**

Saved by a spider

Theo Minsk remembers the day that a spider saved his life. 'If it **hadn't rained**, I **would have gone** to the beach. However, it rained all day, so I tidied my garage instead. While I was doing it, a spider bit my neck. My wife was worried about me, because some spiders in Australia are very poisonous. So we went to the hospital. When the doctors examined me, they noticed a lump on my neck. But it wasn't the spider's bite. Tests showed that I was suffering from cancer.' Today, after several months of treatment, the cancer has gone. 'Life can be strange,' says Theo. 'My wife **wouldn't have taken** me to the hospital if the spider **hadn't bitten me**. Then we probably wouldn't have found the lump in time. If I **had left** it for a few more months, it **would have been** too late. That spider saved my life!'

2 **Read the examples. Study the rules on page 114.**

Third conditional

We use the third conditional to imagine past events, and their results, happening differently.

Real event
It rained, so I didn't go to the beach.
Imagined event
If it **hadn't rained**, I **would have gone** to the beach.

Real event
My wife took me to the hospital because the spider bit me.
Imagined event
My wife **wouldn't have taken** me to the hospital if the spider **hadn't bitten** me.

3a **Complete the third conditional sentences. Use** *had/hadn't* **and** *would have/wouldn't have.*

1 Susan ate too much, so she felt sick.
   If she _hadn't_ eaten too much, she _wouldn't have_ felt sick.
2 Marco missed his appointment, because he didn't get up on time.
   He _wouldn't have_ missed his appointment if he _had_ got up on time.
3 I went to a party and I met my boyfriend.
   If I _____ gone to the party, I _____ met my boyfriend.
4 I complained about the taxi, because it arrived late.
   I _____ complained about the taxi if it _____ arrived late.
5 It wasn't very warm, so we didn't go out.
   If it _____ been warm, we _____ gone out.
6 You didn't work hard, so you didn't pass your exams.
   If you _____ worked hard, you _____ passed your exams.

b ⬛ 70.2 **Listen, check, and repeat.**

4 **Look at the series of events in Theo's story. Make conditional sentences.**

1 The weather wasn't nice.
2 He didn't go to the beach.
3 He tidied the garage.
4 A spider bit him.
5 His wife took him to the hospital.
6 The doctors found a lump on his neck.
7 They started cancer treatment.
8 He didn't die from the disease.

1 *If the weather had been nice, he would have gone to the beach.*
2 *If he had gone to the beach, he wouldn't have tidied the garage.*

5a **Your life** **Think of a turning point in your life, when something changed. Make a flow chart of the events.**

1 *I had toothache.*
2 *I went to the dentist's.*
3 *I read a magazine there.*
4 *I saw an advert for a job.*
   ...

b **Change the events into third conditionals.**

1 *If I hadn't had toothache, I wouldn't have gone to the dentist's.*
2 *If I hadn't gone to the dentist's, I wouldn't have read ...*

 Now I can ... *talk about the results of events that didn't actually happen.*

1 Read the texts. Which person ... ?

a didn't like school _____   b has got three children _____   c had a software company _____

No regrets

Erica, 34, computer programmer	Leroy, 42, production manager with an engineering company	Marianne, 37, housewife and part-time librarian

I was tired of working for somebody else. I wanted to have my own business. Eight years ago I decided to start my own computer software company. I needed a lot of money for it, so I sold my flat and I borrowed money from my friends, too. __ __

I've got a good job now, but I did it the hard way. I left school when I was 17. I was bored with school and I wanted to earn some money. I had a lot of jobs, but they were all boring and low-paid. __ __

I got married to a guy I met at university. I was 21 and we were in love. We had our first child a year later and we've got three children now.

__ __

2a Complete the texts above with these paragraphs. Make sure they are in the correct order.

a But I don't regret it. If I hadn't got married then, I wouldn't have had my three lovely children. I love my family, so I wouldn't change anything really.

b Sometimes I wish that I'd done more and seen more of life before I got married. I feel jealous when friends talk about the things they did in their twenties. While they were travelling and going to parties, I was looking after babies.

c I wish I had worked harder at school now. If I hadn't been so lazy then, things would have been easier. But I don't really regret it. I really enjoy my job and I think that I'm a better person because I had to fight for it.

d Do I regret it? Yes and no. I wish I hadn't borrowed money from my friends. But if I hadn't done it, I would have regretted it all my life. Things don't always work out, but if you don't try, you'll never know.

e Unfortunately, the business wasn't successful and after five years I was bankrupt. I lost everything, including my friends' money.

f I needed qualifications to get a good job, so I went to evening classes and then I applied for a place at university. It was difficult. When I wasn't studying, I was working.

b **71.1** Listen and check.

3 Answer the questions.

1 How did Erica get the money for her business?
2 How long did the business survive?
3 Why couldn't Leroy get a good job when he left school?
4 How did he pay for his education?
5 How old was Marianne when she got married?
6 Why does she feel jealous of her friends?

> **Language note Expressing regret**
>
> **I wish I had worked** harder at school.
> = I didn't work hard at school and I regret it.
> **She wishes she hadn't borrowed** money.
> = She borrowed money and she regrets it.

4 Find this information for each person.

1 What did he/she do?
2 What was the result?
3 What does he/she wish he/she had(n't) done?
4 How does he/she feel about it now?

5a Complete the text about Leroy. Use your answers to the questions in exercise 4.

Leroy ¹_____ . As a result, he ²_____ .
He wishes he ³_____ . However, he doesn't
really regret it, because ⁴_____ .

b **Write a similar text about Erica or Marianne.**

6a Your life What do you wish about your past life?

I wish I had learnt French at school.

b **Compare your ideas with a partner.**

> ✓ Now I can ...
> *talk about regrets.*

1 `72.1` **Read and listen. Which people ... ?**
– are having a party _____
– can't come to the party _____
– are going to the party _____

Our new home

We're having a housewarming party on Friday 29 March (8 for 8.30). We'd be very pleased if you could join us.

Look forward to seeing you.

Bruce and Tina

RSVP: 0117 496 0532/bructin45@wizz.com

47 Walden Road, Bristol, BS6 4DK

To: bructin45@wizz.com

Subject: Party invitation

Dear Tina and Bruce

Thank you very much for your invitation. We'd love to come.

Hope all's going well with your new home. Looking forward to seeing you on the 29th.

All the best,

Ari and Ingrid

---

20 Regal Street

Bath

28 February

Dear Bruce and Tina

Thank you very much for the invitation to your housewarming. Unfortunately, I'm afraid we're going to be on holiday that week.

We hope the party goes well. Sorry we won't be able to make it.

Best wishes,

Petra and Liam

2 **Answer the questions.**
1 Where do Bruce and Tina live?
2 Why are they having a party?
3 What date is it going to be?
4 What time will it start?
5 What are Petra and Liam doing that week?

3a **Complete the expressions.**

Everyday expressions **Invitations**
Inviting
We're _____ a party on Friday 29 March.
We'd be very _____ if you could join us.
Look(ing) forward to _____ you.
Responding
Thank you very much for the _____ to your party.
We'd _____ to come.
Sorry/I'm afraid we won't be _____ to make it.

b **Check your answers in the invitation and replies in exercise 1.**

4 `72.2` **Listen to the messages on Bruce and Tina's voicemail. Complete the table.**

	Name	Can come?	Details
1	Sullivan		
2	Viv and Frank		
3	Natasha		
4	Neil and Erin		

5a Writing **Write an invitation to a party.**

b **Give your invitation to a partner. He/She writes a response.**

English in the world
Invitations

These are some expressions you might see on an invitation.

RSVP	Please reply.
7 for 7.30	Please arrive between 7 and 7.30 in the evening.
Bring a bottle.	Please bring a bottle of wine with you.
Black tie	Formal dress. Men should wear a dinner suit and women a long dress.

Compare this to your country.

Now I can ...
write and respond to invitations.

1a | 73.1 | **Read and listen.**

When you arrive at the airport, make sure you go to the correct **terminal**. A lot of airports have more than one. First, you **check in** at the check-in desk. When you've got your **boarding card**, you go through **passport control** (for international flights). Then you have to **go through security**, where they **check** your bags and coats. After that you wait in **the departure lounge**. When your flight is called, you go to **the departure gate** and **board the plane**.

On the plane, you find your seat, put your **hand luggage** in **an overhead locker**, then sit down and **fasten your seatbelt**. When all **the passengers** are on the plane and everything is ready, **the plane takes off**. During the flight, **the flight attendants** serve drinks and meals. **The pilot** usually gives some information about the flight and the weather, too. Before **the plane lands**, **the cabin crew** check all the passengers' seatbelts again.

b | 73.2 | **Listen and repeat the bold words and expressions.**

2a **What other words connected with air travel do you know?**
a ticket, to fly, …

b **Look at the pictures. What people and things can you name?**

> **Language note** *control* and *check*
>
> **Noun** You have to go through passport **control**.
> **Verb** Someone **checks** your passport.
> NOT ~~Someone controls your passport.~~

3 **Find the bold words or expressions in exercise 1 to match these definitions.**
1 the flight attendants
2 to get on the plane
3 you put your hand luggage here
4 this person flies the plane
5 the plane leaves the airport
6 they check your passports here
7 the place where you wait before flying
8 the people travelling on the plane
9 the plane arrives
10 you wear this for take off and landing

4a | 73.3 | **Listen to Mark's travel story. Why was he worried in Milan? Why did the story have a happy ending?**

b **Listen again and find this information.**
1 How long was the flight to Brussels delayed?
2 What did he do when he got to Brussels?
3 When did he remember his coat?
4 What gate did he need for the flight to Manchester?
5 How did he get to the plane?

5a | Your life | **Answer the questions.**
1 How often do you travel by air?
2 Do you enjoy flying? Why? Why not?
3 Has anything interesting happened to you while flying?

b **Compare your answers with a partner.**

> **English in the world**
> Signs at an airport
> ....
> **What are these signs in your language?**
>
> 1 Check-in
> 2 Connecting flights
> 3 Arrivals
> 4 Customs
> 5 Baggage reclaim
> 6 Departures

 Now I can …
talk about air travel.

1 `74.1` **Read and listen.**

1 Peter has been away on a business trip.

Lucy Do you know **if Peter's plane has landed yet**?

Sarah Yes, it has. He texted me about half an hour ago.

Lucy Well, would you like to go for a meal together this evening?

Sarah Good idea. I wonder **what time Peter will be back**. I'll phone and see **where he is**.

Peter Hi, Sarah. Yes, I'm in the car park at the moment.

Sarah Great. Lucy wants to know **whether we'd like to go for a meal this evening**.

Peter Yes, sure, but I don't know **what time I'll be back**.

Sarah Why? What's the problem?

Peter I can't remember **where I parked my car**!

2 **Read the examples. Study the rules on page 114.**

Indirect questions	
We use indirect questions when we talk <u>about</u> a question.	
Direct	What time **will Peter** be back?
Indirect	I wonder what time **Peter will** be back.
	NOT ~~I wonder what time will Peter be back?~~
Direct	Where **did I park** the car?
Indirect	I can't remember where **I parked** the car.
	NOT ~~I can't remember where did I park the car?~~

3a **Do you know the answers? Ask and answer with a partner.**

A *Do you know what the capital of Vietnam is?*

B *No, I don't./I can't remember./Yes, I do. It's …*

1 What's the capital of Vietnam?
2 What do people usually call a Boeing 747 aeroplane?
3 Where is Lake Titicaca?
4 When did Princess Diana die?
5 Who was the first Roman emperor?
6 Where does the French president live?
7 What did Lazlo Biro invent?

b **Say what your partner knows.**

… doesn't know/can't remember/knows what the capital of Vietnam is.

4 **Read the examples. Study the rules on page 114.**

Indirect questions: *yes/no* questions
With *yes/no* questions we use *if* or *whether*.
Has Peter's plane landed yet?
I'd like to know **if/whether** Peter's plane has landed yet.

5 `74.2` **Drill. Listen. Give the indirect question. Use *I wonder if*.**

1 Have they arrived?
I wonder if they've arrived.

6a `Your life` **Choose someone in your class. Ask a partner what he/she knows about the person. Use these cues.**

1 A *Do you know where Carlos lives?*
B *No, I don't, but I think he lives in the city centre.*

2 A *Do you know whether he's married?*
B *Yes, he is.*

1	where/live	4	good at sport
2	married	5	where/born
3	what/do	6	can/play

b **Tell the person what your partner knows about him/her.**

1 She doesn't know where you live, but she thinks it's in the city centre.

2 She knows that you're married.

 Now I can …
use indirect questions.

1a 75.1 **Listen to the message on Rosa's voicemail. Choose the correct words.**

1 The caller's name is *Sandy/Henry*.
2 The flight is to *Athens/Chicago*.
3 He says that something has *come up/changed*.
4 He can't leave now till *Friday/Thursday*.

b Rosa's secretary leaves her a note about the telephone call. Complete the note. Use your answers to exercise 1a.

> ## Rosa
> ¹_____ rang just before 2 p.m. He wants to know whether you've booked the flight to ²_____ , because something has ³_____ , and he can't leave now till ⁴_____ . Please give him a call.

2a 75.2 **Listen to some more messages in Rosa's voicemail. Match the callers with the questions they ask.**

~~Serena~~ Wallace Yasmin Jack Millie Bob

Name	Question	Reason for asking
	a What time does the meeting start?	
	b Will you be in Cairo on Friday evening?	
	c Where did you stay in Rome?	
Serena	d Can you play tennis on Saturday morning?	*can't make the afternoon*
	e Have you got the phone number of the car insurance company?	
	f When are the visitors arriving?	

b Listen again. What reasons do the people give for their questions? Complete the table.

Language note **Passing on messages**

We use indirect questions to pass on a question in a message.
He wants to know **where the meeting is**.
She would like to know **if you've booked the flight**.
Mike needs to know **how long you're going to stay**.

3 Writing Use the information in the table in exercise 2. Write notes to give Rosa the messages. Follow this pattern.

... phoned. He/She wants to know if/when/what time ... , because he/she ...

4a Write a question about another student.

Where does Kristof work?

b Give your question to a partner. Your partner relays the message to the class.

Anya would like to know where Kristof works.

Pronunciation
Emphatic stress
....

1 75.3 **Listen. Underline the word in each question that is stressed.**

1 Can you play on Saturday morning?
  a Not Saturday afternoon. ✓
  b Not Sunday morning.
2 Are we meeting at half past two?
  a Not half past three.
  b Not quarter past two.
3 I'm in the supermarket car park.
  a Not by the checkout.
  b Not the cinema car park.
4 Is his name Klaus Jensen?
  a Not Klaus Hansen.
  b Not Hans Jensen.
5 Is your office number sixty-four?
  a Not sixty-five.
  b Not seventy-four.

2 Choose the correct meaning of the stress – a or b.

3 Listen again and repeat.

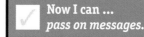
Now I can ...
pass on messages.

1 Look back at Episodes 8 and 9. What happened?

2 76.1 Read and listen to the story.

3 Match the sentence halves.

1 Jordan wants to ___
2 Felton says that ___
3 Jordan goes to the café ___
4 Sarah doesn't know ___
5 Lucy isn't ___
6 Jordan decides to go ___
7 Jordan thinks that ___

a where Lucy is.
b he understands the situation.
c to look for Lucy.
d answering her phone.
e change the schedule.
f Lucy's had an accident.
g to Lucy's house.

4a Complete the expressions.

> **Everyday expressions**
> **Discussing a problem**
>
> Can I _____ a word?
> What's _____ your mind?
> Thanks. I really appreciate _____ .
> I _____ the situation.
> (That's) _____ enough.

b Use the expressions to complete the conversation.

A Hello. Come in. How are you?
B Fine, thanks. Look. ¹_____ ?
A Sure. Sit down. ²_____ ?
B I can't make the meeting on Wednesday. It's my son's graduation.
A ³_____ . We can change the meeting.
B ⁴_____ .
A That's OK. ⁵_____ . You can't miss an important occasion like that.

c Practise the conversation with a partner.

5 Language check. <u>Underline</u> all the examples of indirect questions in the story.

6 Work in a group. Practise the story.

Jordan Hi, Felton. Can I have a word?
Felton Sure. What's on your mind?
Jordan I wonder whether we can change the schedule for these two weekends.
Felton Change the schedule? I hope you realize that won't be very easy.
Jordan Yes, and I'm very sorry, but I have other commitments which are really important to me.
Felton OK. Well, tell me what the problem is and I'll see what I can do.
Later ...
Jordan Thanks, Felton. I really appreciate it.
Felton It's OK. I understand the situation, but I wish you'd told me sooner.
Jordan That's fair enough. I'll know next time. Thanks again.

2 Later ...

Jordan Hi, Sarah. Have you got any idea where Lucy is?
Sarah She was here earlier, but I don't know where she's gone now.
Jordan Do you know whether she's asked anyone else to go to Paris with her?
Sarah I don't think so. She was very upset about it, Jordan.
Jordan Yes, I know, but I've sorted it all out now, so I need to talk to her.
Sarah She's probably gone home.
Jordan Maybe, but she isn't answering her phone or her mobile. I'll go round and see if she's there.

I'm outside Lucy's house and I think she's had an accident!

> ✓ Now I can ...
> *discuss a problem.*

1 `77.1` **Read and listen.**

My name's Nina and I work in an office. I get my **salary** monthly. It's **paid into** my bank account directly by my **employer**. I **spend** most of my salary on **essentials** like rent, food, clothes, and transport. There isn't a lot left after that for **luxuries**, and I try to save something every month.

I keep my **savings** in a different account, where I **earn interest** on my money. **I'm saving up** for a car at the moment. It's taking a long time, so I might apply for **a loan**, but **the interest rate** is quite high and **I can't afford it** at the moment.

I don't go to the bank very often. I **pay bills** by **direct debit**, so the bank pays them automatically. I use my card to **withdraw** money at **a cash machine**. I usually **check my account balance** and **transfer** money from one account to the other online. When I buy things or eat in restaurants I normally pay by credit card.

2 **Find the bold words or expressions in exercise 1 to match these definitions.**

1 to take out money from the bank
2 money that you borrow from the bank
3 you get cash from this
4 money that you save
5 a way of paying bills automatically
6 I haven't got enough money for it
7 to move money from one place to another
8 money that the bank pays to you
9 the money that you earn in your job

> **Language note** *pay*
>
> **pay** a bill/interest/the rent/the waiter
> **pay for** a meal/some clothes
> **pay** money **into** a bank account
> **pay off** a loan
> **pay by** credit card/**in** cash

3 **Complete the sentences with the correct prepositions.**

> in   on (x 2)   for   from   by   ~~at~~   into

1 You can use your card _at_ any cash machine.
2 I don't spend a lot of money _____ clothes.
3 You have to pay interest _____ a loan.
4 My employer pays my salary _____ my account.
5 I don't often withdraw money _____ my account.
6 I keep my savings _____ an Internet account.
7 In restaurants I usually pay _____ credit card.
8 Are you saving up _____ your holidays?

4 `77.2` **Listen. Boris is talking about his finances. Answer the questions.**

1 What does he spend most of his money on? Why?
2 Why doesn't he pay any rent?
3 Where does he keep his money? Why?
4 What things can he do with his Internet account?
5 What can't he do with it?
6 How does he withdraw cash from his account?
7 How does he receive his salary?

5a `Your life` **Answer the questions.**

1 What things are paid directly into your bank account?
2 What do you spend most money on?
3 How do you usually ... ?
   – pay bills
   – withdraw money
   – check your account balance
   – pay for things in shops and restaurants
4 Are you saving up for anything at the moment?

b **Compare your answers with a partner.**

> **English in the world**
> Taxes
> ·····
> The main taxes in most countries are:
> **Income tax:** Employers **deduct** this from the money you earn. Rates vary a lot – from, for example, 15% in Hong Kong to 51% in Norway.
> **Sales tax** or **VAT** (Value Added Tax): You pay this on things you buy. In most countries this is 10% – 25%.
> **Local tax** (In Britain this is called **Council tax**): You pay this to the local government for services like streetlights and rubbish collection.
> In the United Arab Emirates (the UAE) there is no income tax or sales tax!
>
> **What taxes do you pay in your country?**

> ✓ **Now I can ...**
> *talk about personal finance.*

1 78.1 **Read and listen.**

Friday afternoon …

Cindy Ryan, we need some olive oil.

Ryan OK. I'm going out so I'll get some.

Two hours later …

Cindy Well, where is it?

Ryan Oh, I haven't bought the oil. I saw an old friend and I completely forgot about it.

Later that day …

Sarah Have you and Ryan had an argument?

Cindy Yes, we have. This afternoon **I said that we needed** some olive oil. Ryan **said that he was going out**, so **he would get** some. Well, when he came back two hours later, he **said he hadn't bought** the oil!

Sarah Why not?

Cindy He **said he had seen** an old friend and **he had completely forgotten** about it. He was smiling, too!

Sarah Well, they probably had a lot to talk about.

Cindy I'm sure they did, because it wasn't just *any* old friend. It was an old girlfriend!

Sarah Oh, I see.

2 **Read the examples. Study the rules on page 114.**

Reported speech
We use reported speech to say what somebody said.
In reported speech:
1 pronouns normally change to the third person.
2 tenses normally move into the past.

Direct	**I'm going out** so **I'll get** some.
Reported	Ryan **said (that) he was going out** so **he would get** some.
Direct	**I saw** an old friend.
Reported	He **said (that) he had seen** an old friend.

3 **Complete the reported speech with the correct pronouns and possessive adjectives.**

1 Lucy: 'I'm going to see my boss.'
Lucy said that <u>she</u> was going to see <u>her</u> boss.

2 Jordan: 'I'm really enjoying my new job.'
Jordan said that _____ was really enjoying _____ new job.

3 Peter and Sarah: 'We're saving up for our wedding.'
Peter and Sarah said that _____ were saving up for _____ wedding.

4 Cindy: 'I've had an argument with my husband.'
Cindy said that _____ had had an argument with _____ husband.

4a **Complete Ryan's reports of what his ex-girlfriend said.**

1 She said that she had just moved to London.

1 I've just moved to London.

2 I was in France with my husband for ten years.

3 We're divorced now.

4 I came back so that I can be near my parents.

5 They're getting very old.

6 You still look the same.

7 I'm trying to find a flat.

8 I want to buy a house, but I can't afford it.

9 I've seen The Coffee Shop.

10 I'll call in to see you at the café sometime.

b 78.2 **Listen and check.**

5 78.3 **Drill. Listen. Peter phoned his office. Report what he said.**

1 I feel ill.
He said he felt ill.

6 Your life **Think about some conversations that you had yesterday. Tell a partner what people said to you.**

> I've decided to look for a new job.

My son said that he had decided to look for a new job.

Now I can …
report what people said.

1a `79.1` **Read and listen. Match the names with the descriptions.**

1 Fred ___   a   an identity thief
2 Angela ___   b   an expert on identity theft
3 Martin ___   c   a victim of identity theft

b What did Fred lose?

Who's using your identity?

One afternoon last year Fred Payne had a phone call. He tells us what happened: 'It was a young woman. She said her name was Angela, I think, and that she was from my bank. She told me that they'd had a problem with their computers, so they were checking all their customers' accounts. She was so friendly and polite, and she already knew my full name and address, the name of my bank, and even my account number. She said that she just needed to check my date of birth, my mother's maiden name, and my PIN. She asked for my Internet password, too, but I told her that I didn't use the Internet. Well, I gave her the information and she said that I'd been very helpful.'

Two weeks later, however, Fred went to his bank. 'I told the cashier that I wanted to transfer some money, but she said that there wasn't enough money in my account. She said that almost everything – £2,000 – had been withdrawn ten days before. Then, of course, I remembered the phone call. The cashier said that the bank never phoned or emailed people for information like that. I couldn't believe that I had been so stupid.'

Fred had been the victim of identity theft – a crime that costs billions of dollars worldwide every year. Martin Smart is an expert on this modern crime: 'People should be very careful with any information about themselves. Criminals can use it to withdraw money from accounts, buy things on the Internet, and even open new accounts in someone else's name. Sometimes they steal documents, like passports and driving licences. But we also make things very easy for them. For example, Fred told me that he didn't destroy old bank statements, credit card receipts, gas, telephone and electricity bills, etc., but just threw them in the rubbish bin. That's probably how the thieves got his name, address, and account number. People also dump old computers with all their personal and financial information still on them, because they don't delete the data first. Your identity is very important. Protect it!'

2a Which of these things ... ?
– did the caller already know
– did the caller ask for
– did Fred give her

> his PIN   the name of his bank
> his date of birth   his Internet password
> his account number   his full name
> his mother's maiden name   his address

b How do criminals get personal information? How do we make things easy for them?

> **Language note** *say* and *tell*
>
> *say* (*that*) + reported speech
> She **said** her name was Angela.
> NOT ~~She said me her name was Angela.~~
>
> *tell* + person + (*that*) + reported speech
> She **told me** that they'd had a problem.
> NOT ~~She told that they'd had a problem.~~
> NOT ~~She told to me that ...~~

3a Who said these things?

1 The cashier said that there wasn't enough money in Fred's account.

1 There isn't enough money in your account.
2 I want to transfer some money, please.
3 We're checking our customers' accounts.
4 The bank never phones or emails people for information like that.
5 I don't destroy old bank statements.
6 I just need to check your date of birth.
7 I don't use the Internet.
8 You've been very helpful.

b Who did they tell?

1 The cashier told Fred that there wasn't enough money in his account.

4a Writing How can people protect their identity? Discuss ideas with a partner.

b Write five or six pieces of advice for people. Use these expressions.

Don't throw ...
Always check ...
Make sure that you destroy ...
Never give ...
You should delete ...

> **Now I can ...** *report a problem and give advice to prevent it.*

1a `80.1` **Read and listen. What two things does the man want to do? What must he do for one of the things?**

Announcement	*Cashier number three, please.*
Cashier	Good morning. What can I do for you today?
Customer	Hello. Could I pay this cheque into my account, please?
Cashier	Certainly. Have you got the card for your account?
Customer	Yes, here you are.
Cashier	Thank you. ... OK. That's paid in now. Here's your receipt. Is there anything else I can help you with?
Customer	Yes, I'd like to open a savings account, please.
Cashier	You'll need to speak to one of our customer service advisers about that.
Customer	Oh, I see.
Cashier	If you take a seat over there, somebody will be with you shortly.
Customer	Thank you.

b **Practise the conversation with a partner.**

2a **Complete the expressions.**

Everyday expressions At the bank
Cashier _____ three, please.
What can I _____ for you today?
_____ I pay this cheque _____ my account, please?
Is there _____ else I can help you _____?
I'd _____ to open a savings _____ , please.
You'll _____ to speak to one of our advisers _____ that.
If you _____ a seat over there ...
Somebody will be _____ you shortly.

b **Check your answers in the conversation.**

3a `80.2` **Listen. Which of these things do the people want to do? Write the dialogue number. (Not all of the things are mentioned.)**

___ transfer some money abroad
___ know the interest rate
___ pay a cheque in
_1_ withdraw some cash
___ set up a direct debit
___ open a new account
___ change some money into US dollars
___ apply for a loan

b **Listen again. How does the cashier respond? Match the responses with the requests in exercise 3a.**

a ___ Could you sign the form, please?
b ___ It's 2.5%.
c _1_ How much would you like?
d ___ You'll need to speak to an adviser.
e ___ Have you got the details of your account?

4 **Work with a partner. Make the requests and responses from exercise 3.**

A *I'd like to withdraw some cash, please.*
B *Certainly. How much would you like?*

5 **Make conversations with a partner. One person is a customer and one is a cashier. Choose two activities from exercise 3a. Use the conversation in exercise 1 as a model.**

Pronunciation
Sentence rhythm

1 `80.3` **Listen. Underline the syllables with the stress. There are three in each sentence.**

I'd <u>like</u> to ap<u>ply</u> for a <u>loan</u>.
I'd like to withdraw some money.
I'd like to open an account.
I'd like to speak to an adviser.
I'd like to pay this bill.

2 **Listen again and repeat. Keep the rhythm.**

Now I can ...
conduct activities at the bank.

1 **Look back at Episodes 8, 9, and 10. What happened?**

2 `81.1` **Read and listen to the story.**

3a **What do you think has happened to Lucy?**

b `81.2` **Listen and check your ideas.**

Sarah Jordan. What's happened?
Jordan I think Lucy's had an accident.
Peter How do you know?
Jordan Well, I knocked at the door, but there was no reply. So I looked through the letterbox and I saw her lying on the floor. Look.

Sarah Oh, yes. That's her bridesmaid's dress. She was probably trying it on.
Jordan Do you think she's fallen downstairs?
Sarah Maybe. The dress was a bit too long. Perhaps she tripped on it. Oh, I hope she's all right.
Jordan Her mobile's on the floor there, too. That must be why she isn't answering it.
Peter And she's closed the curtains, so we can't see anything through the window.

Sarah Have you phoned the emergency services?
Jordan Yes, I have.
Peter But the traffic's terrible this evening. They might take ages to get here.
Jordan Well, in that case there's only one thing we can do. We'll have to break down the front door.
Sarah You can't do that!
Peter We haven't got any choice. Come on, Jordan! One, two, three!

81

STUDY AND REFERENCE SECTION
Contents

REVIEW AND WORDLISTS

GRAMMAR REFERENCE

AUDIO SCRIPTS

IRREGULAR VERB LIST

PRONUNCIATION CHART

Review 1–8

Vocabulary

1 Complete the introduction.

daughter	engineer	football	married	~~name~~
nurse	swimming	~~thirty~~	~~town~~	watching

Hi. My [1] _name_ 's Osman. I'm [2] _thirty_ years old and
I live in the [3] _town_ of Alanya in the south of Turkey.
I'm an [4] _engineer_ and I work for a car company.
I'm [5] _married_. My wife, Naila, is a [6] _nurse_. We've got
one [7] _daughter_ Miriam. In my free time I play [8] _football_
and I go [9] _swimming_ I like [10] _watching_ old films, too.

2 Match the sentence halves.

1 It got cold so _d_   a from Jing today.
2 I got an email _a_   b getting better now.
3 They got lost because   c got divorced last year.
4 I was ill, but I'm   d I put my coat on.
5 We're getting the train   e to London tomorrow.
6 Tim's single now. He   f they didn't take a map.

Grammar

3 Complete the sentences. Use the correct form of the words in brackets.

1 I _don't know_ (not / know) where my glasses are.
2 The children _doing_ (do) their homework now.
3 We _re going_ (go) home now. See you tomorrow.
4 Harry _doesn't_ (not / like) tennis.
5 It _isn't raining_ (not / rain) at the moment.
6 I usually _wear_ (wear) jeans at the weekend.

4 Put the words in the correct order to make questions.

1 Was the party good?

1 good   the   Was   party   ?
2 sports   you   Were   the   at   yesterday   centre ?
3 they   Did   to   the   cinema   go   ?
4 did   What   on   do   Saturday   Gino   ?
5 jazz   When   the   was   concert   ?

5a Make sentences with the past simple. Use the cues.

1 I was at work yesterday.

1 I / be / at work yesterday.
2 Phil and Julie / see / a play on Saturday.
3 Thanh / go / to a concert last week.
4 You / be / at home last night.
5 We / have / an English test on Monday.

b Make the sentences negative.

1 I wasn't at work yesterday.

Skills

6 Read the text. Are the statements true (T) or false (F)?

Last Thursday, Mark's train was late, and he missed an important meeting. He was angry, and he shouted at his secretary. She went home because she was upset, so Mark had to do all of her work. He made a cup of coffee, and then his phone started to ring. Because his secretary wasn't there, Mark had to answer the phone. He forgot about the coffee and knocked it over his computer. He had to get a new computer and work until midnight to finish his report. The next day he had to apologize to his secretary, too!

1 Mark missed his train. _F_
2 He shouted at his secretary.
3 His secretary left because she was angry.
4 Mark had to do less work.
5 Mark spilt coffee on his computer.
6 He had to clean the computer.
7 Mark had to work late.
8 He had to say 'Sorry' to his secretary.

English for Everyday Life

7 Put the sentences in the correct order to make a conversation.

a _7_ Well, have a good time.
b _3_ How are you getting to Madrid?
c _1_ Hi, Tanya. Are you coming to the party on Friday?
d _4_ I'm using John's car.
e _6_ He's working on Saturday.
f _2_ Sorry, I can't. I'm visiting my family in Madrid.
g _5_ Why isn't John going with you?

8 Choose the correct word.

1 Who do these books belong *to* / *for*?
2 *Whose* / *Who's* bike is this?
3 Is this book *yours* / *your*?
4 This bag is *Toms* / *Tom's*.
5 That cat *belong* / *belongs* to our neighbours.
6 *Our* / *Ours* new camera takes great photos.
7 I think *this* / *these* keys belong to you.
8 The CDs *don't belong* / *doesn't belong* to me.
9 That pen is *my* / *mine*.
10 *Their* / *Theirs* flat is in the town centre.

1
location (n)	/ləʊˈkeɪʃn/
north-west (n)	/ˌnɔːθˈwest/
south (n)	/saʊθ/
accountant (n)	/əˈkaʊntənt/
activity (n)	/ækˈtɪvəti/
city (n)	/ˈsɪti/
country (n)	/ˈkʌntri/
employer (n)	/ɪmˈplɔɪə(r)/
free time (n)	/ˌfriː ˈtaɪm/
interest (n)	/ˈɪntrəst/
marital status (n)	/ˈmærɪtl ˌsteɪtəs/
lawyer (n)	/ˈlɔːjə(r)/
radiologist (n)	/ˌreɪdiˈɒlədʒɪst/
relationship (n)	/rɪˈleɪʃnʃɪp/
greeting (n)	/ˈɡriːtɪŋ/
kiss (v)	/kɪs/
shake hands (v)	/ˌʃeɪk ˈhænz/

2
bridge (n)	/brɪdʒ/
build (v)	/bɪld/
certainly (adv)	/ˈsɜːtnli/
cross (v)	/krɒs/
leadership (n)	/ˈliːdəʃɪp/
manager (n)	/ˈmænɪdʒə(r)/
put up (v)	/ˌpʊt ˈʌp/
tent (n)	/tent/

3
book tickets (v)	/ˈbʊk ˈtɪkɪts/
download music (v)	/ˌdaʊnˈləʊd ˈmjuːzɪk/
edit photographs (v)	/ˌedɪt ˈfəʊtəɡrɑːfs/
print photographs (v)	/prɪnt ˈfəʊtəɡrɑːfs/
shop online (v)	/ʃɒp ˌɒnˈlaɪn/
send emails (v)	/ˈsend ˈiːmeɪlz/
visit a chatroom (v)	/ˌvɪzɪt ə ˈtʃætruːm/
desktop (n)	/ˈdesktɒp/
laptop (n)	/ˈlæptɒp/
leisure (n)	/ˈleʒə(r)/
occupation (n)	/ˌɒkjuˈpeɪʃn/
study (n)	/ˈstʌdi/
survey (n)	/ˈsɜːveɪ/

4
advert (n)	/ˈædvɜːt/
advertising agency (n)	/ˈædvətaɪzɪŋ ˌeɪdʒənsi/
coast (n)	/kəʊst/
definitely (adv)	/ˈdefɪnətli/
emergency call (n)	/iˈmɜːdʒənsi kɔːl/
engineer (n)	/ˌendʒɪˈnɪə(r)/
film (v)	/fɪlm/
fix (v)	/fɪks/
Internet café (n)	/ˌɪntənet ˈkæfeɪ/
postgraduate (adj)	/ˌpəʊstˈɡrædʒuət/
own (v)	/əʊn/
really (adv)	/ˈriːəli/
arrangement (n)	/əˈreɪndʒmənt/

5
get cold (v)	/ˌɡet ˈkəʊld/
get dark (v)	/ˌɡet ˈdɑːk/
get hot (v)	/ˌɡet ˈhɒt/
get hungry (v)	/ˌɡet ˈhʌŋɡri/
get light (v)	/ˌɡet ˈlaɪt/
get ready (v)	/ˌɡet ˈredi/
get a letter (v)	/ˌɡet ə ˈletə(r)/
get a car (v)	/ˌɡet ə ˈkɑː(r)/
get home (v)	/ˌɡet ˈhəʊm/
get to work (v)	/ˌɡet tə ˈwɜːk/
get the bus (v)	/ˌɡet ðə ˈbʌs/
get changed (v)	/ˌɡet ˈtʃeɪndʒd/
get divorced (v)	/ˌɡet dɪˈvɔːst/
get dressed (v)	/ˌɡet ˈdrest/
get lost (v)	/ˌɡet ˈlɒst/
get undressed (v)	/ˌɡet ʌnˈdrest/
get better (v)	/ˌɡet ˈbetə(r)/
get bigger (v)	/ˌɡet ˈbɪɡə(r)/
get closer (v)	/ˌɡet ˈkləʊsə(r)/
get further away (v)	/ɡet ˌfɜːðə(r) əˈweɪ/
get louder (v)	/ˌɡet ˈlaʊdə(r)/
get quieter (v)	/ˌɡet ˈkwaɪətə(r)/
get smaller (v)	/ˌɡet ˈsmɔːlə(r)/

6
concert (n)	/ˈkɒnsət/
fall asleep (v)	/fɔːl əˈsliːp/
straight (adv)	/streɪt/
last (adj)	/lɑːst/
(There weren't any) left (exp)	/left/
look tired (v)	/ˌlʊk ˈtaɪəd/
miss (v)	/mɪs/
queue (v)	/kjuː/
Wow! (exp)	/waʊ/

7
accident (n)	/ˈæksɪdənt/
control (v)	/kənˈtrəʊl/
cry (v)	/kraɪ/
deal with (v)	/ˈdiːl wɪð/
get annoyed (v)	/ˌɡet əˈnɔɪd/
go wrong (v)	/ˌɡəʊ ˈrɒŋ/
knock over (v)	/ˌnɒk ˈəʊvə(r)/
in a hurry (exp)	/ɪn ə ˈhʌri/
secret (n)	/ˈsiːkrət/
shout (v)	/ʃaʊt/
spill (v)	/spɪl/
traditional (adj)	/trəˈdɪʃənl/
typical (adj)	/ˈtɪpɪkl/
upset (adj)	/ʌpˈset/
wedding (n)	/ˈwedɪŋ/

8
neighbour (n)	/ˈneɪbə(r)/
possession (n)	/pəˈzeʃn/
belong to (v)	/bɪˈlɒŋ tuː/
whose (det, pron)	/huːz/

Review 9–16

Vocabulary

1 Complete the advert.

Accommodation	Convenient	Fitted	floor
heating	~~let~~	Rent	

To ¹_let_

First ² ~~floor~~ flat.
³ ~~Accommodation~~ for town centre.
⁴ ~~fitted~~ kitchen.
Gas central ⁵ _heating_.
⁶ _Rent_ €700 per month.
Contact Acorn ⁷ _convenient_ Agency.
Tel: 07784 593162

2 Write the adjective for each noun.

1 luck _lucky_
2 beauty _____
3 danger _____
4 intelligence _____
5 honesty _____
6 pain _Painful_

3 Write the noun for each adjective.

1 successful _success_
2 famous _____
3 angry _anger_
4 difficult _____
5 important _____
6 secure _____

Grammar

4 Choose the correct article.

Duane's bought ¹a/~~the~~ new flat in ²~~a~~/the centre of town. It's on ³~~a~~/the fourth floor, and it's in ⁴an/~~the~~ old building, so it hasn't got ⁵a/the lift. However, it's very convenient for ⁶a/the new shopping centre and for ⁷a/~~the~~ school that his daughter, Filipa, goes to. There's ⁸a/the small park near ⁹a/the flat, where Filipa and her friends play, and ¹⁰~~an~~/the Italian café where they can buy ice cream.

5 Make sentences and questions with the present perfect. Use the cues.

1 They've bought the tickets for the concert.
1 They / buy / the tickets for the concert.
2 I / never / have an accident in my car.
3 you / ever / lost something important?
4 Bruno / not / break / his arm.
5 the children / tidy / their rooms?
6 We / move / into a lovely flat.

Skills

6 Read the text. Answer the questions.

Manuel Fernandez, a 27-year-old scuba-diving instructor from Mexico, has an unusual hobby. When he isn't teaching tourists to dive in the warm waters of Mexico, he goes ice-diving. Some of the best places for ice-diving are Antarctica, Newfoundland, and the White Sea in Russia, and Manuel has dived in all three places. Ice-diving is a dangerous sport – divers cut a hole in the ice so they can get in and out of the freezing cold water, and it's easy to get lost under the ice. This is why ice-divers usually work in teams of six. Manuel has only had one bad accident so far – he was getting out of the water when he slipped on some ice and broke his leg.

1 How old is Manuel?
2 Where does he come from?
3 What is his job?
4 Where does he work?
5 What sport does Manuel do in his free time?
6 Why do ice-divers dive in teams?
7 Where has Manuel dived?
8 How many accidents has Manuel had?
9 What bones has he broken?

English for Everyday Life

7 Complete the conversations.

1 **A** Atishoo!
  B B _l e s s_ you!
2 **A** Franz and Anna have lost their dog.
  B Oh, d _ _ _.
3 **A** I think I've got a cold.
  B P _ _ _ you.
4 **A** Jack was angry when we crashed his car.
  B I c _ _ imagine.
5 **A** I failed my music exam again.
  B That's a s _ _ _ _.

8 Write the numbers as words.

1 365	4 980	7 13.3
2 2,000,000	5 ⅓	8 1,000,000,000
3 74%	6 4,000	9 5,300

9 accommodation (n) /əˌkɒməˈdeɪʃn/
accommodation agency (n) /əˌkɒməˈdeɪʃn ˌeɪdʒənsi/
air conditioning (n) /ˌeə(r) kənˈdɪʃənɪŋ/
central heating (n) /ˌsentrəl ˈhiːtɪŋ/
convenient (adj) /kənˈviːniənt/
facilities (n pl) /fəˈsɪlətiz/
first floor (adj) /fɜːst flɔː(r)/
fitted kitchen (n) /ˌfɪtɪd ˈkɪtʃɪn/
flat (n) /flæt/
flatmate (n) /ˈflætmeɪt/
furnished (adj) /ˈfɜːnɪʃt/
ground floor (adj) /ɡraʊnd flɔː(r)/
landlord (n) /ˈlændlɔːd/
let (v) /let/
noisy (adj) /ˈnɔɪzi/
pay (v) /peɪ/
property (n) /ˈprɒpəti/
quiet (adj) /ˈkwaɪət/
rent (n + v) /rent/
share (v) /ʃeə(r)/
spacious (adj) /ˈspeɪʃəs/
tenant (n) /ˈtenənt/
unfurnished (adj) /ʌnˈfɜːnɪʃt/

10 area (n) /ˈeəriə/
block of flats (n) /ˌblɒk əv ˈflæts/
date (n) /deɪt/
lift (n) /lɪft/
out of order (exp) /ˌaʊt əv ˈɔːdə(r)/
stairs (n pl) /steəz/
throw (v) /θrəʊ/

11 bungalow (n) /ˈbʌŋɡələʊ/
detached house (n) /dɪˈtætʃt haʊs/
semi-detached house (n) /ˌsemi dɪˈtætʃt ˌhaʊs/
terraced house (n) /ˈterəst ˌhaʊs/
available (adj) /əˈveɪləbl/
condition (n) /kənˈdɪʃn/
consist (v) /kənˈsɪst/
deposit (n) /dɪˈpɒzɪt/
fully furnished (adj) /ˌfʊli ˈfɜːnɪʃt/
local amenity (n) /ˌləʊkl əˈmiːnəti/

12 sympathy (n) /ˈsɪmpəθi/
Bless you! (exp) /ˈbles ju/
I can imagine. (exp) /ˌaɪ kən ɪˈmædʒɪn/
Oh, dear. (exp) /ˌəʊ ˈdɪə(r)/
Poor you! (exp) /ˌpɔː(r) ˈjuː/
That's a shame. (exp) /ˌðæts ə ˈʃeɪm/
What a pity. (exp) /ˌwɒt ə ˈpɪti/
annoyed (adj) /əˈnɔɪd/
hit the roof (exp) /ˌhɪt ðə ˈruːf/
at short notice (exp) /æt ˌʃɔːt ˈnəʊtɪs/
waste of time (exp) /ˌweɪst əv ˈtaɪm/
You bet. (exp) /ˌjuː ˈbet/

13 anger (n) /ˈæŋɡə(r)/
angry (adj) /ˈæŋɡri/
beauty (n) /ˈbjuːti/
difficult (adj) /ˈdɪfɪkəlt/
difficulty (n) /ˈdɪfɪkəlti/
fame (n) /feɪm/
famous (adj) /ˈfeɪməs/
health (n) /helθ/
healthy (adj) /ˈhelθi/
honesty (n) /ˈɒnɪsti/
humorous (adj) /ˈhjuːmərəs/
humour (n) /ˈhjuːmə(r)/
importance (n) /ɪmˈpɔːtns/
important (adj) /ɪmˈpɔːtnt/
intelligence (n) /ɪnˈtelɪdʒəns/
intelligent (adj) /ɪnˈtelɪdʒənt/
luck (n) /lʌk/
lucky (adj) /ˈlʌki/
pain (n) /peɪn/
painful (adj) /ˈpeɪnfl/
patience (n) /ˈpeɪʃns/
patient (adj) /ˈpeɪʃnt/
safety (n) /ˈseɪfti/
secure (adj) /sɪˈkjʊə(r)/
security (n) /sɪˈkjʊərəti/
success (n) /səkˈses/
successful (adj) /səkˈsesfl/
sound (v) /saʊnd/

14 book (v) /bʊk/
bruise (v) /bruːz/
fault (n) /fɔːlt/
look round (v) /ˌlʊk ˈraʊnd/
reverse (v) /rɪˈvɜːs/

15 be in trouble (v) /ˌbi ɪn ˈtrʌbl/
be locked out (v) /bi ˌlɒkt ˈaʊt/
break the law (v) /ˌbreɪk ðə ˈlɔː/
gamble (v) /ˈɡæmbl/
helmet (n) /ˈhelmɪt/
knock (v) /nɒk/
mountaineering (n) /ˌmaʊntəˈnɪərɪŋ/
prison (n) /ˈprɪzn/
skyscraper (n) /ˈskaɪskreɪpə(r)/
storey (n) /ˈstɔːri/

16 billion (n) /ˈbɪljən/
half (n) /hɑːf/
hundred (n) /ˈhʌndrəd/
million (n) /ˈmɪljən/
per cent (adv) /pə ˈsent/
point (n) /pɔɪnt/
quarter (n) /ˈkwɔːtə(r)/
third (n) /θɜːd/
thousand (n) /ˈθaʊznd/

Vocabulary

1 Choose the correct word.

1 She needs to lose *weight* / ~~fit~~.
2 I think I've *pulled* / *kept* a muscle.
3 Try to *do* / *get* a good night's sleep.
4 *Warm* / *Lift* up before you exercise.
5 Ding *lost* / *gave up* smoking last year.
6 I'm trying to cut *up* / *down* on sugar.

2 Match the sentence halves.

1 We were stuck in a traffic _b_   a works.
2 My car broke ___   b jam.
3 There are road ___   c delayed.
4 Where is the ticket ___   d lights.
5 Turn right at the traffic ___   e flooded.
6 The flight to Beijing is ___   f office?
7 It's raining and many roads are ___ g down.

Grammar

3 Complete the sentences. Use *will* or *going to* and the verbs in brackets.

1 **A** Have you made any plans for the summer?
   B Yes, We*'re going to travel* (travel) around Europe.
2 **A** Do you want tea or coffee?
   B Oh, I _____ (have) tea, please.
3 **A** I'm going to the supermarket now.
   B What _____ (you / buy)?
4 **A** Do you want to watch this DVD?
   B I'm quite tired. I think I _____ (go) to bed now.
5 **A** Why is John wearing shorts?
   B He _____ (play) tennis.
6 **A** I can't do this exercise.
   B Don't worry. I _____ (help) you.

4 Complete the sentences. Use the past perfect.

| go | ~~leave~~ | lose | park |
| take | not see | start | not remember |

1 Sal realized that she _'d left_ her purse at home.
2 We forgot where we _____ our car.
3 He couldn't phone you because he _____ your number.
4 I couldn't go out because you _____ my car keys.
5 The classroom was empty. Everyone _____ home.
6 We arrived late, and the play _____ already _____ .
7 My wife was angry that I _____ our anniversary.
8 I _____ Ang for ten years, so I didn't recognize him.

Skills

5 Read the text. Answer the questions.

A common problem today is that office workers spend most of their day sitting at a desk. They even eat their lunch at their desks. If you sit down for long periods of time, your spine will become weaker and you will start to have back problems, and eating lunch at your desk can result in poor digestion. If you have a desk job, you should take some time to do some exercises to strengthen your spine. Stop work at lunchtime and go for a walk. This will help you to digest your food, and it will make you feel healthier.

1 What is wrong with the way that office workers work?
2 What health problems can this cause?
3 What should you do?
4 How will this help you?

English for Everyday Life

6 Put the words in the correct order to make expressions.

1 She's my best friend.

1 my She's friend best .
2 relationship got You've great a .
3 happy I you'll together be hope .
4 enjoy each really company other's We .
5 other get each know They to will .

7 Complete the sentences. Use *on*, *in*, or *at*.

1 Our flight is _on_ Monday _____ 10.30.
2 It rained _____ Sunday morning, but the sun came out _____ the afternoon.
3 I don't often go out _____ night _____ the winter.
4 Kim's birthday isn't _____ May. It's _____ 10th July.
5 Are you doing anything _____ the weekend?

17 health (n) /helθ/
fitness (n) /ˈfɪtnəs/
take exercise (v) /ˌteɪk ˈeksəsaɪz/
do stretching exercises (v) /du ˈstretʃɪŋ ˌeksəsaɪzɪz/
injure a joint (v) /ˌɪndʒə(r) ə ˈdʒɔɪnt/
keep fit (v) /ˌkiːp ˈfɪt/
lift weights (v) /ˌlɪft ˈweɪts/
pull a muscle (v) /ˌpʊl ə ˈmʌsl/
warm up (v) /ˌwɔːm ˈʌp/
lifestyle (n) /ˈlaɪfstaɪl/
cut down on fat (v) /kʌt ˌdaʊn ɒn ˈfæt/
cut down on sugar (v) /kʌt ˌdaʊn ɒn ˈʃʊgə(r)/
eat a healthy diet (v) /ˌiːt ə ˈhelθi ˈdaɪət/
get a good night's sleep (v) /ˌget ə ˌgʊd naɪts ˈsliːp/
give up junk food (v) /ˌgɪv ʌp ˈdʒʌŋk ˈfuːd/
give up smoking (v) /ˌgɪv ʌp ˈsməʊkɪŋ/
lose weight (v) /ˌluːz ˈweɪt/
put on weight (v) /ˌpʊt ɒn ˈweɪt/
take vitamins (v) /ˌteɪk ˈvɪtəmɪnz/
personal measurement (n) /ˌpɜːsənl ˈmeʒəmənt/
height (n) /haɪt/
weigh (v) /weɪ/
weight (n) /weɪt/

18 human emotion (n) /ˌhjuːmən ɪˈməʊʃn/
make a difference (exp) /ˌmeɪk ə ˈdɪfrəns/
robot (n) /ˈrəʊbɒt/

19 backache (n) /ˈbækeɪk/
brain (n) /breɪn/
breathing exercise (n) /ˈbriːðɪŋ ˌeksəsaɪz/
digest (v) /daɪˈdʒest/
fresh (adj) /freʃ/
get fat (v) /ˌget ˈfæt/
get fit (v) /ˌget ˈfɪt/
heavy (adj) /ˈhevi/
in good shape (exp) /ɪn ˌgʊd ˈʃeɪp/
lower (v) /ˈləʊə(r)/
nap (n) /næp/
on the go (exp) /ˌɒn ðə ˈgəʊ/
palm (n) /pɑːm/
rush (v) /rʌʃ/
spine (n) /spaɪn/

20 best friend (n) /ˌbest ˈfrend/
get to know each other (exp) /ˌget tə ˈnəʊ iːtʃ ˌʌðə(r)/
each other's company (exp) /iːtʃ ˌʌðəz ˈkʌmpəni/
a great relationship (n) /ə ˌgreɪt rɪˈleɪʃnʃɪp/
celebration (n) /ˈselɪbreɪʃn/
come over (v) /kʌm ˈəʊvə(r)/
exhausted (adj) /ɪgˈzɔːstɪd/
round the world trip (n) /ˌraʊnd ðə ˌwɜːld ˈtrɪp/
the States (n) /ðə ˈsteɪts/
wedding plans (n pl) /ˈwedɪŋ ˌplænz/

21 transport problem (n) /ˈtrænspɔːt ˌprɒbləm/
accident (n) /ˈæksɪdənt/
ahead (adv) /əˈhed/
blocked (adj) /blɒkt/
break down (v) /ˌbreɪk ˈdaʊn/
bridge (n) /brɪdʒ/
cancelled /ˈkænsld/
delayed (adj) /dɪˈleɪd/
diversion (n) /daɪˈvɜːʃn/
emergency sign (n) /ɪˈmɜːdʒənsi ˌsaɪn/
flooded (adj) /ˈflʌdɪd/
inconvenience (n) /ˌɪnkənˈviːniəns/
queue (n) /kjuː/
slow down (v) /ˌsləʊ ˈdaʊn/
stuck (adj) /stʌk/
roadworks (n pl) /ˈrəʊdwɜːks/
strike (n) /straɪk/
ticket office (n) /ˈtɪkɪt ˌɒfɪs/
traffic jam (n) /ˈtræfɪk ˌdʒæm/
traffic lights (n pl) /ˈtræfɪk ˌlaɪts/
tunnel (n) /ˈtʌnl/
Underground (n) /ˈʌndəgraʊnd/

22 coincidence (n) /kəʊˈɪnsɪdəns/
lock (sb) out (v) /ˌlɒk ˈaʊt/
post (v) /pəʊst/
previous (adj) /ˈpriːviəs/
return (sth) (v) /rɪˈtɜːn/
strange (adj) /streɪndʒ/

23 catch (v) /kætʃ/
fine (n) /faɪn/
grab (v) /græb/
hurry (v) /ˈhʌri/
nearby (adv) /ˌnɪəˈbaɪ/
not believe your eyes (exp) /ˌnɒt bɪˌliːv jɔː(r) ˈaɪz/
passenger (n) /ˈpæsɪndʒə(r)/
realize (v) /ˈriːəlaɪz/
silence (n) /ˈsaɪləns/
speeding (n) /spiːdɪŋ/
stay awake (v) /ˌsteɪ əˈweɪk/
still (adv) /stɪl/

24 earlier (adj) /ˈɜːliə(r)/
later (adj) /ˈleɪtə(r)/
business class (n) /ˈbɪznəs klɑːs/
economy class (n) /ɪˈkɒnəmi klɑːs/
book a flight (exp) /ˌbʊk ə ˈflaɪt/
via (prep) /ˈvaɪə/
return flight (n) /rɪˈtɜːn flaɪt/
fully booked (adj) /ˌfʊli ˈbʊkt/
bit (n) /bɪt/
check (v) /tʃek/
come back (v) /ˌkʌm ˈbæk/
direct (adj) /dəˈrekt/

Vocabulary

1 Complete the sentences.

| crisp | mild | off | rare | ~~sweet~~ |

1 No sugar for me. I don't like _sweet_ tea.
2 I like my steak _____.
3 This fish isn't fresh. It's _____.
4 Do you prefer strong or _____ cheese?
5 We bought some lovely _____ apples.

2 Write five more adjectives to describe food.

3 Match the disaster words with the definitions.

| a famine | an earthquake | a hurricane |
| ~~a drought~~ | an avalanche | a war |

1 a long period with little or no rain _a drought_
2 a bad storm with strong winds _____
3 a period with little or no food _____
4 snow or rocks falling down a mountain _____
5 a fight between two countries or groups _____
6 movement of the Earth's surface _____

Grammar

4 Tick ✓ or correct the tag questions.

1 You don't like tea, ~~don't you?~~ _do you_
2 It's going to rain, isn't it? _____
3 Gianni works in Rome, don't he? _____
4 You've been to Russia, aren't you? _____
5 We weren't late, weren't we? _____
6 She'd had breakfast, hadn't she? _____
7 They phoned you, don't they? _____
8 I gave you my address, didn't I? _____

5 Put the verbs in the correct form.

1 If it _rains_ (rain) tomorrow, the river will flood.
2 If I _____ (work) at home, I wouldn't need a car.
3 People _____ (die) if the drought continues.
4 We _____ (not travel) abroad if flights were more expensive.
5 If I was the president, public transport _____ (be) free.
6 I _____ (not cycle) to work tomorrow if it's windy.
7 If people _____ (turn off) their computers, they'd save electricity.
8 He'll go to the bank if he _____ (have) time.

Skills

6 Read the text. Answer the questions.

Camilla Marx climbs volcanoes in her free time. She started her unusual hobby in 1998, after she saw a TV programme about a volcanic eruption in the Indian Ocean. Since then she has been to 28 volcanoes and climbed 19 of them. Camilla is a geography teacher and wants to learn more about volcanoes. She wants to know if it is possible to predict when a volcano will erupt and how strong the eruption will be. Many people live near volcanoes, and if they had more information, it would be easier to move before they were in danger.

1 What is Camilla's job?
2 What is her hobby?
3 How many volcanoes has Camilla visited?
4 How could Camilla's hobby help people who live near volcanoes?

English for Everyday Life

7 Put the sentences in the correct order to make a conversation.

a ___ **Jane** That's right. I thought I recognized you.
b ___ **Hiro** Yes, I think we have. You look familiar.
c ___ **Jane** Hello, Hiro. We haven't met before, have we?
d ___ **Hiro** I know. It was at Ben's party.
e _1_ **Mika** Jane, this is my brother, Hiro.
f ___ **Jane** Yes, I know your face, too.

8 Put the words in the correct order to make expressions.

1 I'd like a non-smoking room, please.

1 like room please non-smoking I'd a .
2 luggage need Do any your with help you ?
3 stay a Have pleasant .
4 is from Breakfast served 8 to 9.30 .
5 please your fill you details form on in the Could ?
6 wake-up Would like a call you ?

25 flavour (n) /'fleɪvə(r)/
hot (adj) /hɒt/
mild (adj) /maɪld/
salty (adj) /'sɔːlti/
spicy (adj) /'spaɪsi/
sour (adj) /'saʊə(r)/
strong (adj) /strɒŋ/
sweet (adj) /swiːt/
crisp (adj) /krɪsp/
dry (adj) /draɪ/
fresh (adj) /freʃ/
juicy (adj) /'dʒuːsi/
off (adj) /ɒf/
soft (adj) /sɒft/
burnt (adj) /bɜːnt/
meat (n) /miːt/
medium (adj) /'miːdiəm/
rare (adj) /reə(r)/
raw (adj) /rɔː/
well-done (adj) /wel'dʌn/

26 couple (n) /'kʌpl/
vegetarian (adj) /ˌvedʒə'teəriən/

27 banana (n) /bə'nɑːnə/
dish (n) /dɪʃ/
Hungary (n) /'hʌŋgəri/
India (n) /'ɪndiə/
Indian (adj) /'ɪndiən/
lime juice (n) /'laɪm dʒuːs/
naan (n) /nɑːn/
rice (n) /raɪs/
tasty (adj) /'teɪsti/
chemical (n) /'kemɪkl/
fair price (n) /'feə 'praɪs/
fair trade (adj) /'feə 'treɪd/
free range (adj) /'friː 'reɪndʒ/
label (n) /'leɪbl/
low fat (adj) /ˌləʊ 'fæt/
organic (adj) /ɔː'gænɪk/
outdoors (adv) /ˌaʊt'dɔːz/
produce (v) /prə'djuːs/
producer (n) /prə'djuːsə(r)/
sell by date (n) /'sel baɪ deɪt/
use by date (n) /'juːz baɪ deɪt/

28 forget (v) /fə'get/
recognize (v) /'rekəgnaɪz/
familiar (adj) /fə'mɪliə(r)/
audition (n) /ɔː'dɪʃn/
be in touch (exp) /ˌbi ɪn 'tʌtʃ/
cut (v) /kʌt/
ideal (adj) /aɪ'diːəl/
part (n) /pɑːt/
soap opera (n) /'səʊp ˌɒprə/

29 disaster (n) /dɪ'zɑːstə(r)/
avalanche (n) /'ævəlɑːnʃ/
drought (n) /draʊt/
earthquake (n) /'ɜːθkweɪk/
explosion (n) /ɪk'spləʊʒn/
famine (n) /'fæmɪn/
flood (n) /flʌd/
forest fire (n) /'fɒrɪst ˌfaɪə(r)/
hurricane (n) /'hʌrɪkən/
pollution (n) /pə'luːʃn/
volcanic eruption (n) /vɒlˌkænɪk ɪ'rʌpʃn/
tsunami (n) /tsuː'nɑːmi/
war (n) /wɔː(r)/

30 disappear (v) /ˌdɪsə'pɪə(r)/
global warming (n) /ˌgləʊbl 'wɔːmɪŋ/
island (n) /'aɪlənd/
mind (v) /maɪnd/
rise (v) /raɪz/
scientist (n) /'saɪəntɪst/
sea level (n) /'siː levl/
worried (adj) /'wʌrid/

31 agriculture (n) /'ægrɪkʌltʃə(r)/
approach (v) /ə'prəʊtʃ/
cause (v) /kɔːz/
chase (v) /tʃeɪs/
danger (n) /'deɪndʒə(r)/
destroy (v) /dɪ'strɔɪ/
indoors (adv) /ˌɪn'dɔːz/
in seconds (exp) /ɪn 'sekəndz/
lightning (n) /'laɪtnɪŋ/
meteorologist (n) /ˌmiːtiə'rɒlədʒɪst/
survive (v) /sə'vaɪv/
temperature (n) /'temprətʃə(r)/
thunderstorm (n) /'θʌndəstɔːm/
tornado (n) /tɔː'neɪdəʊ/
TV station (n) /ˌtiː 'viː ˌsteɪʃn/
weather forecast (n) /'weðə ˌfɔːkɑːst/

32 served from … to … (exp) /'sɜːvd frəm tu/
take a credit card (exp) /ˌteɪk ə 'kredɪt ˌkɑːd/
fill in your details (exp) /ˌfɪl ɪn jɔː 'diːteɪlz/
sign it at the bottom (exp) /ˌsaɪn ɪt ət ðə 'bɒtəm/
luggage (n) /'lʌgɪdʒ/
stay (n) /steɪ/
a reservation in the name of … (exp) /ə ˌrezə'veɪʃn ɪn ðə 'neɪm əv/
non-smoking room (n) /nɒn 'sməʊkɪŋ ruːm/
check in (v) /ˌtʃek 'ɪn/
checkout time (n) /'tʃekaʊt ˌtaɪm/
emergency exit (n) /ɪ'mɜːdʒənsi ˌeksɪt/
reception (n) /rɪ'sepʃn/
room service (n) /'ruːm ˌsɜːvɪs/

Vocabulary

1 Choose the correct word.

1 You've got a lot of *luggage / luggages*.
2 We need *information / informations* about Chile.
3 Did you see the *new / news* last night?
4 Darius is wearing his new *jean / jeans*.
5 I can't see without my *glass / glasses*.
6 Put your *litter / litters* in the bin.

2 Complete the table.

crime	criminal	verb
murder	[1] a murderer	[2]
[3]	[4]	burgle
blackmail	[5]	[6]
[7]	[8]	vandalize
[9]	a robber	[10]

Grammar

3 Complete the sentences. Use the correct form of *used to* and the verb.

A Your English is very good.
B Thank you. It [1] *didn't use to be* very good. (not/be)
A Where did you learn it?
B Well, I [2]_____ English at school in Brazil. (study)
A What was your teacher like?
B Horrible! He [3]_____ us lots of homework. (give)
A [4]_____ you _____ good marks? (get)
B No, I [5]_____ the homework. (not/do)
A So how did you learn English?
B My brother and I [6]_____ our holidays in the USA. (spend)

4 Choose the correct form.

A man [1]*fell / was falling* asleep while he [2]*'d burgled / was burgling* a house in Manchester. The police [3]*found / were finding* Mick Molt in the house the next morning. He [4]*had slept / was sleeping* on the sofa when they [5]*'d arrived / arrived*. The owner of the house, Sandy Jones, [6]*heard / was hearing* a noise from the living room while she [7]*got dressed / was getting dressed*, so she [8]*called / was calling* the police. 'It [9]*was / was being* the first good night's sleep I [10]*was having / 'd had* for weeks,' Molt said when he was arrested.

Skills

5 Read the text. Are the statements true (T) or false (F)?

French bus driver Michel Brun retired from his job when he was 65 and bought an old bus. For the next two years he travelled around Africa. He started in Egypt, then went to Sudan, Ethiopia, and Kenya. He worked in a school in Zambia for two months and a hotel in Botswana. He didn't earn much money, but he made lots of new friends. When the hotel closed for winter Michel drove to Namibia and helped to build a new hospital. Michel had the best time of his life in Africa, but he's not ready to relax yet – next year he's going to sail to New York and drive his bus across the USA!

1 Michel is a young man. *F*
2 He's from France.
3 He travelled around Africa alone.
4 He worked as a bus driver in Africa.
5 He visited six countries.
6 He earned a lot of money.
7 He met lots of people and made friends with them.
8 He enjoyed his time in Africa.
9 He's going to drive to Australia.

English for Everyday Life

6 Complete the text.

I saw Brian King last week. He's really [1]c h *a n g e*d a lot. I can [2]r _ _ _ _ _ _r when he sat next to me at school. In those [3]d _ _ s he used to hate school, now he's a teacher! School [4]s _ _ _s a long time ago now. I can't believe it's 20 years since we left. Doesn't [5]t _ _ e fly? I wonder what's [6]h _ _ _ _ _ _d to our old teacher, Mr Smith?

7 Write C for complaints and R for responses.

1 That's no good. *C*
2 I can only apologize.
3 This is very inconvenient.
4 I'm sorry about that.
5 I'm afraid there's nothing I can do.
6 This is completely unacceptable.

Wordlist 33–40

33	advice (n)	/əd'vaɪs/
	clothes (n pl)	/kləʊðz/
	equipment (n)	/ɪ'kwɪpmənt/
	glasses (n pl)	/'glɑːsɪz/
	headphones (n pl)	/'hedfəʊnz/
	information (n)	/ˌɪnfə'meɪʃn/
	jeans (n pl)	/dʒiːnz/
	litter (n)	/'lɪtə(r)/
	luggage (n)	/'lʌgɪdʒ/
	news (n)	/njuːz/
	scales (n pl)	/skeɪlz/
	scissors (n pl)	/'sɪzəz/
	stairs (n pl)	/steəz/
	work (n)	/wɜːk/
	allow (v)	/ə'laʊ/
	drop (v)	/drɒp/
	illegal (adj)	/ɪ'liːgl/
	offence (n)	/ə'fens/
	prohibited (adj)	/prə'hɪbɪtɪd/
	skateboarding (n)	/'skeɪtbɔːdɪŋ/
	unattended (adj)	/ˌʌnə'tendɪd/
	warning sign (n)	/'wɔːnɪŋ saɪn/
	yellow line (n)	/ˌjeləʊ 'laɪn/

34	karaoke (n)	/ˌkæri'əʊki/
	singer (n)	/'sɪŋə(r)/
	suppose (v)	/sə'pəʊz/
	used to (v)	/'juːst tə/

35	a chance of a lifetime (exp)	/ə ˌtʃɑːns əv ə 'laɪftaɪm/
	afterwards (adv)	/'ɑːftəwədz/
	a golden opportunity (exp)	/ə ˌgəʊldən ˌɒpə'tjuːnəti/
	assistant (n)	/ə'sɪstənt/
	professional (adj)	/prə'feʃənl/
	sports equipment (n)	/'spɔːts ɪˌkwɪpmənt/
	sports reporter (n)	/'spɔːts rɪˌpɔːtə(r)/
	tennis player (n)	/'tenɪs ˌpleɪə(r)/
	TV company (n)	/ˌtiː 'viː ˌkʌmpəni/

36	Doesn't time fly? (exp)	/'dʌznt taɪm 'flaɪ/
	remember (v)	/rɪ'membə(r)/
	in those days (exp)	/ɪn 'ðəʊz deɪz/
	has changed a lot (exp)	/həz 'tʃeɪndʒd ə lɒt/
	seems a long time ago now (exp)	/siːmz ə ˌlɒŋ taɪm ə'gəʊ naʊ/
	What's happened to that guy …? (exp)	/wɒts 'hæpənd tə ðæt 'gaɪ/
	What's he up to these days? (exp)	/wɒts hiː 'ʌp tu ˌðiːz deɪz/
	any more (adv)	/eni'mɔː(r)/
	apparently (adv)	/ə'pærəntli/
	Cool! (exp)	/kuːl/
	recognize (v)	/'rekəgnaɪz/
	repair (v)	/rɪ'peə(r)/

37	assault (n + v)	/ə'sɔːlt/
	attacker (n)	/ə'tækə(r)/
	blackmail (n + v)	/'blækmeɪl/
	blackmailer (n)	/'blækmeɪlə(r)/
	burglar (n)	/'bɜːglə(r)/
	burglary (n)	/'bɜːgləri/
	burgle (v)	/'bɜːgl/
	commit a crime (v)	/kəˌmɪt ə 'kraɪm/
	criminal (n)	/'krɪmɪnl/
	go to prison (v)	/ˌgəʊ tə 'prɪzn/
	identity theft (n)	/aɪ'dentəti θeft/
	identity thief (n)	/aɪ'dentəti θiːf/
	murder (n + v)	/'mɜːdə(r)/
	murderer (n)	/'mɜːdərə(r)/
	rob (v)	/rɒb/
	robber (n)	/'rɒbə(r)/
	steal (v)	/stiːl/
	vandal (n)	/'vændl/
	vandalism (n)	/'vændəlɪzəm/
	vandalize (v)	/'vændəlaɪz/
	victim (n)	/'vɪktɪm/
	witness (n)	/'wɪtnəs/

38	burn (v)	/bɜːn/
	grateful (adj)	/'greɪtfl/
	put out (v)	/pʊt 'aʊt/
	smell (v)	/smel/
	smoke (n)	/sməʊk/

39	alibi (n)	/'æləbaɪ/
	commit suicide (v)	/kəˌmɪt 'suːɪsaɪd/
	dead (adj)	/ded/
	find out (v)	/ˌfaɪnd 'aʊt/
	fingerprint (n)	/'fɪŋgəprɪnt/
	gun (n)	/gʌn/
	motive (n)	/'məʊtɪv/
	shoot (v)	/ʃuːt/
	shot (n)	/ʃɒt/
	character (n)	/'kærəktə(r)/
	crime novel (n)	/'kraɪm ˌnɒvl/
	detective (n)	/dɪ'tektɪv/
	fictional (adj)	/'fɪkʃənl/
	literature (n)	/'lɪtrətʃə(r)/
	whodunit (n)	/ˌhuː'dʌnɪt/

40	make a formal complaint (v)	/meɪk ə ˌfɔːml kəm'pleɪnt/
	That's no good. (exp)	/ˌðætz nəʊ 'gʊd/
	completely unacceptable (exp)	/kəm'pliːtli ˌʌnək'septəbl/
	inconvenient (adj)	/ˌɪnkən'viːniənt/
	I can only apologize. (exp)	/aɪ kən ˌəʊnli ə'pɒlədʒaɪz/
	I'm afraid … . (exp)	/aɪm ə'freɪd/
	available (adj)	/ə'veɪləbl/
	record (n)	/'rekɔːd/

Review 41–48

Vocabulary

1 Complete the sentences. Use the phrasal verbs.

fill in	get on	pick up
take off	turn off	~~turn up~~

1 I can't hear the TV. Can you _turn_ it _up_?
2 Can you _____ _____ this form, please?
3 Why don't you _____ your coat _____?
4 Don't drop litter on the floor. _____ it _____.
5 Please _____ the lights _____ when you leave.
6 _____ _____ the bus and find a seat.

2 Make the opposites. Use un-, dis-, in-, im-.

1 kind _unkind_
2 polite _____
3 tidy _____
4 loyal _____
5 honest _____
6 sensitive _____
7 reliable _____
8 patient _____

Grammar

3 Complete the sentences with the passive form. Use the verb and the tense in brackets.

1 A lot of food in our supermarkets _is produced_ in other countries. (produce – present simple)
2 Many of our rivers _____ by chemicals. (pollute – present simple)
3 These cakes _____ in France. (make – past simple)
4 Those toys _____ here by the children. (carry – past simple)
5 The problem _____ by the government. (study – present perfect)
6 The island _____ by a storm. (hit – present perfect)
7 Food _____ by people, so what is the solution? (need – future *will*)
8 We think that more gardens _____ to grow fruit and vegetables. (use – future *will*)

4 Complete the sentences. Use should, shouldn't, might, or might not.

1 Take an umbrella. It _might_ rain.
2 You _____ smoke. It's bad for your health.
3 Don't phone before six because I _____ be in.
4 You _____ always lock your doors at night.
5 Don't wait for us. We _____ be late.
6 You _____ revise for the English test.
7 You _____ use your mobile when you're driving.
8 I'm very busy, so I _____ have time for lunch.

Skills

5 Put the stages of the tea-producing process in the correct order.

A worker in India picks tea leaves.

a __ When the tea plants are ready, the leaves are picked by workers.
b __ In the factory the leaves are dried and cut into smaller pieces by a machine.
c __ The dried tea is sorted and packed into bags or special boxes
d __ Finally, the tea is bought and served by tea-drinkers.
e __ The leaves are sent to tea factories for processing.
f __ After it is packed, the tea is shipped to tea companies, and then to shops around the world.
g _1_ Most tea leaves are produced by tea farmers in China and India.

English for Everyday Life

6 Put the words in the correct order.

1 I hear that Martina is getting married.

1 Martina married that I hear getting is .
2 has Apparently got girlfriend a Kazuki new .
3 understand Lyn working Vietnam I is in .
4 seems It Danny that job new likes his .
5 Jing me she's that tells a flat buying .

7 Match the statements with the responses.

1 I was ill last week. __
2 I can play the guitar. __
3 I love Thai food. __
4 I don't like my job. __
5 I'm not going out. __
6 I didn't enjoy the play. __

a Neither do I.
b Oh, I am.
c Neither did I.
d Oh, I can't.
e So was I.
f So do I.

41	cut down (v)	/ˌkʌt ˈdaʊn/
	cut out (v)	/ˌkʌt ˈaʊt/
	fill in (v)	/ˌfɪl ˈɪn/
	get off (v)	/ˌget ˈɒf/
	get on (v)	/ˌget ˈɒn/
	give back (v)	/ˌgɪv ˈbæk/
	look back (v)	/ˌlʊk ˈbæk/
	pick up (v)	/ˌpɪk ˈʌp/
	put in (v)	/ˌpʊt ˈɪn/
	put on (v)	/ˌpʊt ˈɒn/
	take off (v)	/ˌteɪk ˈɒf/
	take out (v)	/ˌteɪk ˈaʊt/
	throw away (v)	/ˌθrəʊ əˈweɪ/

42	bath toy (n)	/ˈbɑːθ tɔɪ/
	break up (v)	/ˌbreɪk ˈʌp/
	cargo ship (n)	/ˈkɑːgəʊ ʃɪp/
	container (n)	/kənˈteɪnə(r)/
	current (n)	/ˈkʌrənt/
	Pacific Ocean (n)	/pəˌsɪfɪk ˈəʊʃn/
	plastic (n)	/ˈplæstɪk/
	pollute (v)	/pəˈluːt/
	wave (n)	/weɪv/
	artificial (adj)	/ˌɑːtɪˈfɪʃl/
	bio-degradable (adj)	/ˌbaɪəʊdɪˈgreɪdəbl/
	chlorine-free (adj)	/ˌklɔːriːn ˈfriː/
	colouring (n)	/ˈkʌlərɪŋ/
	damage (v)	/ˈdæmɪdʒ/
	eco-friendly (adj)	/ˌiːkəʊ ˈfrendli/
	environment (n)	/ɪnˈvaɪrənmənt/
	flavouring (adj)	/ˈfleɪvərɪŋ/
	phosphate-free (adj)	/ˌfɒsfeɪt ˈfriː/
	preservative (adj)	/prɪˈzɜːvətɪv/
	recycled material (n)	/ˌriːˈsaɪkld məˈtɪəriəl/
	sustainable source (n)	/səˈsteɪnəbl ˌsɔːs/

43	diver (n)	/ˈdaɪvə(r)/
	oyster (n)	/ˈɔɪstə(r)/
	make into (v)	/ˌmeɪk ˈɪntə/
	mother of pearl (n)	/ˌmʌðər əv ˈpɜːl/
	pearl (n)	/pɜːl/
	round (adj)	/raʊnd/
	shell (n)	/ʃel/
	sort (v)	/sɔːt/

44	Apparently ... (exp)	/əˈpærəntli/
	I hear (that) ... (exp)	/aɪ ˈhɪə ðət/
	I understand (that) ...	/aɪ ˌʌndəˈstænd ðət/
	It seems (that)... (exp)	/ɪt ˈsiːmz ðət/
	She tells me (that) ... (exp)	/ʃiː ˈtelz mi ðət/
	down in the dumps (exp)	/ˌdaʊn ɪn ðə ˈdʌmps/
	feel sorry for yourself (exp)	/ˌfiːl ˈsɒri fə jəself/
	leave behind (v)	/ˌliːv bɪˈhaɪnd/
	move on (v)	/ˌmuːv ˈɒn/
	transfer (v)	/trænsˈfɜː(r)/

45	personality (n)	/ˌpɜːsəˈnæləti/
	ambitious (adj)	/æmˈbɪʃəs/
	big-headed (adj)	/ˌbɪg ˈhedɪd/
	cheerful (adj)	/ˈtʃɪəfl/
	dishonest (adj)	/dɪsˈɒnɪst/
	disloyal (adj)	/dɪsˈlɔɪəl/
	easy-going (adj)	/ˌiːziˈgəʊɪŋ/
	impatient (adj)	/ɪmˈpeɪʃnt/
	insensitive (adj)	/ɪnˈsensətɪv/
	loyal (adj)	/ˈlɔɪəl/
	modest (adj)	/ˈmɒdɪst/
	patient (adj)	/ˈpeɪʃnt/
	polite (adj)	/pəˈlaɪt/
	reliable (adj)	/rɪˈlaɪəbl/
	sensible (adj)	/ˈsensəbl/
	sensitive (adj)	/ˈsensətɪv/
	silly (adj)	/ˈsɪli/
	sociable (adj)	/ˈsəʊʃəbl/
	tense (adj)	/tens/
	unambitious (adj)	/ˌʌnæmˈbɪʃəs/
	unkind (adj)	/ˌʌnˈkaɪnd/
	unreliable (adj)	/ˌʌnrɪˈlaɪəbl/
	unsociable (adj)	/ˌʌnˈsəʊʃəbl/
	untidy (adj)	/ˌʌnˈtaɪdi/

46	might (modal)	/maɪt/
	pessimistic (adj)	/ˌpesɪˈmɪstɪk/
	blow your nose (v)	/ˌbləʊ jɔː ˈnəʊz/
	offend (v)	/əˈfend/
	taboo (n)	/təˈbuː/
	sole (n)	/səʊl/

47	amuse (v)	/əˈmjuːz/
	brave (adj)	/breɪv/
	chin (n)	/tʃɪn/
	correctly (adv)	/kəˈrektli/
	dream (n)	/driːm/
	fold your arms (v)	/ˌfəʊld jɔː ˈɑːmz/
	moderately (adv)	/ˈmɒdərətli/
	noisily (adv)	/ˈnɔɪzəli/
	laugh (v)	/lɑːf/
	loudly (adv)	/ˈlaʊdli/
	pleasant (adj)	/ˈpleznt/
	quickly (adv)	/ˈkwɪkli/
	quietly (adv)	/ˈkwaɪətli/
	serious (adj)	/ˈsɪəriəs/
	side (n)	/saɪd/
	slowly (adv)	/ˈsləʊli/
	smile (v)	/smaɪl/
	strong (adj)	/strɒŋ/

48	Neither ... I. (exp)	/ˈnaɪðə(r) ... ˈaɪ/
	Nor ... I. (exp)	/ˌnɔː(r) ... ˈaɪ/
	Oh, I ... (exp)	/əʊ ˈaɪ/
	So ... I. (exp)	/ˌsəʊ ... ˈaɪ/

Vocabulary

1 Match the words with the definitions.

bride	~~groom~~	honeymoon
reception	registry office	

1 A man who is going to get married. _groom_
2 A place where people can get married. _____
3 A holiday for a newly-married man and woman. _____
4 A party to celebrate a marriage. _____
5 A woman who is going to get married. _____

2 Choose the correct word.

1 I'm studying for a *degree / ~~course~~* in History.
2 Do most students live on *campus / seminar*?
3 We attend *assignments / lectures* every day.
4 Paulo *passed / graduated* from the University of Rome.
5 The graduation *ceremony / certificate* was held in June.

Grammar

3 Rewrite the sentences. Put the words in brackets in the correct place.

1 Did you send a postcard to your dad?

1 Did you send a postcard? (to your dad)
2 Will you email the report tonight? (to the boss)
3 Have they shown their photos? (you)
4 I've lent my lecture notes. (Stefan)
5 Do you give presents at Christmas? (to friends)
6 We posted a card from Canada. (Patricia)

4 Complete the conversation. Use the present perfect continuous.

Katia Sorry I'm late.
Pedro It's OK. I [1]*haven't been waiting* (not / wait) long.
Katia You look tired. [2]_____ (you / work) hard?
Pedro Yes, I [3]_____ (not / sleep) well.
Katia Why not?
Pedro I [4]_____ studying for my exams.

5 Choose the correct form.

1 We've *driven / ~~been driving~~* 200 kms today.
2 I'm tired because I've *driven / been driving* all day.
3 How long have they *learned / been learning* English?
4 How many new words have you *learned / been learning*?
5 She's *written / been writing* six emails this morning.
6 I've *written / been writing* my assignment, but I can't finish it today.

Skills

6 Read the text. Answer the questions.

Anna and Dimitri had a traditional Greek wedding in a church in Athens. At the end of the ceremony the best man put the *stefanas* (rings of flowers) on Anna and Dimitri's heads to symbolize they were married. Then the bride and groom gave their guests *koufeta* – nuts covered in sugar.

The reception lasted all night and started with a *money dance*, when guests attached money to Anna's dress. After that, there was Greek dancing. During the dancing people started to break plates on the floor – this is supposed to bring the bride and groom good luck.

1 Where did Anna and Dimitri get married?
2 Why do the bride and groom wear *stefana*?
3 Who receives *koufeta* at a wedding?
4 What happens during a *money dance*?
5 What tradition brings good luck?

7 Match the halves of the expressions.

1 I would like to apply __   a for a new challenge.
2 Tim's in charge __   b in computing.
3 We're responsible __   c of the sales office.
4 She has a qualification __   d for the post of lecturer.
5 I feel the need __   e for advertising.

English for Everyday Life

8 Put the sentences in the correct order to make a conversation.

a __ I hope you're right. He's at the door now.
b __ What do you think he wants?
c _1_ There's a man looking at our house.
d __ Maybe, but I think it's more likely that he's lost.
e __ I've got no idea. Perhaps he's a burglar.
f __ Well, whatever he wants, we'll know soon.

9 Read the news. Choose the best response.

1 Guess what? I've got a new job.
  a Oh, dear.   b That's wonderful news.
2 Have you heard? Paola's getting married.
  a That's wonderful news. b That's so sad.
3 I'm afraid I've been sacked.
  a Congratulations.   b I'm sorry to hear that.

Wordlist 49-56

49

best man (n)	/ˌbest 'mæn/
bouquet (n)	/bʊ'keɪ/
bride (n)	/braɪd/
bridesmaid (n)	/'braɪdzmeɪd/
confetti (n)	/kən'feti/
get married (v)	/ˌget 'mærid/
go on honeymoon (v)	/ˌgəʊ ɒn 'hʌnimuːn/
groom (n)	/gruːm/
have a wedding (v)	/ˌhæv ə 'wedɪŋ/
marriage (n)	/'mærɪdʒ/
reception (n)	/rɪ'sepʃn/
registry office (n)	/'redʒɪstri ˌɒfɪs/
relationship (n)	/rɪ'leɪʃnʃɪp/
ex-wife (n)	/ˌeks'waɪf/
parents-in-law (n pl)	/'peərəntsɪn ˌlɔː/
stepdaughter (n)	/'stepdɔːtə(r)/

50

Christmas (n)	/'krɪsməs/
gift (n)	/gɪft/
greedy (adj)	/'griːdi/
immediately (adv)	/ɪ'miːdiətli/
pleased (adj)	/pliːzd/
present (n)	/'preznt/
receive (v)	/rɪ'siːv/
take (someone) out (v)	/ˌteɪk sʌmwʌn 'aʊt/
unclean (adj)	/ˌʌn'kliːn/
Valentine's Day (n)	/'væləntaɪnz ˌdeɪ/
vase (n)	/vɑːz/

51

coin (n)	/kɔɪn/
cow (n)	/kaʊ/
garland of flowers (n)	/ˌgɑːlənd əv 'flaʊəz/
plant (n)	/plɑːnt/
ribbon (n)	/'rɪbən/
symbolize (v)	/'sɪmbəlaɪz/
Mexico (n)	/'meksɪkəʊ/
Sudan (n)	/su'dæn/
Syria (n)	/'sɪriə/
Uruguay (n)	/'jʊərəgwaɪ/
Vietnam (n)	/ˌviət'næm/

52

It's more likely that ... (exp)	/ɪts mɔː 'laɪkli ðət/
I've got no idea. (exp)	/aɪv gɒt ˌnəʊ aɪ'dɪə/
maybe (adv)	/'meɪbi/
perhaps (adv)	/pə'hæps/
possibly (adv)	/'pɒsəbli/
whatever he wants (exp)	/wɒtˌevə hi 'wɒnts/
advertise (v)	/'ædvətaɪz/
certificate (n)	/sə'tɪfɪkət/
employee (n)	/ɪm'plɔɪiː/
fire (v)	/'faɪə(r)/
give (someone) the sack (v)	/ˌgɪv sʌmwʌn ðə 'sæk/
post (n)	/pəʊst/
prize (n)	/praɪz/
quit (v)	/kwɪt/

53

university (n)	/ˌjuːnɪ'vɜːsəti/
assignment (n)	/ə'saɪnmənt/
campus (n)	/'kæmpəs/
course (n)	/kɔːs/
degree (n)	/dɪ'griː/
degree certificate (n)	/dɪ'griː səˌtɪfɪkət/
final examination (n)	/ˌfaɪnl ɪgˌzæmɪ'neɪʃn/
graduate (v)	/'grædʒueɪt/
graduation ceremony (n)	/ˌgrædʒu'eɪʃn ˌserəməni/
lecture (n)	/'lektʃə(r)/
lecturer (n)	/'lektʃərə(r)/
seminar (n)	/'semɪnɑː(r)/
undergraduate (n)	/ˌʌndə'grædʒuət/
author (n)	/'ɔːθə(r)/
century (n)	/'sentʃəri/
Nobel Prize (n)	/nəʊˌbel 'praɪz/
prime minister (n)	/ˌpraɪm 'mɪnɪstə(r)/
professor (n)	/prə'fesə(r)/

54

improve (v)	/ɪm'pruːv/
look for (v)	/'lʊk fɔː/
memory (n)	/'meməri/
show (n)	/ʃəʊ/
wait (v)	/weɪt/

55

apply for (v)	/ə'plaɪ fɔː/
challenge (n)	/'tʃæləndʒ/
CV (n)	/ˌsiː 'viː/
experience (n)	/ɪk'spɪəriəns/
human resources (n)	/ˌhjuːmən rɪ'zɔːsɪz/
I look forward to hearing from you. (exp)	/aɪ lʊk 'fɔːwəd tə 'hɪərɪŋ frəm ju/
in charge of (adj)	/ɪn 'tʃɑːdʒ əv/
marketing (n)	/'mɑːkɪtɪŋ/
position (n)	/pə'zɪʃn/
promote (v)	/prə'məʊt/
publicity (n)	/pʌb'lɪsəti/
qualification (n)	/ˌkwɒlɪfɪ'keɪʃn/
responsible for (adj)	/rɪ'spɒnsəbl fɔː/
telecommunications (n pl)	/ˌtelikəˌmjuːnɪ'keɪʃnz/
work placement (n)	/'wɜːk ˌpleɪsmənt/
Yours faithfully (exp)	/ˌjɔːz 'feɪθfəli/

56

Guess what? (exp)	/ˌges 'wɒt/
Have you heard ...? (exp)	/ˌhæv jə 'hɜːd/
good news (n)	/ˌgʊd 'njuːz/
bad news (n)	/ˌbæd 'njuːz/
Congratulations. (exp)	/kənˌgrætʃu'leɪʃnz/
wonderful news (n)	/'wʌndəfl 'njuːz/
I'm sorry to hear that. (exp)	/aɪm ˌsɒri tə 'hɪə ðæt/
Oh, dear. (exp)	/ˌəʊ 'dɪə(r)/
That's very sad. (exp)	/ðæts ˌveri 'sæd/
expecting a baby (v)	/ɪkˌspektɪŋ ə 'beɪbi/
lose your job (v)	/ˌluːz jɔː 'dʒɒb/
split up (v)	/ˌsplɪt 'ʌp/

Review 57–64

Vocabulary

1a Write the phrases in the correct column.

| a phone call | the housework | a course |
| a drink | judo | a mistake |

make	do
a phone call	

b Write two more phrases in each column.

2 Complete the sentences. Use the correct form of the verb in brackets.

1 Do you enjoy *travelling* by train? (travel)
2 We've decided _____ to New York. (move)
3 Have you managed _____ your assignment? (finish)
4 Malek gave up _____ last month. (smoke)
5 Do you fancy _____ tonight? (go out)
6 Huong is planning _____ French at university. (study)

Grammar

3 Choose the correct form.

1 We ~~couldn't~~ / can't help you. We're busy.
2 They *won't* / *didn't* have to go to school tomorrow.
3 He *can* / *could* read when he was three years old.
4 You *must* / *had to* phone the doctor now.
5 I *couldn't* / *won't be able to* go to the cinema next week.
6 The police *must* / *had to* close the motorway yesterday.

4 Put the words in the correct order to make sentences and questions.

1 I can smell fish cooking.

1 I   cooking   can   smell   fish   .
2 There   a   was   selling   man   ice cream   .
3 you   Can   mobile   hear   a   ringing   phone   ?
4 I   a   wearing   blue   saw   woman   a   dress   .
5 two   sitting   people   river   There   the   are   by   .
6 children   some   watched   football   playing   We   .

Skills

5 Read the text. Answer the questions.

James Bond is a spy from a series of books by Ian Fleming. Several of the novels have been made into films, and I love watching them. There have been over 20 Bond films, and they usually involve the leading character trying to save the world from disaster. My favourite is *Die Another Day*, which starred Pierce Brosnan, and was directed by Lee Tamahori. The story starts off in North Korea. Then Bond travels to Hong Kong, Cuba, and London. The story is a bit silly, but the film is very exciting because the special effects are amazing. It's not surprising though. The film cost nearly $150,000,000 to make!

1 What sort of films are James Bond films?
2 What usually happens in a Bond film?
3 Who are these people?
   a James Bond   c Pierce Brosnan
   b Ian Fleming   d Lee Tamahori
4 Where does *Die Another Day* take place?
5 What makes the film exciting?
6 How much did it cost to film *Die Another Day*?

English for Everyday Life

6 Read the sentences. Complete the words.

1 Does that m *e a n* that you're working late?
2 Yes, it l _ _ _ _ like it.
3 Are you s _ _ _ _ _ that the report isn't ready?
4 Yes, I'm a _ _ _ _ _ so.
5 Don't tell me t _ _ _ you forgot to phone Nico.
6 Yes, un _ _ _ _ _ _ _ _ _ _ _.

7 Put the words in the correct order to make expressions.

1 Would you like to see a film tonight?

1 film   like   see   a   tonight   Would   to   you   ?
2 tonight   don't   going   I   really   like   feel   out   .
3 Monday   you   having   Do   a   drink   on   fancy   ?
4 Monday   sorry,   I'm   manage   can't   I   .
5 don't   Why   club   we   that   try   new   ?
6 don't   to   I   go   want   really   .

Wordlist 57–64

57 do a course (v) /ˌduː ə ˈkɔːs/
do judo (v) /ˌduː ˈdʒuːdəʊ/
do some damage (v) /ˌduː səm ˈdæmɪdʒ/
do some photocopying (v) /ˌduː səm ˈfəʊtəʊkɒpiɪŋ/
do the housework (v) /ˌduː ðə ˈhaʊswɜːk/
do the shopping (v) /ˌduː ðə ˈʃɒpɪŋ/
make a decision (v) /ˌmeɪk ə dɪˈsɪʒn/
make a drink (v) /ˌmeɪk ə ˈdrɪŋk/
make a film (v) /ˌmeɪk ə ˈfɪlm/
make a mistake (v) /ˌmeɪk ə mɪˈsteɪk/
make a phone call (v) /ˌmeɪk ə ˈfəʊn kɔːl/
make friends (v) /ˌmeɪk ˈfrendz/

58 able to (adj) /ˈeɪbl tə/
can (modal) /kæn/
can't (modal) /kɑːnt/
coffee machine (n) /ˈkɒfi məˌʃiːn/
dangerous (adj) /ˈdeɪndʒərəs/
don't have to (modal) /ˌdəʊnt ˈhæv tə/
have to (modal) /hæv tə/
in stock (adj) /ˌɪn ˈstɒk/
must (modal) /mʌst/
mustn't (modal) /ˈmʌsnt/

59 adventure film (n) /ədˈventʃə ˌfɪlm/
cartoon (n) /kɑːˈtuːn/
comedy (n) /ˈkɒmədi/
horror film (n) /ˈhɒrə ˌfɪlm/
musical (n) /ˈmjuːzɪkl/
romance (n) /rəʊˈmæns/
science fiction film (n) /ˌsaɪəns ˈfɪkʃn ˌfɪlm/
western (n) /ˈwestən/
colour film (n) /ˈkʌlə ˌfɪlm/
silent film (n) /ˈsaɪlənt ˌfɪlm/
sound film (n) /ˈsaʊnd ˌfɪlm/
special effects (n pl) /ˌspeʃl ɪˈfekts/
Bollywood (n) /ˈbɒliwʊd/
city life (n) /ˈsɪti ˌlaɪf/
film industry (n) /ˈfɪlm ˌɪndəstri/
hero (n) /ˈhɪərəʊ/
Hindi (n) /ˈhɪndi/
internationally (adv) /ˌɪntəˈnæʃnəli/
traditional (adj) /trəˈdɪʃənl/
villain (n) /ˈvɪlən/

60 Are you saying /ˌɑː ju ˈseɪŋ ðət/
(that) ... ? (exp)
Does that mean /dʌz ˌðæt ˈmiːn ðət/
(that) ...? (exp)
Don't tell me (that) ... (exp) /ˌdəʊnt tel mi ðət/
it looks like ... (exp) /ɪt ˈlʊks laɪk/
unfortunately (exp) /ʌnˈfɔːtʃənətli/
fire (n) /ˈfaɪə(r)/
schedule (n) /ˈʃedjuːl/
studio (n) /ˈstjuːdiəʊ/

61 avoid (v) /əˈvɔɪd/
decide (v) /dɪˈsaɪd/
enjoy (v) /ɪnˈdʒɔɪ/
expect (v) /ɪkˈspekt/
fancy (v) /ˈfænsi/
finish (v) /ˈfɪnɪʃ/
give up (v) /ˌɡɪv ˈʌp/
hope (v) /həʊp/
I can't stand ... (exp) /aɪ ˌkɑːnt ˈstænd/
I don't mind ... (exp) /aɪ ˌdəʊnt ˈmaɪnd/
imagine (v) /ɪˈmædʒɪn/
manage (v) /ˈmænɪdʒ/
need (v) /niːd/
offer (v) /ˈɒfə(r)/
plan (v) /plæn/
promise (v) /ˈprɒmɪs/
want (v) /wɒnt/

62 bark (v) /bɑːk/
hang (v) /hæŋ/
helicopter (n) /ˈhelɪkɒptə(r)/
jump off (v) /ˌdʒʌmp ˈɒf/
paragliding (n) /ˈpærəɡlaɪdɪŋ/
take up (v) /ˌteɪk ˈʌp/
upside down (adj) /ˌʌpsaɪd ˈdaʊn/

63 bone (n) /bəʊn/
butterfly (n) /ˈbʌtəflaɪ/
chew (v) /tʃuː/
delicious (adj) /dɪˈlɪʃəs/
follow (v) /ˈfɒləʊ/
ground (n) /ɡraʊnd/
have a rest (v) /ˌhæv ə ˈrest/
in trouble (exp) /ɪn ˈtrʌbl/
leopard (n) /ˈlepəd/
monkey (n) /ˈmʌŋki/
towards (prep) /təˈwɔːdz/
trick (v) /trɪk/
wander (v) /ˈwɒndə(r)/
bush (n) /bʊʃ/
hatch (v) /hætʃ/
proverb (n) /ˈprɒvɜːb/
spot (n) /spɒt/
worm (n) /wɜːm/
worth (adj) /wɜːθ/

64 Do you fancy ...? (exp) /ˌduː jə ˈfænsi/
Do you want ...? (exp) /ˌduː jə ˈwɒnt/
How about ...? (exp) /ˌhaʊ əˈbaʊt/
Shall we ...? (exp) /ˈʃæl wi/
Why don't we ...? (exp) /ˈwaɪ dəʊnt wi/
Would you like ...? (exp) /ˌwʊd jə ˈlaɪk/
I can't make that. (exp) /aɪ ˌkɑːnt ˈmek ˌðæt/
I can't manage that. (exp) /aɪ ˌkɑːnt ˈmænɪdʒ ˌðæt/
I don't feel like ... (exp) /aɪ ˌdəʊnt ˈfiːl laɪk/

Review 65–72

Vocabulary

1a Read the definitions. Unscramble the anagrams to find the words.

1 A group of people who play a sport together.
mate   team
2 A place to play football.   *hpict*
3 A piece of tennis equipment.   *atkrec*
4 Win a point or a goal.   *reocs*
5 The person who is in charge of a game.   *erereef*
6 Use your arm to send a ball through the air.   *owtrh*

b Write one more place, person, piece of equipment, and verb connected with sport.

2 Complete the sentences. Use the correct preposition.

about	for	in	of	to	~~with~~

1 Do you agree __with__ me?
2 I'm waiting _____ a phone call.
3 Does Thuyen take part _____ any sports?
4 We're worried _____ our exams.
5 Are you afraid _____ spiders?
6 Faisal and Ali are talking _____ their teacher.

Grammar

3 Choose the correct relative pronoun.

Did you see the photos ¹*who / that* Laura took in Tunisia? She had a great time. The hotel ²*who / which* she stayed in was really beautiful. And the couple ³*which / that* own the hotel have a son ⁴*who / which* is a famous footballer. He's the player ⁵*who / which* scored the winning goal in the championship match.

4 Tick the sentences which do not need a relative pronoun.

1 Moscow is a place that we'd like to visit. ✓
2 People who play loud music annoy me.
3 The man who you met is my father-in-law.
4 Homework is something which no one likes doing.
5 Music is the thing which is most important to me.

5 Rewrite the sentences. Use the third conditional.

1 If Suzi had taken her umbrella, she wouldn't have got wet.
1 Suzi didn't take her umbrella and she got wet.
2 We didn't have breakfast, so we were hungry.
3 I felt ill, so I went to the doctor's.
4 They arrived late and they missed the meeting.
5 It wasn't a nice day, so we stayed at home.

Skills

6 Read the text. Are the sentences true (T) or false (F)?

Now I've reached fifty I don't enjoy my birthdays. I wish I'd done more with my life. For example, I left school when I was sixteen, and I didn't go to university, which is something I've always regretted. I wanted to travel, so I joined the army, but I didn't really enjoy it. When I left I was offered a job in a factory. I'm glad I took the job. If I hadn't taken it, I wouldn't have met my wife. She says you shouldn't regret things. You can't change the past, so it's better to think about the future. Perhaps she's right.

1 The writer is going to be fifty soon.   F
2 He thinks he has done a lot during his life.
3 He wishes he had gone to university.
4 He didn't enjoy the army.
5 Taking the factory job was a good decision.

English for Everyday Life

7 Put the words in the correct order to make expressions.

1 Jing I meet tomorrow promised to .
2 Sheila don't to want down let I .
3 already I'm something tonight doing .
4 without to You'll me do have .

8 Complete the invitation.

forward	~~having~~	invitation	join	make	best

Dear Oliver,
I'm ¹*having* a dinner party on Saturday, and I'd be very pleased if you could ² _____ us.
Looking ³ _____ to seeing you.
Maxine xx

Hi Maxine
Thank you very much for the ⁴ _____ . I'm sorry, but I'm going to be away, so I won't be able to
⁵ _____ it.
Hope the party goes well.
All the ⁶ _____
Oliver

65 sport (n) /spɔːt/
ball (n) /bɔːl/
bat (n) /bæt/
beat (v) /biːt/
catch (v) /kætʃ/
court (n) /kɔːt/
draw (n) /drɔː/
goal (n) /gəʊl/
half-time (n) /ˌhɑːfˈtaɪm/
hit (v) /hɪt/
kick (v) /kɪk/
lose to (v) /ˈluːz tə/
net (n) /net/
nil (n) /nɪl/
pitch (n) /pɪtʃ/
player (n) /ˈpleɪə(r)/
racket (n) /ˈrækɪt/
referee (n) /ˌrefəˈriː/
score (n + v) /skɔː(r)/
team (n) /tiːm/
throw (v) /θrəʊ/
win (v) /wɪn/

66 below (prep) /bɪˈləʊ/
complain (v) /kəmˈpleɪn/
invite (v) /ɪnˈvaɪt/
keep (someone) awake (v) /ˌkiːp sʌmwʌn əˈweɪk/
keep noise down (v) /ˌkiːp ˈnɔɪz daʊn/
keep (someone) happy (v) /ˌkiːp sʌmwʌn ˈhæpi/
reach an agreement (v) /ˌriːtʃ ən əˈgriːmənt/

67 full (adj) /fʊl/
golf ball (n) /ˈgɒlf bɔːl/
jar (n) /dʒɑː(r)/
philosophy (n) /fəˈlɒsəfi/
pour (v) /pɔː(r)/
sand (n) /sænd/
space (n) /speɪs/
stone (n) /stəʊn/
unusual (adj) /ʌnˈjuːʒuəl/
wonder (v) /ˈwʌndə(r)/

68 commitment (n) /kəˈmɪtmənt/
priority (n) /praɪˈɒrəti/
let (someone) down (exp) /ˌlet sʌmwʌn ˈdaʊn/
already doing something (exp) /ˌɔːlredi ˈduːɪŋ ˌsʌmθɪŋ/
I promised to go. (v) /aɪ ˈprɒmɪst tə ˌgəʊ/
It can wait. (exp) /ɪt kən ˈweɪt/
They'll have to do without me. (exp) /ðeɪl ˌhæv tə ˌdu wɪˈðaʊt mi/
alter (v) /ˈɔːltə(r)/
entertain (v) /ˌentəˈteɪn/
play (a part) (v) /ˌpleɪ ə ˈpɑːt/
sewing (n) /ˈsəʊɪŋ/

69 apply for (v) /əˈplaɪ fə/
afraid of (adj) /əˈfreɪd əv/
agree with (v) /əˈgriː wɪð/
bored with (adj) /ˈbɔːd wɪð/
different from (adj) /ˈdɪfrənt frəm/
good at (adj) /ˈgʊd ət/
interested in (adj) /ˈɪntrəstɪd ɪn/
look at (v) /ˈlʊk ət/
similar to (adj) /ˈsɪmələ tə/
suffer from (v) /ˈsʌfə frəm/
take part in (v) /ˌteɪk ˈpɑːt ɪn/
talk to (v) /ˈtɔːk tə/
think about (v) /ˈθɪŋk əˌbaʊt/
tired of (adj) /ˈtaɪəd əv/
wait for (v) /ˈweɪt fə/
worry about (v) /ˈwʌri əˌbaʊt/

70 bite (n) /baɪt/
cancer (n) /ˈkænsə(r)/
examine (v) /ɪgˈzæmɪn/
notice (v) /ˈnəʊtɪs/
lump (n) /lʌmp/
poisonous (adj) /ˈpɔɪzənəs/
save (someone's) life (v) /ˌseɪv sʌmwʌnz ˈlaɪf/
spider (n) /ˈspaɪdə(r)/
treatment (n) /ˈtriːtmənt/

71 bankrupt (adj) /ˈbæŋkrʌpt/
borrow (v) /ˈbɒrəʊ/
computer software company (n) /kəmˌpjuːtə ˈsɒftweə ˌkʌmpəni/
evening classes (n pl) /ˈiːvnɪŋ ˌklɑːsɪz/
fight (v) /faɪt/
guy (n) /gaɪ/
jealous (adj) /ˈdʒeləs/
librarian (n) /laɪˈbreəriən/
look after (v) /ˌlʊk ˈɑːftə/
low-paid (adj) /ˌləʊˈpeɪd/
part-time (adj) /ˌpɑːtˈtaɪm/
regret (v) /rɪˈgret/

72 Look(ing) forward to seeing you. (exp) /ˌlʊkɪŋ ˌfɔːwəd tə ˈsiːɪŋ ju/
We'd be very pleased if ... (exp) /wiːd bi ˌveri ˈpliːzd ɪf/
not be able to make it (exp) /ˌnɒt bi ˌeɪbl tə ˈmeɪk ɪt/
invitation (n) /ˌɪnvɪˈteɪʃn/
We'd love to come. (exp) /wiːd ˈlʌv tə ˈkʌm/
housewarming (adj) /ˈhaʊs wɔːmɪŋ/
7 for 7.30 (exp) /ˌsevn fə ˌsevnˈθɜːti/
black tie (exp) /ˌblæk ˈtaɪ/
Bring a bottle. (exp) /ˌbrɪŋ ə ˈbɒtl/
dinner suit (n) /ˈdɪnə ˌsuːt/
formal dress (n) /ˈfɔːml ˌdres/
RSVP (exp) /ˌɑːr es viː ˈpiː/

Vocabulary

1 Put the stages of the journey in the correct order.

a ___ fasten your seatbelt
b ___ check in
c ___ land
d _1_ drive to the terminal
e ___ board the plane
f ___ take off
g ___ go through security
h ___ wait in the departure lounge

2 Match the sentence halves.

1 We don't spend a lot on _e_   a bank account.
2 You can use your card at this ___   b interest.
3 His salary is paid into his ___   c debit.
4 I need to check my account ___   d balance.
5 A savings account earns ___   e luxuries.
6 We pay all our bills by direct ___   f cash machine.

Grammar

3 Put the words in the correct order to make indirect questions.

1 Do you know where Timbuktu is?

1 where   know   you   is   Timbuktu   Do   ?
2 Anita   how   wonder   old   is   I   ?
3 whether   speaks   Sam   Do   know   Arabic   you   ?
4 it   wonder   snow   will   I   if   tomorrow   .
5 They   where   don't   Jamal   know   works   .
6 We'd   the   starts   like   know   to   time
   what   film   .
7 remember   I   what   his   can't   is   name   .
8 wants   Mike   know   to   if   leaving   you're   .

4 Rewrite the sentences. Use reported speech.

1 I left my job at the factory.
   Marcus said *he'd left his job at the factory*.
2 I'm not working now.
   He said _____ .
3 I've decided to go back to university.
   He said _____ .
4 I'm going to study business.
   He said _____ .
5 I want to have my own company.
   He said _____ .
6 You can work for me.
   He said _____ .
7 I'll pay you a lot of money.
   He said _____ .

Skills

5 Complete the messages.

| come up | make | ~~rang~~ | tickets | whether |

Hamida [1] _rang_ . She wants to know [2]_____ you've booked the theatre [3]_____ . Something has [4]_____ and she can't [5]_____ Friday.

| because | called | if | meeting | would |

Mr Khunpol [6]_____ . He [7]_____ like to know [8]_____ it's possible to change the time of his dental appointment, [9]_____ he has an important [10]_____ on Monday.

6 Match the sentences halves.

1 Don't make things   a in the rubbish bin.
   easy for ___   b old bank statements.
2 Never give your PIN ___   c credit card bills carefully.
3 You should destroy ___   d to anyone.
4 Make sure you delete   e before dumping an old
   all the data ___   computer.
5 Always check your ___   f identity thieves.
6 Don't throw old bills ___

English for Everyday Life

7 Match the sentences with the responses.

1 Can I have a word? ___
2 What's on your mind? ___
3 I'll see what I can do. ___
4 Thanks for your help. ___

a I really appreciate that.
b It's OK. I understand the situation.
c I wonder if we can change our meeting.
d Sure.

8 Who says these sentences at the bank? Write *cashier* or *customer*.

1 Is there anything else I can help you with? *cashier*
2 I'd like to open an account.
3 Someone will be with you shortly.
4 Can I pay this cheque into my account, please?
5 You'll need to speak to one of our advisers for that.
6 What can I do for you today?

73	baggage reclaim (n)	/ˈbægɪdʒ rɪˌkleɪm/
	board the plane (v)	/ˌbɔːd ðə ˈpleɪn/
	boarding card (n)	/ˈbɔːdɪŋ ˌkɑːd/
	cabin crew (n)	/ˈkæbɪn ˌkruː/
	check in (v)	/ˌtʃek ˈɪn/
	customs (n pl)	/ˈkʌstəmz/
	departure lounge (v)	/dɪˈpɑːtʃə ˌlaʊndʒ/
	domestic departures (n pl)	/dəˈmestɪk dɪˌpɑːtʃəz/
	fasten your seatbelt (v)	/ˌfɑːsn jɔː ˈsiːtbelt/
	flight attendant (n)	/ˈflaɪt əˌtendənt/
	flight connections (n pl)	/ˌflaɪt kəˈnekʃnz/
	go through passport control (v)	/ˌgəʊ θruː ˌpɑːspɔːt kənˈtrəʊl/
	go through security (v)	/ˌgəʊ θruː sɪˈkjʊərəti/
	hand luggage (n)	/ˈhænd ˌlʌgɪdʒ/
	land (v)	/lænd/
	overhead locker (n)	/ˌəʊvəhed ˈlɒkə(r)/
	passenger (n)	/ˈpæsɪndʒə(r)/
	pilot (n)	/ˈpaɪlət/
	take off (v)	/ˌteɪk ˈɒf/
	terminal (n)	/ˈtɜːmɪnl/
	travelling by air (exp)	/ˌtrævəlɪŋ baɪ ˈeə(r)/
74	back (adv)	/bæk/
	text (v)	/tekst/
	whether (conj)	/ˈweðə(r)/
	yet (adv)	/jet/
75	come up (v)	/ˌkʌm ˈʌp/
	flight (n)	/flaɪt/
	ring (v)	/rɪŋ/
	till (prep)	/tɪl/
76	Can I have a word? (exp)	/ˌkən aɪ hæv ə ˈwɜːd/
	I really appreciate it. (exp)	/aɪ ˈriːəli əˈpriːʃieɪt ɪt/
	I understand the situation. (exp)	/aɪ ˌʌndəˈstænd ðə ˌsɪtʃuˈeɪʃn/
	(That's) fair enough. (exp)	/ˌðæts ˌfeər ɪˈnʌf/
	What's on your mind (exp)	/ˈwɒts ɒn jɔː ˈmaɪnd/
	go round (v)	/ˌgəʊ ˈraʊnd/
	sort something out (v)	/ˌsɔːt ˌsʌmθɪŋ ˈaʊt/
	Sure. (exp)	/ʃʊə(r)/

77	personal finance (n)	/ˌpɜːsənl ˈfaɪnæns/
	account balance (n)	/əˈkaʊnt ˌbæləns/
	direct debit (n)	/dəˌrekt ˈdebɪt/
	earn interest (v)	/ˌɜːn ˈɪntrəst/
	essential (n)	/ɪˈsenʃl/
	interest rate (n)	/ˈɪntrəst ˌreɪt/
	loan (n)	/ləʊn/
	luxury (n)	/ˈlʌkʃəri/
	pay a bill (v)	/ˌpeɪ ə ˈbɪl/
	pay into (v)	/ˌpeɪ ˈɪntə/
	save up (v)	/ˌseɪv ˈʌp/
	savings (n pl)	/ˈseɪvɪŋz/
	transfer (v)	/trænsˈfɜː(r)/
	withdraw (v)	/wɪðˈdrɔː/
	council tax (n)	/ˈkaʊnsl ˌtæks/
	deduct (v)	/dɪˈdʌkt/
	income tax (n)	/ˈɪnkʌm ˌtæks/
	local government (n)	/ˌləʊkl ˈgʌvənmənt/
	local tax (n)	/ˌləʊkl ˈtæks/
	rate (n)	/reɪt/
	rubbish collection (n)	/ˈrʌbɪʃ kəˌlekʃn/
	sales tax (n)	/ˈseɪlz ˌtæks/
	streetlights (n pl)	/ˈstriːtlaɪts/
	vary (v)	/ˈveəri/
	VAT – Value Added Tax (n)	/ˌviː eɪ ˈtiː - ˌvæljuː ˈædɪd ˌtæks/
78	completely (adv)	/kəmˈpliːtli/
	olive oil (n)	/ˌɒlɪv ˈɔɪl/
	understandable (adj)	/ˌʌndəˈstændəbl/
79	bank statement (n)	/ˈbæŋk ˌsteɪtmənt/
	data (n)	/ˈdeɪtə/
	delete (v)	/dɪˈliːt/
	dump (v)	/dʌmp/
	email (v)	/ˈiːmeɪl/
	expert (n)	/ˈekspɜːt/
	maiden name (n)	/ˈmeɪdn ˌneɪm/
	password (n)	/ˈpɑːswɜːd/
	protect (v)	/prəˈtekt/

80 & Epilogue

cashier	/kæˈʃɪə(r)/
Is there anything else I can help you with? (exp)	/ɪz ðeər ˈeniθɪŋ ˈels aɪ kən ˈhelp jə wɪð/
Somebody will be with you shortly. (exp)	/ˈsʌmbədi wɪl bi ˈwɪð ju ˈʃɔːtli/
What can I do for you today? (exp)	/ˈwɒt kən aɪ ˈdu fə ju təˈdeɪ/
adviser (n)	/ədˈvaɪzə(r)/
curtain (n)	/ˈkɜːtn/
emergency services (n pl)	/iˈmɜːdʒənsi ˈsɜːvɪsɪz/
letterbox (n)	/ˈletəbɒks/
trip (v)	/trɪp/
try on (v)	/ˌtraɪ ˈɒn/

Grammar reference

Lessons 1–4

Present simple

1 We use the present simple for:
- **permanent or general states**
We **live** in a village.
She **doesn't work** here.
- **regular activities**
I **play** basketball on Thursdays.
He usually **finishes** at 5.30.

Positive statements

I/You/We/They	I **play** tennis.
He/She/It	He **plays** tennis.

Negative statements

I/You/We/They	We **don't** (do not) **play** tennis.
He/She/It	She **doesn't** (does not) **play** tennis.

NOTE After *doesn't* we use the infinitive form of the verb NOT the third person form.
He doesn't **like** his job.
NOT ~~He doesn't likes his job.~~

2 We often use these expressions with the present simple:
usually, often, always, every day, on Saturdays

Spelling

1 When the verb ends in -ss, -sh, -ch, or -o, we add -es.
miss   misses   catch   catches
rush   rushes   go   goes

2 When the verb ends in -y, we change the -y to -ies.
hurry   hurries

Present continuous

1 We use the present continuous for:
- **temporary states**
He **isn't wearing** a suit today.
We**'re doing** a leadership course this week.
- **what is happening at the time of speaking**
She**'s talking** on her mobile at the moment
I**'m not using** the Internet now.

2 We often use these expressions with the present continuous:
now, at the moment, today, this week

3 We make the present continuous tense with the verb *to be* and the *-ing* form of the verb (the present participle).

Positive and negative statements

I	I**'m** (am) **watching** TV. I**'m not** (am not) **having** dinner.
He/She It	She**'s** (is) **cycling**. She **isn't** (is not) **running**.
We/You/They	They**'re** (are) **taking** the bus. They **aren't** (are not) **walking**.

Spelling

1 For verbs that end in -e, we remove the -e and add -ing.
take   taking   drive   driving

2 For verbs with a short vowel and only one consonant, we double the consonant and add -ing.
get   getting   stop   stopping

Describing states (stative verbs)

Some verbs describe states, not actions. We don't normally use these verbs in the present continuous, even when we are talking about the present moment:
need, want, think, believe, know, like, prefer, love

I **don't want** to watch TV at the moment.
NOT ~~I'm not wanting to watch TV at the moment.~~

Present simple and present continuous: question forms

1 Present simple

yes/no questions and short answers

I/You/We/They	**Do** you **use** a laptop?	Yes, I do. No, I don't.
He/She/It	**Does** he **use** a laptop?	Yes, he does. No, he doesn't.

NOTE In questions we use the infinitive form of the verb.
Does she use a laptop?
NOT ~~Does she uses a laptop?~~

wh- questions
In *wh-* questions we use the normal question form.
Where **do you work**?
How often **does she shop** online?

2 Present continuous

To make questions we put the verb *to be* in front of the subject.

yes / no questions and short answers

Statement   **He is** downloading a song.

Question   **Is he** downloading a song?   Yes, he is.
No, he isn't.

Statement   **They are** having lunch.

Question   **Are they** having lunch?   Yes, they are.
No, they aren't.

wh- questions
In *wh-* questions we use the question word order.
What **are you doing**?
NOT ~~What you are doing?~~

Present continuous with future meaning

We also use the present continuous + a future time expression to talk about arrangements.
We**'re meeting** for dinner on Friday.
I**'m working** this weekend.

Lessons 5–8

Past simple

We use the past simple to talk about completed events in the past.

1 *to be*

Positive and negative statements	
I / He / She / It	I **was** ill yesterday. She **wasn't** (was not) ill yesterday.
We / You / They	We **were** away last week. They **weren't** (were not) away last week.

To make questions with *to be*, we put the verb in front of the subject.

yes / no questions and short answers

Statement   **She was** ill.

Question   **Was she** ill?   Yes, she was.
No, she wasn't.

Statement   **They were** on holiday.

Question   **Were they** on holiday?   Yes, they were.
No, they weren't.

wh- questions
When **were you** away?
Where **was the meeting**?

2 Regular verbs

NOTE The past simple is the same for all subjects.

With most verbs we add *-ed*.

look	looked
miss	missed

When the verb ends in *-e*, we add *-d*.

arrive	arrived
believe	believed

When the verb ends in a short vowel and a single consonant, we double the consonant and add *-ed*.

stop	stopped
jog	jogged

When the verb ends in *-y*, we change the *-y* to *-ied*.

study	studied

NOTE When the verb ends in *-t* or *-d* we pronounce the final syllable /ɪd/.
waited /ɪd/, needed /ɪd/

3 Irregular verbs

Many common verbs have an irregular past form.

take	They **took** the bus.
leave	I **left** at 10.15.

See the list of irregular verbs on page 123.

4 Negative statements

The negative form is the same for all subjects and for both regular and irregular verbs.

We **didn't** (did not) **like** the film.
She **didn't** (did not) **go** to work.

NOTE After *didn't* we use the infinitive form of the verb.
We didn't **watch** the game.
NOT ~~We didn't watched the game.~~
I didn't **get** any letters.
NOT ~~I didn't got any letters.~~

5 Questions

The question form is the same for all subjects and for both regular and irregular verbs.

yes / no questions and short answers
Did you **have** a good time?   Yes, we did.
No, we didn't.

wh- questions
Where **did you go**?
When **did she arrive**?

Grammar reference

NOTE In questions, we use the infinitive form of the verb.

Did you **go** to the party?

NOT ~~Did you went to the party?~~

What did you **do**?

NOT ~~What did you did?~~

have to

We use *have to* to show that something is necessary.

Present	
I **have to** go to work.	= It's necessary.
She **has to** book a hotel.	
I **don't have to** go to work.	= It isn't necessary.
She **doesn't have to** book a hotel.	
Do you **have to** go to work?	= Is it necessary?
Does she **have to** book a hotel?	
Past	
He **had to** go home again.	= It was necessary.
He **didn't have to** take Emily to school.	= It wasn't necessary.
Did it **have to** be a bad start?	= Was it necessary?

Possessive pronouns

We use a possessive pronoun to replace a possessive adjective + noun. Possessive pronouns are the same for singular and plural.

This is my book.   This is **mine**.
They're my books.   They're **mine**.

Possessive adjective	my	your	his	her	its	our	their
Possessive pronoun	mine	yours	his	hers	its	ours	theirs

Lessons 9–12

Articles

1 A singular noun normally has an indefinite article (*a / an*) or a definite article (*the*).

An engineer is fixing **the** computer.

NOT ~~Engineer is fixing computer.~~

2 The indefinite article: *a / an*

We use the indefinite article for something that is not specific.

I bought **a** shirt.

You'll need **an** umbrella.

NOTE Plural nouns don't always need an indefinite article.

We're going to **a** party.   article + singular noun

BUT We like parties.   no article + plural noun

3 The definite article: *the*

We use the definite article for something specific:

– when we have mentioned a thing before

We went to **a** concert.

Was **the** concert good?

NOTE Plural nouns need a definite article in this situation, too.

She's wearing new shoes. **The** shoes aren't very comfortable.

– when there is probably only one

I'll meet you at **the** station.

The boss wants to see you.

– with ordinal numbers and superlatives

on **the** second floor

the best restaurant

Lessons 13–16

Nouns and adjectives

We can make a lot of adjectives by adding a suffix to a noun.

Suffix	Noun	Adjective
-ous	danger	dangerous
	fame	famous
-ful	success	successful
	beauty	beautiful
-ent / -ant	intelligence	intelligent
	importance	important
-y	luck	lucky
	anger	angry

NOTE *-y* is a common adjective ending, but words ending in *-ty* are often nouns.

Noun	difficul**ty**	safe**ty**	securi**ty**	hones**ty**
Adjective	difficult	safe	secure	honest

Grammar reference

Present perfect

1 The present perfect connects the past with the present. We use it:
– when we're interested in the present result of an event
I'**ve cooked** the dinner. (So we can eat now.)
– to talk about experiences up to now (often with *ever* and *never*)
I'**ve never eaten** sushi.
Have you **ever been** sailing?

2 We make the present perfect with *have / has* and a past participle.

Positive and negative statements

I / You / We / They	We'**ve** (have) **seen** that film. I **haven't** (have not) **booked** a table.
He / She / It	He'**s** (has) **been** to Australia. She **hasn't** (has not) **had** lunch.

3 To form regular past participles, we add *-ed* to the verb stem.

watch   watched
arrive   arrived

This is the same as the regular past tense (see Lessons 5–8 above for spelling rules).

Verbs with an irregular past tense also have an irregular past participle.

Infinitive	Past simple	Past participle
give	gave	given
buy	bought	bought
forget	forgot	forgotten

See the list of irregular verbs on page 123.

4 To make questions with the present perfect, we put *have / has* in front of the subject.

yes / no questions and short answers
Statement   **He has** finished work.

Question   **Has he** finished work?   Yes, he has.
                                     No, he hasn't.

Statement   **You have** eaten it.

Question   **Have you** eaten it?   Yes, I have.
                                     No, I haven't.

wh- questions
What **has he done**?
Where **have you been**?

5 *been* and *gone*

In the present perfect tense, we use *been* instead of *gone* when we are talking about our experiences.
Have you ever **been** to Iceland?
No, I haven't.
We've never **been** skiing.

Been means *go and come back*
I've **been** to the bank. = I'm not at the bank now.
She's **gone** to the bank. = She's at the bank now.

Present perfect and past simple

The present perfect and the past simple both tell us about events in the past.

1 We use the present perfect to talk about:
– the effect of the event on the present
I'**ve broken** my arm. (So I can't go swimming.)

– general experiences when we don't give the time
John **has broken** his arm three times.

2 We use the past simple to talk about:
– the details of the event
How **did you break** your arm?
NOT ~~How have you broken your arm?~~
I **fell** downstairs.
NOT ~~I've fallen downstairs.~~

– the time or place of the event
When **did that happen**?
NOT ~~When has that happened?~~
I **did** it last Friday.
NOT ~~I've done it last Friday.~~

3 We often use the present perfect followed by the past simple to give some news and then give details about the event.
I'**ve broken** my arm. I **fell** downstairs. I **did** it last Friday.

Numbers

1 We say large numbers like this:
400 cars = four **hundred** cars
NOT ~~four hundred of cars~~ or ~~four hundreds cars~~

2 In large numbers we say *and* before tens and units.
620 = six hundred **and** twenty
NOT ~~six hundred twenty~~
7005 = seven thousand **and** five
NOT ~~seven thousand five~~
310,000 = three hundred **and** ten thousand
NOT ~~three hundred ten thousand~~

Grammar reference

3 When we write large numbers we separate them with commas.
twenty million = 20,000,000
NOT ~~20.000.000~~
nine thousand = 9,000
NOT ~~9.000~~

4 We separate decimals with a full stop.
eight **point** five   = 8.5   NOT ~~8,5~~
twelve **point** seven three = 12.73 NOT ~~12,73~~

5 To make fractions, we normally use ordinal numbers.
$^1/_3$ = a third $^3/_5$ = three fifths
BUT
½ = a half   ¼ = a quarter

6 After percentages and fractions, we use *of*.
Thirty per cent **of** people
60% **of** the population
a third **of** all houses
Three quarters **of** the money
BUT we don't normally use *of* after *half*.
half the population

Lessons 17–20

The future

We can express the future in different ways.
1 *will*
We use *will* + a verb for:
– general predictions
In the future, most people **will work** at home. They **won't work** in offices.

– spontaneous decisions
A I haven't got time to post this letter.
B It's OK. I**'ll post** it for you.

2 *going to*
We use *be going to* + a verb for:
– predictions when it's clear now that something is certain in the future
Look at those clouds. It**'s going to** rain.

– fixed plans and decisions
We**'re going to** watch the football match on TV.

probably

We often use *probably* with the *will* future.
With a positive verb, it goes after *will* and before the main verb.

I'll **probably** get a sandwich.
NOT ~~I'll get probably a sandwich.~~

With a negative verb it goes before *won't*.
I **probably** won't go to the cinema.
NOT ~~I won't probably go to the cinema.~~

First conditional

We use the first conditional to show a real or likely result.
1 A conditional sentence always has two clauses.
an *if* clause   a main clause
If you **do** this exercise, your back **will be** flexible.

When the *if* clause comes second, there is no comma between the clauses.
Your back **will be** flexible if you **do** this exercise.

2 We use the present simple tense in the *if* clause and the *will* future in the main clause.
If you **have** a nap, you**'ll feel** better.
NOT ~~If you'll have a nap, you'll feel better.~~

3 We use the same form with time clauses.
You**'ll feel** very tired when you **go** home.
I**'ll join** you in the café after I **finish** these letters.

Lessons 21–24

Past perfect

1 We use the past perfect to look back from one past event to events that happened before that time.
When Sally **arrived** at work, she **was** annoyed, because she **had forgotten** her briefcase.
When Sally **arrived** at work, she **was** annoyed.
(past simple – it happened in the past.)
She **had forgotten** her briefcase.
(past perfect – it happened before she arrived.)

2 We make the past perfect with *had* and a past participle. (See Lessons 13–16 for past participles.)

Positive and negative statements		
I He She It You We They	had 'd had not hadn't	phoned the police. been in a traffic jam. taken the train. had a meeting.

Grammar reference

3 To make questions with the past perfect, we put *had* in front of the subject.

yes / no **questions and short answers**

Statement   **He had** sent the email.

Question   **Had he** sent the email?   Yes, he had.
                                                          No, he hadn't.

Statement   **They had** broken it.

Question   **Had they** broken it?   Yes, they had.
                                                      No, they hadn't.

wh- **questions**

Where **had she gone**?

Why **had they written** the letter?

Sentence linkers

We use sentence linkers to connect clauses in a sentence. The linker shows the relationship between the clauses.

1 *because* **shows a cause.**

I was late **because** I missed the train.

2 *so* **shows a result.**

I missed the train **so** I was late.

3 *when* **connects two things that happen at the same time or one immediately after the other.**

When I arrived at the station, I bought my ticket.

4 *and* **connects similar things or a sequence of events.**

I got on the train **and** sat down.

5 *but* **shows a contrast.**

I hurried to the station **but** the train had gone.

Time prepositions

1 We use *on* **with:**

– days	**on** Monday, **on** my birthday, **on** New Year's Day
– dates	**on** 21 March, **on** Thursday 4 September
– parts of a specific day	**on** Sunday morning, **on** Friday night

2 We use *at* **with:**

– times	**at** 12.15, **at** ten past three
– *the weekend / night*	**at** the weekend, **at** night
– festivals	**at** Christmas, **at** New Year

3 We use *in* **with:**

– months	**in** November, **in** January
– seasons	**in** spring / summer / autumn / winter
– parts of the day	**in** the morning / the afternoon / the evening BUT **at** night
– years / centuries	**in** 2008, **in** the nineteenth century

Lessons 25–28

Nouns and adjectives

1 We can make adjectives from some nouns by adding *-y*.

There's a lot of **cream** in it. It tastes very **creamy**.

2 Spelling

	Noun	Adjective
+ y	salt	salty
-e + y	juice	juicy
double consonant *+ y*	fat	fatty

Tag questions

1 We use tag questions to check or confirm information.

He doesn't like coffee, **does he**?

We've seen that film, **haven't we**?

2 After a negative verb we use a positive tag.

It isn't raining, **is it**?

After a positive verb we use a negative tag.

It's raining, **isn't it**?

3 With the verb *to be* **(***is, was***, etc.) and auxiliary verbs (***can, will, have, does, did,* **etc.) we use the verb** *to be* **or the auxiliary verb to make the tag.**

She **was** ill, **wasn't she**?

They**'ll** be here at ten, **won't they**?

We **aren't** leaving today, **are we**?

He **hasn't** got a car, **has he**?

4 With positive present simple and past simple verbs, we use *don't / doesn't* **or** *didn't* **to make a negative tag.**

She lives near here, **doesn't she**?

You bought the tickets, **didn't you**?

5 When the subject of the sentence is a noun, we use a pronoun in the tag.

Mike works in a hospital, doesn't **he**?

NOT ~~Mike works in a hospital, doesn't Mike?~~

108

Grammar reference

Lessons 29–32

First and second conditional

1 We use a conditional sentence to describe the results of an action or event.

| *if* clause | main clause |

first conditional: If it **rains** later, we **won't play** tennis.
second conditional: If I **lived** in Australia, I**'d go** surfing every day.

2 We use the first conditional for a real or possible situation and its results.
If global warming **continues**, it **will cause** a lot of problems.

For first conditionals, we use the present simple in the *if* clause and the future with *will* in the main clause.

3 We use the second conditional for an unlikely or imaginary situation and its results.

If we **were** younger, we **would move** to a safer place.
(= imaginary, because we can't be younger.)
We **wouldn't stay** here if we **had** more money.
(= unlikely, because we can't get more money.)

For second conditionals, we use the past simple in the *if* clause and the conditional with *would* in the main clause.

Lessons 33–36

Uncountable nouns

1 Some common nouns that refer to more than one thing are uncountable, e.g.:
equipment, luggage, information, news, furniture, litter, accommodation, advice, work

2 These nouns have no plural form, and they take a singular verb.
This information is very useful.
NOT ~~These informations are very useful.~~

3 We use *some / any* and *this / that* with these nouns.
We need **some equipment**.
NOT ~~We need an equipment.~~
That luggage is mine.
NOT ~~Those luggages are mine.~~

4 When we use numbers with these nouns, we must use *a piece of / ... pieces of*.
some advice or **a piece of** advice
NOT ~~an advice~~
three pieces of furniture
NOT ~~three furnitures~~

Plural nouns

1 Some nouns that refer to a single thing are always plural, e.g.:
scissors, glasses, stairs, headphones, scales, clothes, jeans, trousers, shorts, pliers

2 These nouns have no singular form, and they take a plural verb.
These glasses are very nice.
NOT ~~This glasses is very nice.~~

3 We use *some / any* and *these / those* with these nouns.
We need **some scissors**.
NOT ~~We need a scissors.~~
Those jeans are mine.
NOT ~~That jeans is mine.~~

4 When we use numbers with these nouns, we must use *a pair of / ... pairs of*.
some headphones or **a pair of** headphones
NOT ~~a headphones~~
three pairs of trousers
NOT ~~three trousers~~

used to

1 We use *used to* for regular activities and states that were true in the past but are not now.
I **used to work** in Milan.
= I worked in Milan in the past, but I don't work there now.
He **used to play** rugby.
= He played rugby in the past, but he doesn't play it now.

2 To make a negative statement, we use *didn't use to*.
I **didn't use to like** cheese. (= but I like it now.)
She **didn't use to have** long hair. (= but she's got long hair now.)

3 To make questions with *used to* we use *did ... use to*.
Did you use to have a beard?   Yes, I **did**.
                              NOT ~~Yes, I used.~~
                              No, I **didn't**.
Where **did they use to live**?

4 *Used to / didn't use to / did ... use to* are the same for all subjects.

Grammar reference

Lessons 37–40

Narrative tenses

1 **We use these three tenses to tell a story in the past.**
Past perfect   Bill **had gone out.**
Past continuous Two people **were watching** the house.
Past simple   They **burgled** the house.
The three tenses show us whether something happened at the same time as, after, or before another event.

2 **We use the past perfect for an event that happened before another event or situation in the past.**
The house was empty because Bill **had gone out.**
= Bill went out and after that the house was empty.

3 **We use the past continuous for a continuing action or situation that is happening at the same time as another event.**
When Bill went out, two people **were watching** the house.
= The people were watching the house, and while they were doing that, Bill went out.

4 **We use the past simple for actions that happened one after the other.**
Bill **left** the house, **got into** his car, and **drove away.**
= He left the house. Then he got into the car. Then he drove away.

Lessons 41–44

Separable and inseparable phrasal verbs

1 **A lot of common English verbs have got two parts: a verb and a particle, e.g.:**

Verb	Particle
put	on
run	away

2 **When a phrasal verb has an object, we can normally put the particle before or after the object.**
I **took off** my coat.
I **took** my coat **off.**

3 **When the object is a pronoun, the particle <u>must</u> go after the object.**
I **took** it **off.**
NOT ~~I took off it.~~

4 **We can't separate all phrasal verbs. These phrasal verbs are inseparable:**
look for, look after, look round, get on, get off, get in, get out (of), wait for, listen to
I **'m looking for** my keys.
NOT ~~I'm looking my keys for.~~

The passive voice

1 **These two sentences have the same meaning:**
Active voice   Ships **transport** containers.
Passive voice   Containers **are transported** by ships.
Ships is the subject of the active sentence.
Containers is the subject of the passive sentence.

2 **We normally use the passive when we are more interested in the action than the person or thing that does the action.**
Containers **are transported** to other countries.
We don't know (or need to know) who or what transports them.

3 **We make the passive voice with the verb *to be* and a past participle. (See Lessons 13–16 for past participles.)**
The sea **is polluted** by chemicals.
Some containers **are lost.**

4 **We can make the passive in any tense. To change the tense, we change the tense of the verb *to be*.**
Past simple   Thousands of containers **were lost** last year.
Present perfect Two containers **have been lost** today.
Present simple   Every year containers **are lost.**
Future   More containers **will be lost** this year.

5 **When we want to know who or what does the action in a passive verb, we use *by* + an agent.**

	Subject	Verb	Object
Active	A storm	hit	the ship.
	Subject	**Verb**	**Agent**
Passive	The ship	was hit	**by** a storm.

6 **To make questions in the passive, we use the normal question form of the verb *to be*.**
yes / no questions
Statement Pearls are made by oysters.

Question   Are pearls made by oysters?   Yes, they are.
                                                                    No, they aren't.
NOT ~~Yes, they do. / No, they don't.~~

Grammar reference

wh- **questions**
When **were they** produced?
How **will they be** transported?
Where **have they been** taken?

Lessons 45–48

might

1 We use *might / might not* to express possibility.
   There's a lot of traffic. We **might be** late.
   = It's possible that we will be late.
   We **might not be** at the meeting.
   = It's possible that we won't be at the meeting.

2 We use *might* when something is possible. We use *will* when something is definite.
   We're stuck in a traffic jam. We**'ll be** late.
   = It's definite that we will be late.
   We **won't be** at the meeting.
   = It's definite that we won't be at the meeting.

Giving advice

We often use *should / shouldn't* with *might / might not* to give advice.
   You **should** take an umbrella. It **might** rain.
   You **shouldn't** close the door. You **might not** hear the phone.

Adjectives and adverbs

1 We use an adjective to describe a noun. We use an adverb to describe a verb.

adjective	adverb
He's a **sensible** person.	He always acts **sensibly**.

2 To make most adverbs we add *-ly*. Note these spelling rules.

	Adjective	Adverb
+ *ly*	quiet	quietly
-le + *ly*	reliable	reliably
-y + *ily*	tidy	tidily

3 These adverbs are irregular.

Adjective	Adverb
good	well
fast	fast
hard	hard

Comparing experiences

To say that our own experiences are the same as someone else's we use:

So		
Neither / Nor	+ auxiliary verb	+ *I / we*

If our experience is different we use:
(Oh) + subject + auxiliary verb

To compare with a positive statement we use *So*.

Positive statement	Same experience	Different experience
I was ill last week.	So was I.	(Oh,) I wasn't.
I like classical music.	So do I.	(Oh,) I don't.
We went to the theatre.	So did we.	(Oh), we didn't.

With a negative statement we use *Neither* or *Nor*.

Negative statement	Same experience	Different experience
I'm not going out.	Neither am I.	(Oh,) I am.
I can't swim.	Nor can I.	(Oh,) I can.
We won't be at the party.	Nor will we.	(Oh), we will.

Lessons 49–52

Direct and indirect objects

1 We use direct and indirect objects with verbs like:
   give, send, email, write, post, lend

   The direct object is the thing that is given. The indirect object is the person that it is given to.

	Verb	Direct object	*to* + indirect object
I	gave	some money	to my brother.
She	wrote	a letter	to the bank.

2 The indirect object can go:
   – after the direct object and with *to*
   – before the direct object and without *to*

	Verb	Direct object	*to* + indirect object
I	gave	some money	to my brother.

		Indirect object	Direct object
I	gave	my brother	some money.
NOT	~~I gave to my brother some money.~~		

Grammar reference

Lessons 53–56

Present perfect continuous

1 We use the present perfect continuous for:
   – a recent activity when we want to emphasize the duration
   I**'ve been playing** tennis all afternoon.
   He**'s been looking for** somewhere to park.
   (= and it took a long time)

   – an activity that has lasted a long time and still continues in the present
   She**'s been living** there for twenty years.
   (= and she still lives there now.)
   We**'ve been studying** Chinese for a six months now.
   (= and we're still studying it.)

2 We make the present perfect continuous with *have / has been* and a present participle. (See Lessons 1–4 for present participles.)

Positive and negative statements			
I You We They	have 've have not haven't	been	watching a film. having lunch. jogging in the park. looking for a flat.
He She It	has 's has not hasn't		

3 To make questions with the present perfect continuous, we put *have / has* in front of the subject.

yes / no questions and short answers
Statement   **She has** been using the computer.

Question   **Has she** been using   Yes, she has.
                the computer?   No, she hasn't.
Statement   **You have** been waiting long.

Question   **Have you** been   Yes, we have.
                waiting long?   No, we haven't.

wh- questions
What **has he been doing**?
Where **have you been studying**?

Present perfect simple and present perfect continuous

1 We often use the present perfect continuous for an activity that is still continuing now.
   I**'ve been reading** that book.   (I haven't finished it.)
   I**'ve read** that book.   (I've finished it.)

2 However, the two tenses can often mean the same. We normally use the continuous form to emphasize the duration.
   I've worked here for ten years.
   I've been working here for ten years.

for / since

1 We use *for* + a period of time.
   I've been living here **for** three years / **for** a month.

2 We use *since* + a point of time.
   I've been living here **since** February / **since** 2007.

Lessons 57–60

Modal verbs: *can / must* (future and past forms)

1 *Can* only has a present and a past form. It has no future form. For the future, we use *will / won't be able to*.
   Past   There was no gas, so we **couldn't** cook.
   Present   There's no gas, so we **can't** cook.
   Future   There won't be any gas, so we **won't be able to** cook.

2 *Must* has no past or future form. We use the past or future form of *have to*.
   Past   We couldn't cook, so we **had to** go to a restaurant.
   Present   We can't cook, so we **must** go to a restaurant.
   Future   We won't be able to cook, so we**'ll have to** go to a restaurant.

3 NOTE *Must* has two negative forms:
   – *mustn't*
   You **mustn't** touch it. = Don't touch it. It's dangerous.
   We can only use *mustn't* in the present tense.

   – *not have to*
   We **don't have to** go out. = It isn't necessary.
   We can use *not have to* in the past and future (*didn't have to / won't have to*).
   We **didn't have to** go out.
   We **won't have to** go out.

Grammar reference

Lessons 61–64

Verb + -ing or infinitive

1 **Some verbs are followed by the -ing form:**
enjoy, give up, can't stand, don't mind, finish, avoid, fancy, imagine

I enjoy **watching** sport.
NOT ~~I enjoy to watch sport.~~

2 **Some verbs are followed by the infinitive:**
decide, want, need, hope, offer, expect, manage, plan, promise

I've decided **to go** by train.
NOT ~~I've decided going by train.~~

3 **Some verbs can take either the -ing form or the infinitive. The meaning is similar:**
like, love, hate, prefer, start

We love **dancing**. OR We love **to dance**.

4 **Some verbs can take either the -ing form or the infinitive, but the meaning is different:**
stop, remember

He stopped **to eat**.
= He stopped because he wanted to eat.
He stopped **eating**.
= He was eating and then he stopped.

She remembered **to lock** the door.
= She remembered and then she locked the door.
She remembered **locking** the door.
= She locked the door. Later she remembered that she had done it.

Verb + noun + -ing

We use verb + noun + -ing to describe a scene:

1 **After *There is / are / was / were***
There were two people. They were waiting for the bus.
There were two people waiting for the bus.

There's someone. He's looking through the window.
There's someone looking through the window.

2 **After *see / hear / feel / smell*, etc.**
I saw a plane. It was taking off.
I saw **a plane taking off**.

I can smell something. It's burning.
I can smell **something burning**.

Lessons 65–68

Relative clauses

1 **Relative clauses show which thing / person we are talking about.**
They're the people. They bought our house.
They're the people **that bought our house**.

This is the car. I want this car.
This is the car **that I want**.
NOT ~~This is the car that I want it.~~

2 **A relative clause usually starts with a relative pronoun. We use:**
who for people
which for things
that for people or things

They're the people **who** bought our house.
This is the car **which** I want.

3 **A relative pronoun can be the subject or the object of the relative clause. The relative pronoun (*who*, *which*, *that*) is the same for both the subject and the object.**

	subject	verb	object
They're the people	**that**	**bought**	**our house.**

(= *that* is the subject of *bought*.)

	object	subject	verb
This is the car	**that**	**I**	**want.**

(= *that* is the object of *want*.)

Omitting the relative pronoun

When the relative pronoun is the object of the relative clause, we can leave it out.
That's the car **that I want**.
OR That's the car **I want**.

We can't do this when the relative pronoun is the subject of the relative clause.
They're the people **that bought our house**.
NOT ~~They're the people bought our house.~~

Grammar reference

Lessons 69–72

Third conditional

1 We use the third conditional to imagine past events, and their results, happening differently.

| Real event | I got up late, so I missed the train. |
| Imagined event | If I **hadn't got up** late, I **wouldn't have missed** the train. |

| Real event | She didn't get a good job, because she didn't go to university. |
| Imagined event | She **would have got** a good job if she **had gone** to university. |

2 In a third conditional we use:
  – the past perfect in the *if* clause
  – the conditional perfect in the main clause

3 We make the conditional perfect with *would / wouldn't* + *have* + past participle.
We **would have gone** to the party if I hadn't been ill.
He **wouldn't have had** an accident if he had been more careful.

Expressing regret

To express regret, we use *wish / wishes* + the past perfect.

I wish I had learnt to play the piano.
= I didn't learn to play the piano, and I regret it.
He wishes he hadn't given up his job.
= He gave up his job, and he regrets it.

Lessons 73–76

Indirect questions

1 We use indirect questions when we talk <u>about</u> a question. We use it after expressions like:
I wonder ..., Do you know ..., I can't remember ...,
I don't know ..., I'd like to know ...

| Direct question | What time does the film start? |
| Indirect question | I wonder **what time the film starts**. |

2 In an indirect question we use the statement form NOT the question form.
I don't know **what time the film starts**.
NOT ~~I don't know what time does the film start?~~

3 With *yes / no* questions we use *if* or *whether* to introduce the indirect question.
Is Miguel here?
Do you know **if** Miguel's here?

Has the post arrived?
I wonder **whether** the post has arrived.

4 We often use indirect questions to pass on a question in a message.

Original message from Anna: When is the party?
Anna wants to know **when the party is**.

Lessons 77–80

Reported speech

1 We use reported speech to say what somebody said.

| Direct speech | Cindy: I'm going to the shops. |
| Reported speech | Cindy said **she was going to bed**. |

2 In reported speech pronouns and possessive adjectives normally change to the third person.

| Direct speech | Ryan: **I** saw **my** old friend. |
| Reported speech | Ryan said **he** had seen **his** old friend. |

3 When the reporting verb is in the past tense (*said / told*), tenses normally move into the past.

Direct speech	→	Reported speech
present simple	→	past simple
present continuous	→	past continuous
future with *will*	→	conditional with *would*
present perfect	→	past perfect
past simple	→	past perfect

| Direct speech | I'**ll phone** before I **leave**. |
| Reported speech | He said (that) he **would phone** before he **left**. |

| Direct speech | I **booked** a taxi but it **hasn't arrived**. |
| Reported speech | She said (that) she **had booked** a taxi, but it **hadn't arrived**. |

4 To report speech we use:
said (that) + reported speech
Ryan **said that he was going out**.
NOT ~~Ryan said Cindy that he was going out.~~

told + a person (that) + reported speech
Ryan told Cindy that he was going out.
NOT ~~Ryan told that he was going out.~~

Audio scripts

Hello. My name's Roberto Fonseca. That's F O N S E C A – Fonseca, and I'm from Brazil. I live in the city of Recife in the north-east of Brazil. I'm forty-three years old. I'm a lawyer and I work for an insurance company. I'm divorced. I've got a daughter. Her name's Fernanda and she's a student. What do I do in my free time? Well, I go swimming a lot. I live near the sea, so it's easy. I also play the saxophone and I do some painting, too. Like most Brazilians, of course, I love watching football. Oh, and I like listening to jazz and watching movies.

2.3

1 A I'm going to the shop now. We need some bread.
  B Oh, I think the shop closes at four on Sundays.
2 A The Director wants to talk to Katrin, but I don't know where she is.
  B I believe she's having lunch at the moment. She usually goes for lunch at 1.30.
3 A I'm making a cup of coffee now. Do you want one?
  B No, thanks, I don't like coffee. I prefer tea.

3.1

Nicola Hello. My name's Nicola. I'm doing a survey for *Modern Life* magazine, called 'How do people use their computers?' Can I ask you a few questions, please?
Charlie Er, OK.
Nicola Thank you. OK. First. What's your name?
Charlie It's Charlie Bell.
Nicola OK, and what do you do?
Charlie I'm a student.
Nicola What are you studying?
Charlie Biology.
Nicola Oh, that's interesting. Are you using a computer at the moment?
Charlie Yes, I am.
Nicola What sort of computer are you using – a desktop or a laptop?
Charlie A laptop. I always use a laptop.
Nicola I see, and do you use it for work, study or leisure?
Charlie Study and leisure.
Nicola OK. Now, how often do you do these things on your computer – often, sometimes or never? Firstly, do you send emails?
Charlie Yes, I do – every day.
Nicola OK. So that's 'often'. Do you visit chatrooms?
Charlie No, I don't.
Nicola Do you shop online?
Charlie Sometimes.
Nicola What sort of things do you buy?
Charlie Presents – you know, birthday presents and things. Because they send the present directly to the person, it's a lot easier.
Nicola OK. Do you book tickets on the Internet?
Charlie Yes. I often book tickets for rock concerts.
Nicola What about flights?
Charlie No. My girlfriend works for a travel company, so she always does that.
Nicola OK. Do you download music, TV programmes and so on?
Charlie Yes, I do that a lot. In fact, I'm downloading some music at the moment.
Nicola Oh, I see. Do you edit and print photographs?
Charlie No, I don't. I always take them to a shop. It's a lot quicker and the photos look better.
Nicola And do you play computer games?
Charlie Yes, I often do that – especially when the lectures at university are boring!
Nicola Oh, really?
Charlie No, I'm only joking.
Nicola Right. OK. Well, can I ask you now about …

5.3

I usually get up at 6.15. I have a shower and I get dressed. I don't have breakfast, but I get a cup of coffee at the station. I normally get the 7.30 train, and I get to work at 8.45. I always check my emails first. I don't get a lot of emails, fortunately. By 10.30 I start to get hungry, so I usually get a cake or something from the cafeteria. At ten to five I get ready to leave work, but I get home quite late, at about 7 p.m. Then I usually get changed into my jeans. It's a long day. It's OK, but I don't like it in the winter, because it only gets light at about 8 a.m. and then it gets dark again before I leave work.

6.3

1 **Woman** Were you out last night, Axel?
  Axel Yes, I was. I was at the theatre.
  Woman Oh, did you see a play?
  Axel Yes, I did. It was very good.
2 **Man** Were you and Max at home last night, Corrie?
  Corrie No, we weren't. We were at the sports centre.
  Man Oh, really? Did you go swimming?
  Corrie No, we didn't. We played table tennis.
3 **Man** Did you go out last night, Shilpa?
  Shilpa No, I didn't. I was at home all evening.
  Man Oh, did you see that film on Channel 4?
  Shilpa No, I didn't watch TV last night. I did some work.
  Man Oh, I see.
4 **Woman** Did you have a nice evening yesterday?
  Jack Yes, we did. Davina and I were at a friend's house. We had dinner there.
  Woman That sounds nice.
  Jack Yes, it was.
5 **Woman** Were you at Miguel's party last night, George?
  George No, I wasn't. I was away on business, so I was at a hotel.
  Woman Oh, I see.
  George So I didn't do anything interesting. I just fell asleep in front of the TV.
6 **Man** Were you out last night, Leah?
  Leah Yes, I was at the college with Phil. We went to our Spanish lesson.
  Man Oh, I see.

6.4

1 You weren't at the party.
2 I was tired.
3 You were at work.
4 The hotel wasn't expensive.
5 The concert was very good.
6 We were on holiday.
7 She wasn't here last week.
8 They weren't at home.

8.4

1 A Who does this laptop belong to?
  B Not me. Mine's in my briefcase.
  A Well, it must be someone's.
  B Switch it on and find out.
  A OK.
  B It's Deena's.
2 A Are these car keys yours?
  B No. Maybe they're Frank's.
  A No, they can't be his. He drives a BMW.
  B Oh. Well, they must be Eduardo's. He was here earlier.
3 A Whose is this cup of coffee?
  B It's Cecilia's.
  A Who's Cecilia?
  B She's the new girl in the Sales Department.
4 A Who does that motorbike belong to?
  B It belongs to Avril's new boyfriend.
  A Oh? What's his name?
  B Eric.
5 A Whose is this money? It doesn't belong to me.
  B If it's a thousand pounds, it's mine.
  A No, seriously. Whose is it?
  B It belongs to Gus. It's his change from the sandwich bar.

115

9.2

I live in a first-floor flat. I live with two flatmates. We don't own the flat. We rent it. Our landlord lives in the flat above us. The flat's furnished, so the furniture isn't ours. It's in an old house, but it's got central heating, and it's very warm. Unfortunately, it hasn't got air conditioning, so it can get too hot in the summer. We've got a fitted kitchen with plenty of cupboards, and a new oven and fridge. We've all got our own bedrooms, but we share the other rooms. We share the rent, too, of course. The bedrooms are small, but the living room is quite spacious. The flat isn't very convenient for the shops, but it's in a nice location and it isn't noisy.

10.3

1 **A** Is there a toilet near here?
   B Yes, it's on the second floor next to the escalator.
2 **A** Would you like to go for a meal on Thursday?
   B OK. We can try the new restaurant that's near the park.
   A Yes, that's an idea. I think that's the best restaurant in the area now.
3 **A** That's a nice shirt and tie.
   B Thanks. I bought the shirt at a shop in the town centre, but my wife bought the tie at a market in Italy.
4 **A** I went to a play last night. I went with a friend from work. And we went for a meal afterwards.
   B Was the play good?
   A Not really. The main actor wasn't very good, but the meal afterwards was great.

11.1

George OK. Here we are. This is the hall. Now, what does it say here? The accommodation consists of two bedrooms …
Ellie Here's one bedroom and this is the other one.
George OK. And the living room. That's here.
Ellie Uh-huh. So these must be the kitchen and the bathroom.
George Yes. OK. Let's have a look round. Let's start with the bedrooms.
Ellie Mm. There's a good view from the living room. What floor are we on here?
George The third floor. Well, what do you think?
Ellie Well, it's in a quiet location.
George Yes, it certainly isn't noisy.
Ellie It says it's close to local amenities, so I suppose it's convenient for the shops.
George But it isn't very convenient for the station.
Ellie That's true.
George What about the flat itself?
Ellie Well, it's in excellent condition.
George Yes.
Ellie And it's furnished, so we won't need a lot of things.
George There's a fitted kitchen, too.
Ellie Yes, but the room's very dark.
George Yes, I suppose so. What do you think of the other rooms?
Ellie They're nice and spacious.
George But it hasn't got central heating, so it will be expensive to heat.
Ellie That's true, but it isn't cold at the moment.
George Anyway. What do you think?
Ellie I'm not sure. The flat's OK, but I don't like that kitchen — it's too dark — and this is an expensive area, so rents are high.
George Yes. I'm sure we can find somewhere better for the money.
Ellie I agree. So we'll say no, then?
George Yes, OK. I'll call the accommodation agency and see if they've got anything else.

13.3

1 You need a lot of patience for this job. You won't have much success if you get angry easily.
2 With her intelligence and her beauty, she's become one of the most famous people in the country.
3 It's difficult to be successful without a lot of luck.
4 It was very cold, so the last part of the climb was dangerous and painful, but we finally reached the safety of our camp.
5 Honesty and a good sense of humour are very important for a healthy relationship.
6 We all want security and good health, but we need a bit of danger in our lives, too.

14.2

Raj Sorry to hear about your accident.
Jordan Thanks, Raj.
Raj Have you taken the van to the garage?
Jordan Yes, I have, but I haven't collected another van. It wasn't ready.
Raj Oh, OK. Have you phoned the insurance company?
Jordan Yes, I have. And I've downloaded the insurance form, but I haven't filled it in yet. I hate filling in forms.
Raj Me, too.
Jordan But I've written a report about the accident.
Raj Have you emailed it to Head Office?
Jordan No, I haven't. They won't be very pleased.
Raj No, they won't.
Jordan I'm just going to send it now, actually.
Raj And have you seen the doctor about your hand?
Jordan No. I'm going to do that today.

16.2

a three hundred and twenty-five
b five million
c twenty-eight thousand
d ninety-five per cent
e twenty-one point seven
f four thousand, nine hundred and thirty-two
g three million dollars
h forty billion euros
i eight point two per cent
j three quarters
k seven thousand and thirty-six
l a half

16.3

In 1900, there were very few cars. In that year, the USA produced only 4,192 cars. However, in 1908 the first mass-produced car appeared – the Ford *Model T*. Between 1908 and 1927, 16,536,075 *Model Ts* were made. Today there are over 600 million cars in the world and 35 million new cars are produced every year. Of all the cars in the world, ¼ are in the USA, although the USA has only 5% of the world's population.

We all love our cars and the world's car companies spend more than $19 billion a year on advertising. However, cars come at a high cost. They produce 4 billion tonnes of carbon dioxide every year. That's $^1/_5$ of all the CO_2 that is produced. By 2030, this will be over 7.5 billion tonnes. The United Nations says that 1.2 million people a year die on the world's roads. That's 25% of all the deaths from accidents.

17.3

1 I've always tried to keep fit. I go to the gym two or three times a week. I warm up first, then I go on the rowing machine for about twenty minutes. After that I do some stretching exercises. I don't lift weights. I pulled a muscle in my back once when I was lifting weights, so I don't do it now. In the summer I don't usually go to the gym. I go for a run instead. I enjoy taking exercise, because I always feel great afterwards.
2 I had a small heart attack last year, so I had to change my lifestyle. I gave up smoking and I've cut down on fat and sugar. I eat quite a healthy diet now with lots of fruit and vegetables, and I don't eat junk food, like hamburgers and pizzas. That's hard. I didn't take any exercise at all before my heart attack, but I do now. I go for a walk every day, or if the weather's bad I go for a swim at the sports centre. I always try to get a good night's sleep, too, so I go to bed earlier these days.

19.1

We all have very busy lives these days. Today I'm going to talk about some simple things that will keep your body and mind in good shape when you're at work or on the go.

First, we're going to think about our backs. We all spend a lot of time at desks, in cars and aeroplanes, or just in front of the TV. This isn't good for your spine and you'll probably get backache. This simple exercise will help. Lie on the floor on your stomach. Put your arms by your side with your palms on the floor. Now breathe in and lift your head and chest off the floor. Hold for five seconds, then slowly lower your head and chest, as you breathe out. Repeat ten times. The exercise will only take a minute. If you do this exercise, your back will be strong and flexible.

When you rush from one meeting to another, your brain is always busy and you get tired and stressed. Try a power nap. You can do this at your desk. Just sit comfortably, close your eyes and relax for about twenty minutes. When you open your eyes again, you'll feel fresh and ready to go. It's important that you don't fall into deep sleep. If you do, you'll feel worse when you wake up. So hold something in your hand. If you fall asleep, you'll drop it.

Now, I know that a lot of you are going to have lunch at your desk today. So here's the final piece of advice: don't! If your body sends blood to your brain, so that you can work, it won't send enough blood to your stomach. So you'll eat too much and you'll put on weight. Give your brain and your stomach a break. Have lunch in the park and digest your food properly.

If you follow this advice, you'll be fitter and healthier. Tomorrow we're going to look at some breathing exercises. Have a good – and a healthy – day!

Audio scripts

21.3

1 A Oh, hello. This is Jane Smith. I'm afraid I can't make my appointment at 10.30. My train's delayed.
   B Oh, I see. How long …
2 A Oh, no. The road's closed.
   B Yes, I think there's been an accident.
3 A Hello. Can I check in here for Zagreb, please?
   B I'm sorry, but the plane to Zagreb is cancelled.
   A Oh, no. Why?
   B The weather in Zagreb is very bad, and the airport is closed.
4 There are long traffic jams on the M20 at the moment. A lorry has broken down under a bridge, and it's blocking the road.
5 A We need to get our tickets.
   B OK. Oh, dear – there's a long queue at the ticket office.
   A Yes, it's probably because the ticket machines aren't working.
6 A Are we there yet?
   B No. The traffic still isn't moving.
   A But we've been stuck in this traffic jam for half an hour.
   C We know, but there are some roadworks ahead.
7 A Why don't we use the tunnel? It's faster.
   B The tunnel's closed at the moment.
   A Really? Why? Is it flooded after all that rain?
   B No. They're repairing it.
8 All buses in the capital city have been full again today. Drivers of the Underground trains are on strike, so there have been no trains on the Underground.

22.3

John Marsh and his wife own a caravan. Last week two men tried to steal it. They'd seen the caravan two weeks before and they'd decided to take it. At about four o'clock on Wednesday morning they attached the caravan to their car and drove away. However, they didn't know that John was inside it at the time! He'd worked very late the day before and he'd come home at 1 a.m. He hadn't wanted to wake up his wife, so he'd gone to sleep in the caravan. The thieves got a big surprise when a police car stopped them 20 minutes later. When they'd moved the caravan, John had woken up and he'd phoned the police on his mobile.

24.2

Travel agent Good morning. Can I help you?
Customer Yes. I'd like to book a flight to Rio de Janeiro in Brazil, please.
Travel agent OK. When do you want to travel out?
Customer On 22 May.
Travel agent And the return flight?
Customer I'd like to come back on 3 June.
Travel agent OK. Let's see what we can find. Right. Well, the best flight is one that leaves at 19.35 and that arrives at 04.20 the next morning.
Customer That's a bit early in the morning to arrive. Are there any other flights?
Travel agent No. There aren't any direct flights, I'm afraid. There's a later one via Paris.
Customer OK. Let's try the direct flight then.
Travel agent Right. How many people is it for?
Customer Just one.
Travel agent And do you want business class or economy class?
Customer Business, please.
Travel agent OK. There are seats available in economy class, but I'm afraid business class is fully booked.
Customer Oh, I see. Can you check the other flights then, please?
Travel agent OK. Just a minute.

25.3

1 A How would you like your steak?
   B Medium-rare, please.
   A Thank you.
2 A Are those apples nice?
   B Yes. They're very crisp and juicy. Do you want one?
   A Yes, please. … Mmm, they are nice, but a bit sour.
   B Oh, I like them like that.
3 A Is that milk fresh?
   B I don't think so. It smells off to me.
   A I'll have my coffee black, then.
4 A How's the dessert?
   B It's nice – very sweet and creamy. Here. Try it.
   A Mmm. Yes. That's delicious.
5 A Don't you like the soup?
   B No. It tastes a bit too salty for me.
   A Well, we should send it back then.
6 A Is the curry nice?
   B Yes. It's very spicy.
   A Not too hot?
   B No, it's very good.
7 A Could I have a cheese sandwich, please?
   B Certainly. Would you prefer the strong cheese or the mild one?
   A Oh, strong, please.

27.1

Ramesh You've had Indian food before, haven't you, Stefan?
Stefan No, I haven't. It's very hot and spicy, isn't it?
Ramesh Some of it is. India's a very big country, so there are lots of different kinds of food.
Stefan You weren't born in India, were you, Ramesh?
Ramesh No, I wasn't. I was born here in England, but I've visited India several times.
Stefan Anyway. It's OK. I don't mind spicy food. Some of our dishes in Poland are quite hot.
Ramesh Yes, of course. Well, let's have a look at the menu, shall we?
Stefan What do you recommend?
Ramesh Well there's the Chicken Kashmiri. That's chicken in a mild and creamy sauce. The sauce is made with pineapples and bananas, so it's quite sweet, too.
Stefan No, I'm not very fond of bananas.
Ramesh OK. Well I'm not keen on mild dishes. I prefer something hotter.
Stefan Fine. As I said, I'm quite happy with spicy food. What's Lamb Rogan Josh?
Ramesh That's lamb cooked with tomatoes and peppers. It's very tasty, but quite hot.
Stefan I'll have that. It sounds delicious. What are you going to have?
Ramesh I'm going to have the Vegetable Patiya.
Stefan You aren't vegetarian, are you?
Ramesh No, I'm not, but a lot of people in India are, so there are some excellent vegetarian dishes.
Stefan What's Patiya?
Ramesh It's made from tomatoes and lime juice, so it's quite sour.
Stefan It sounds nice.
Ramesh Yes, I really like it – and we can share the two dishes.
Stefan OK.
Ramesh So that's one Lamb Rogan Josh and one Vegetable Patiya. Would you like rice or naan with it?
Stefan What's naan?
Ramesh Oh, sorry. It's a kind of bread.
Stefan I think I'd prefer rice.
Ramesh Me, too. Now, what shall we have to drink?

29.2

1 The problems in East Africa are getting worse. People are dying in the famine here. The famine is the result of a long war. People have left their farms and their animals to escape the war. Now there is no food.
2 There's been an earthquake near the west coast of the USA. The earthquake has damaged buildings and two bridges. It also caused a big avalanche in a popular skiing area.
3 A hurricane has hit the coast of Central America. The high winds have destroyed buildings and the heavy rain has caused floods in many places.
4 There has been a volcanic eruption on a small island in the Philippines. The eruption caused a tsunami, which hit the large island of Luzon this afternoon. Fortunately, most people had already left the coast.
5 The long drought is continuing in Australia. Some parts of the country have had no rain for five years. In the dry conditions, forest fires have broken out in many places. The fires are getting closer to some large cities.
6 Several people in northern India are in hospital after they drank polluted water. The pollution is the result of an explosion at a chemical factory. Dangerous chemicals escaped into a local river.

30.2

1 If I was younger, I'd look for another house.
2 We wouldn't stay here if we were worried about floods.
3 They'd miss their home if they moved.
4 If the weather got better here, we wouldn't go abroad.
5 We wouldn't have a car if we lived in the city.
6 There wouldn't be so much pollution if we all travelled less.
7 If the buses were free, more people would use them.
8 People wouldn't fly so much if air travel became more expensive.

32.2

Receptionist	Good evening.
Guest	Good evening. I've got a reservation in the name of Helen Ross.
Receptionist	Is that R O double S?
Guest	Yes, it is.
Receptionist	OK. Just one moment, Ms Ross. Yes, here we are. A non-smoking room with a sea view.
Guest	Yes, please.
Receptionist	And you're staying for three nights?
Guest	Yes, that's correct.
Receptionist	OK. Could you just check your details on this form, and could I take a credit card, please?
Guest	Certainly. Here you are.
Receptionist	Thank you. And could you sign the form at the bottom, please?
Guest	Yes, of course.
Receptionist	So, here's your credit card. Would you like a newspaper or a wake-up call in the morning?
Guest	Yes, I'd like *The Times*, please, and could I have a wake-up call at 7.15, please?
Receptionist	7.15. Certainly. Here's your key, Ms Ross. You're in room 23. That's on the second floor. Breakfast is served from 7 to 10.30 in the Blue Room on the first floor.
Guest	Thank you.
Receptionist	The lifts are over there. Do you need any help with your luggage?
Guest	Yes, please.
Receptionist	OK. The porter will bring your bag to your room. Have a pleasant stay.
Guest	Thank you. Goodnight.
Receptionist	Goodnight.

33.2

1 How much are the headphones? I like these ones.
2 Some advice is helpful when you buy a computer.
3 We haven't got any homework today.
4 These sunglasses aren't mine.
5 I've got some good news.
6 Do we need all this equipment?
7 Are there any scales in the bathroom?
8 That's our luggage on the trolley.
9 Have you got any scissors?
10 These clothes look very expensive.

35.1

My name's Martin. I'm from England, but when I was a teenager we used to live near Munich in Germany. My father used to work for a car company there.

There was a tennis club near our house and I used to go there most days after school. I didn't play a lot, but I used to collect balls for the players. I learnt a lot about tennis and most of the players used to give me a good tip after a game.

One of the players there – his name was Conrad – was very good. He decided to try his luck as a professional tennis player and he asked me to be his assistant. I jumped at the chance. I was 19 then and I'd just left school. I didn't really want to go straight to university, but I wanted to get away from home for a bit.

For the next year I travelled all over Europe. There were a lot of competitions. For the bigger tournaments, we used to travel on Friday. Saturday and Sunday were usually practice days and the competition itself normally used to start on Monday. I used to come home between competitions. Sometimes, if he lost his first match, I spent a lot of time at home.

My main jobs as an assistant were to carry Conrad's bags and look after his equipment. Before each match or practice session I used to check that everything was ready for him. Then afterwards I used to clean his shoes and all the equipment. It was hard work, and it wasn't all fun. The bags were heavy. We often used to get up very early, too, so that he could practise.

Conrad paid for everything – hotels, transport, meals and so on. I also got 10% of all his prize money. But I didn't make a lot of money, because Conrad didn't win very much, and as a result he decided to give it up at the end of the year. I didn't mind. It was time for me to go to university anyway, and I'd had a great time. The best year of my life.

37.3

In July last year, three people robbed the Goldmine jewellery shop. Two men and a woman stole watches and jewellery worth over £80,000. There was a lot of publicity about the crime, because the robbers violently assaulted the shop's owner, Mr Hall.

Fortunately, several witnesses saw the robbery. The police soon arrested the three people. They went to prison for robbery and assault. The victim, Mr Hall, said, 'Those people have committed so many crimes. They are very dangerous criminals. I thought they were going to murder me.'

38.3

Yesterday morning I was cooking, when the phone rang. My son had fallen over at school. While I was collecting my son, someone broke into our home. When I arrived home, a man was running away from the house. Then I noticed that smoke was coming from the kitchen window. I suddenly remembered that I hadn't turned off the cooker. I rushed into the house. The saucepan had been on fire, but the burglar had thrown a wet towel over it. He had prevented a serious fire. Unfortunately, he'd stolen my laptop and some jewellery, too.

39.2

Jack	Your attention, please, everyone! Mr Randolph did not commit suicide. Somebody murdered him. And the murderer was you, Mrs Turner. You shot your uncle while he was sleeping. Then you put the gun in his hand. You hoped it would look like suicide.
Aston	That's impossible. Caroline was sending emails when Randolph died. Her laptop shows that.
Jack	Yes, an email was sent from that laptop, but she didn't send it. You did, Mr Turner.
Belinda	But he was with me. The gardener saw us.
Jack	Yes, and the gardener said that Mr Turner was carrying something. It was the laptop, wasn't it? When you heard the shot, you sent the email, came into the house, took the laptop to your room, then went into the study with Ms Wells. Your wife was already there.
Caroline	That's silly. And how did I get the gun? He kept it in the safe and I haven't got a key.
Jack	No, but Ms Wells has. She had taken the gun from the safe before she went for a walk. So, you see, you all murdered him. Ms Wells got the gun, Mrs Turner fired it, and Mr Turner provided an alibi.
Belinda	Huh! Nobody will believe that. It was clearly suicide.
Jack	No, it wasn't, Ms Wells. Your plan was very clever, but you made one rather stupid mistake. Look at that photograph of Mr Randolph.
Aston	What, that one where he's playing tennis?
Jack	Yes. Mrs Turner put the gun in her uncle's right hand, but you can see from the picture that he was in fact left-handed.

41.3

1 We looked round a new house today.
2 It's cold, so you should put a coat on.
3 Are you waiting for the bus?
4 Don't forget to switch your mobile off.
5 Are you looking for your keys?
6 Have you thrown the magazines away?
7 You can't cut that tree down!

Audio scripts

42.2

Plastic is used to make almost anything – toys, tools, shoes, computers. Often these products are made in one part of the world and they are transported to other continents. They are carried in containers on very large ships. Sometimes a ship is hit by a storm and some of the containers are lost.

In 1992, thousands of plastic toys were thrown into the sea when a cargo ship was hit by a storm in the Pacific Ocean. Some of the toys were carried north to the Arctic. Here, they were trapped in ice. The ice was taken into the Atlantic by ocean currents. One plastic duck was seen on a beach in Scotland. Other toys were taken south. Several toys were found in Australia.

43.1

Interviewer With our modern interest in the environment, farming is important. But not all farms produce food. Pierre Kimitete lives in Tahiti. He's a pearl farmer. Are most pearls produced on farms now, Pierre?

Pierre Yes, they are. Pearls have been worn for thousands of years. Divers used to look for them in the sea, but today most are produced by pearl farmers.

Interviewer How is a pearl produced?

Pierre All pearls are made by oysters. A small piece of shell is put inside the oyster. The oyster doesn't like that, so it covers the piece of shell with mother-of-pearl, to protect itself, and slowly the pearl is made.

Interviewer How long does it take?

Pierre About two or three years. The oysters are kept in baskets in the sea, and we turn the baskets regularly to make nice, round pearls.

Interviewer How is the pearl removed from the oyster? Do you break the shell?

Pierre No, we don't. The oyster is opened very gently and the pearl is taken out. These pearls here were collected yesterday.

Interviewer Now, some of these pearls are different colours – black and gold. How are they produced?

Pierre Different colours are produced by different kinds of oyster. The most expensive ones are pink, but we don't produce those here.

Interviewer What will happen to these pearls now? Will they be made into jewellery?

Pierre First, they'll be sorted into different colours, sizes, and shapes. Then they'll be sent to Japan. They'll be made into necklaces, bracelets, and other jewellery there.

Interviewer And what do you do with the oyster after the pearl has been removed? Is it just thrown away?

Pierre No, we use it again to make a new pearl.

Interviewer Oh, I see. How many times is each oyster used?

Pierre Usually three times.

Interviewer And what happens to the oysters after that?

Pierre They're eaten!

Interviewer Oh!

45.4

1 Man What's your new colleague like, Fatima?

Fatima Josh? I don't know him very well, because he's a bit unsociable.

Man Maybe he's just shy.

Fatima Maybe. Anyway, he's very reliable. He finishes everything on time. And he's always very polite.

2 Woman Who was your favourite teacher at school?

Fatima Oh, that was Mrs Bell – our History teacher.

Woman Why did you like her?

Fatima She was very patient and kind. She never got angry and she always tried to help you, so we all wanted to work hard for her. She was always very cheerful, too. She smiled a lot. I used to really enjoy her lessons.

3 Man Is that your boss?

Fatima Yes, it is. His name's Richard.

Man What's he like?

Fatima He's OK. He's very easy-going. He doesn't get tense or take things too seriously.

Man That's good.

Fatima Yes, but he's very untidy, so he can never find anything. He's a bit big-headed, too. He likes sport, and if he wins something, he talks about it all week.

4 Woman Do you live on your own?

Fatima No, I don't. I share a flat with a friend. Her name's Maxine.

Woman What's she like?

Fatima OK. She doesn't talk a lot about herself. She's quite modest. But I think she's very ambitious. She works hard.

Woman Is she easy to live with?

Fatima Yes and no. You wouldn't call her easy-going. She's a bit tense.

47.2

This is how you score the quiz:
For every answer a, give yourself one point.
For every answer b, give yourself two points.
For every answer c, give yourself three points.
So that's one for a, two for b, and three for c.

49.2

Adam Mary and I went to my neighbour's wedding on Saturday. You know – Angela.

Bea Oh, yes. I remember her. Where was it? At a registry office?

Adam No, it was at a church. Anyway, we all arrived. The groom was already there with his younger brother. He was the best man. And then the bride arrived with her father and the bridesmaids.

Bea Well, come on. What was it like? What colour was the dress?

Adam Oh, right. Ah, well it was all very traditional. Her wedding dress was white and the two bridesmaids were wearing ... oh ... yellow.

Bea Hm. Who were they? The bridesmaids.

Adam Erm ... one was the groom's daughter from his first marriage and the other was the bride's niece, I think.

Bea Uh-huh. How old were they?

Adam I don't know – about ten, I think.

Bea Oh, how sweet.

Adam Anyway, after the service we had the photographs and we threw confetti over the happy couple.

Bea What was the weather like?

Adam Oh, it was very good. Nice and sunny. Then we all went off to the reception.

Bea Where did they hold it?

Adam At a hotel in the city centre – The Red Lion. The food was excellent. Then we had the speeches, of course. The best man made a great speech – very funny. Then the bride and groom cut the wedding cake.

Bea Was there dancing afterwards?

Adam Yes, there was, but the bride and groom didn't stay very long. They left for their honeymoon.

Bea Where did they go?

Adam Thailand.

Bea Oh, very nice.

Adam Anyway, why don't you give Mary a ring? She'll know all the details.

Bea Yes, I'll call her this evening.

Audio scripts

Giving and receiving gifts is a traditional part of weddings all over the world. Parents and guests normally give gifts to the couple to help them start their new home, and it's traditional for the bride and groom to give each other rings to symbolize their love. However, some countries have other traditions of giving, too.

1 Coins are part of weddings in many countries. In Mexico it is traditional for the groom to give the bride thirteen coins. The coins mean that the groom promises to support his new wife.
2 In China the groom gives money, too. It's wrapped in red paper or put in a red envelope. However, he doesn't give it to the bride. He gives it to the bride's friends to thank them for letting her go.
3 In Sudan the groom traditionally receives a present from his future mother-in-law. She gives him a garland of flowers to welcome him into the family.
4 In Vietnam, on the other hand, it's the groom's mother who gives presents. She gives them to the bride's parents. She gives a plant. This shows respect. She also gives them something pink. Pink is the colour of happiness.
5 Parents give their children gifts in many countries. In Poland the parents of the bride and groom give the couple bread, salt and vodka at the wedding reception. The bread symbolizes a wish that the couple will never be hungry. The salt is a way of saying that marriage won't always be easy. The vodka symbolizes happiness.
6 In South Africa the groom's family gives a gift to the bride's family. It's traditional to give some cows, but these days money is often given instead. The gift is to show that the marriage isn't just between the bride and the groom, but between the two families.

54.3

1 **Woman** Hi. How's your new bike?
  Ian It's great.
2 **Tom** Phew, that was a good run.
  Amy Yes, excellent.
3 **Sophie** Right and 'Send'. That's the last one. I'll shut it down now.
4 **Jack** Oh, that was good. There's nothing like a good shower.
5 **Max** Did you enjoy that film?
  Kim Yes, it was very good.
6 **Muriel** Good boy! That was a good walk, wasn't it?

55.2

OK, this one looks interesting ... listen ... This application is from Orson Barnes, who lives in Birmingham. He's applying for the post of Publicity Manager with *Happy Holidays*.

He's 32 years old and he's got a degree in Economics from Manchester University. It was a five-year course, and as part of his studies he did a work placement for a year with a small telecommunications company in Spain.

His first job after he left university was with *XL Holidays* and he worked there for four years. After three years he was promoted to the position of Operations Assistant and he was in charge of a team of three people. For the last three years he's been working for *Sky Airlines*. He's responsible there for Marketing.

In addition to his degree, he's got a qualification in Russian. He's been studying Italian since July, too, but he hasn't taken any examinations in it yet. He's also done courses in Human Resources and in Business Law.

He says that he's enjoyed his time at *Sky Airlines*, but he now feels the need for a new experience. He sounds ideal. What do you think?

56.1

1 **A** Guess what? I've got a place at university.
  B I'm very pleased to hear that. Congratulations.
2 **A** Have you heard? Coleen and Mack have split up.
  B They're getting divorced? Well, I know they've been having problems lately.
3 **A** Guess what? Henry's moving. He's bought a flat.
  B That's good. He's been looking for a place since last year.
4 **A** I've got some good news. Tania's expecting a baby.
  B Really? That's great. When's it due?
5 **A** Have you heard the news? I've lost my job.
  B I'm sorry to hear that. How long have you been working there?
6 **A** Guess what? Bill and Jolene are getting married.
  B That's wonderful news. When's the wedding?
7 **A** I've got some bad news, I'm afraid.
  B Oh, dear. What's that?
  A Mr Woods died last week.
  B That's very sad. How old was he?
8 **A** Have you heard? Elizabeth has had her baby.
  B That's great news! Did she have a boy or a girl?
9 **A** Guess what? I've got an interview for a new job today.
  B Great. Well, good luck. I'll keep my fingers crossed for you.
10 **A** Where are Maria and Carlos?
  B Oh, haven't you heard? Carlos has had an accident.
  A I didn't know that. I hope it was nothing serious.

56.4

1 Guess what? We're moving.
2 Jim and Liz are getting married.
3 I've got some news.
4 We've got our final exams today.
5 I'm looking for a new job.
6 Have you heard the news?

57.4

My name's Bella and I work for a film company. I'm an assistant to a director. I do photocopying and make appointments – and I make a lot of cups of coffee, too! I don't make a lot of money, but I'm doing a job that I really enjoy. I've made some good friends, too.

It isn't all fun. At the moment we're making a film about a hospital and we have to do a lot of the work at night.

I really want to be a film director, so in my free time I'm doing a course in film directing. It's quite hard. I had to do a big assignment last week.

I'm not doing anything today. I'm going to do a bit of housework this morning and then I'll probably do some exercise later. But first I'm going to make a few phone calls.

58.3

1 My car broke down yesterday, so I couldn't drive to work. I had to take the bus. It isn't a serious problem, so I won't have to buy a new car. The car will be ready today, so I'll be able to collect it after work, and then I won't have to go by bus again tomorrow.
2 Martin had flu last week, so he couldn't go on holiday. He had to stay in bed for the first few days, because he felt very ill. After that he could get up. He feels OK now, but he isn't happy because he'll have to go back to work on Monday. He won't be able to go on holiday again before next year.

59.2

Interviewer	When did the first real films appear?
Film historian	The first films appeared in 1895. They were shown in Paris by the Lumière brothers. The films were less than one minute long.
Interviewer	Why did Hollywood in California become the centre of the film industry?
Film historian	Well, the weather was very good there, so they could make films outside all year round.
Interviewer	I see. Now, today, films can take years to make, but in the early days film companies made them very quickly, didn't they?
Film historian	Yes, they did. In fact, Charlie Chaplin – the world's first movie star – once made eight films in just two months.
Interviewer	Wow. How were they able to do that?
Film historian	Well, there were two reasons. Firstly, films were still very short – only about six to ten minutes long. And secondly, they were silent. So directors didn't have to worry about noise. In fact, film companies could make two films in the same street at the same time.
Interviewer	When did the first film with sound appear?
Film historian	In 1927. It was a musical called *The Jazz Singer*. It was more difficult to make films with sound, because the microphone had to follow the actors. That was a big problem for films like westerns.
Interviewer	In the late 1970s computers appeared. How did they change things?
Film historian	With computers, directors could create amazing special effects. The science fiction film *Star Wars* was the first film to really use this.
Interviewer	And what about the future?
Film historian	Well, perhaps in the future directors won't have to use actors, because they'll be able to create whole films with computers.
Interviewer	Really? Is that possible?
Film historian	Yes. In the film *Gladiator* one of the actors died while they were making the film. Computers were used to put him into later parts of the film.
Interviewer	Well, we've come a long way since the first short, silent films.
Film historian	Yes, but the magic of the movies will never die.

61.3

Last year, I didn't feel very happy. I decided to change my job. My job was OK, but I just fancied doing something different. I planned to travel round the world. However, I needed to save some money first. So I avoided having lunch in restaurants and I gave up commuting by car. I cycled to work instead. In a year I managed to save a lot of money. I also felt fitter, healthier and happier, and I didn't really want to leave my job any more. I was already doing something different.

64.2

Man	Would you like to go for a meal later?
Woman	No, I don't really want to go out this evening. I'm tired.
Man	OK. How about tomorrow?
Woman	Tomorrow's out for me, I'm afraid. Are you free on Wednesday?
Man	No, I'm sorry. I can't manage Wednesday or Thursday. I'm away. Friday?
Woman	Yes, Friday's OK at the moment. Where shall we go?
Man	Why don't we try that new Lebanese restaurant near the square?
Woman	Yes, that sounds good.
Man	OK. Great. I'll book a table and text you.

65.2

Sue	Do you like sport, Brendan?
Brendan	Yes, I do.
Sue	What sports do you play?
Brendan	I play quite a lot of sports, but my favourite is five-a-side football. I usually play two or three times a week.
Sue	Where do you play it?
Brendan	At the local sports centre.
Sue	How do you play five-a-side?
Brendan	Well, it's like normal football, so there are two teams, but there are only five players in a team. There are eleven in normal football.
Sue	Oh. Are there any other differences?
Brendan	You don't play outside on a big football pitch, you play it indoors. We actually play on the basketball court at the sports centre. The goals are smaller in five-a-side, too. But otherwise it's the same as normal football. There's a goal with a goalkeeper. You have to kick the ball. You can't throw it or touch it with your hands, and so on.
Sue	Why do you like it?
Brendan	Well, it's quite fast, so it's good exercise. You play it indoors, so you can play it all year, and you don't need a lot of expensive equipment like rackets and things like that.
Sue	Who do you normally play with?
Brendan	I play with a group of guys from work. We've got our own team and we play against other local teams.
Sue	Are you any good?
Brendan	Not bad. We won our last game. We beat a very good team. The score was three-two and I scored the winning goal. So that was good.

66.2

I like all kinds of sport, but tennis is the sport that I like best. I'm a member of a club that's very close to my flat, so I play several times a week. In this picture I'm holding a cup that I won two years ago. I was pleased to win it, because the player that I beat in the final was very good. One sport that I can't do at all is ice skating, but I like to watch it on TV. It isn't a big sport here in Spain. It's most popular in countries that have very cold winters. I like to watch football, too. My husband works for a company that makes sports equipment, so he often gets tickets to matches that we want to see.

67.2

'Now,' said the professor, 'this glass jar represents your life. The golf balls represent the things that are really important – your family, your health and your favourite free time activity. If you lost everything else and only had these things, your life would still be full. The stones are the things that are quite important, but replaceable – your house or your job. If you lost them, it would be hard, but it wouldn't be the end of the world. The sand is everything else – the ordinary, everyday things that we all have in our lives, but which aren't really important; things like clothes, housework, TV programmes. If you fill the jar with sand and stones, there's no room for the golf balls. It's the same with life. You should make room for the things that are really important first.'

One of the students then asked, 'But what about the two cups of coffee? What do they represent?' 'The coffee,' said the professor, 'shows that even if your life is very full, there's always time for a cup of coffee with a friend!'

69.4

1 I wanted to talk to Umberto today, but he's suffering from a bad cold.
2 I'm not interested in clothes, so I soon get bored with shopping.
3 I'm tired of taking part in competitions and losing!
4 Our new flat is very different from our old flat. Actually, it's similar to yours.
5 I've looked at your email again, and I'm afraid I don't agree with you.
6 She's very good at her job, but she's thinking about leaving.
7 I'm worried about going on holiday. I'm afraid of flying.
8 Steve has applied for a new job. He's waiting for an interview.

70.2

1 If she hadn't eaten too much, she wouldn't have felt sick.
2 He wouldn't have missed his appointment if he had got up on time.
3 If I hadn't gone to the party, I wouldn't have met my boyfriend.
4 I wouldn't have complained about the taxi if it hadn't arrived late.
5 If it had been warm, we would have gone out.
6 If you had worked hard, you would have passed your exams.

Audio scripts

1 Hi. It's Sullivan. Thanks very much for the invitation to your housewarming party, but I'm afraid I won't be able to be there. I'm going to be away on business. Sorry, but I hope it all goes well. Cheers.

2 Hello. This is Viv here. Thanks ever so much for the invitation. We'll be delighted to come. Would you like us to bring anything? See you then. Bye.

3 Hi. It's Natasha. I'm phoning about your housewarming. Yes, great. I'd love to come. It's a bit cheeky, I know, but my cousin's going to be staying with me that weekend. Is it OK if she comes, too? Bye.

4 Hello, there. This is Neil. Thanks very much for the invitation to your party. I'm sorry, but it's our son's 21st birthday that day and we're going out for dinner. So I'm afraid we won't be able to join you. Thanks, anyway. Bye.

73.3

Last year I flew from Milan to Manchester. It wasn't a direct flight; I had to change in Brussels. I got to the airport and checked in. Then I went through passport control and security. When I got to the departure lounge, I checked the TV screens to find my gate, and my heart sank. The flight was delayed. Would I get to Brussels in time for my flight to Manchester?

Finally, we boarded the plane. I put my coat in the overhead locker, sat down and fastened the seatbelt. We soon took off and we landed in Brussels half an hour late. I hurried off the plane and checked my flight to Manchester. I had arrived at Terminal A, but my next flight was from Terminal B. Luckily, that flight was also delayed.

I walked to Terminal B. It was a long way. When I arrived, I found that there was another security control. I took everything out of my pockets and then I remembered: I'd left my coat on the plane! But it was too late now. So I went through security and looked for my gate. I was standing next to gate B1 and my flight went from gate B93!

I rushed through the terminal to gate B93. There was a bus to go to the plane. I got on the bus. The bus went round Terminal B, past all the planes and then back to Terminal A! We stopped next to a plane. I couldn't believe it. It was the same plane that I travelled on from Milan. When I got on, the flight attendant said, 'Oh, hello, again.' I even sat in the same seat! But there was one good thing: my coat was still in the overhead locker!

75.1

Morning, Rosa. It's Henry. Can you tell me whether you've booked the flight to Athens yet? Something's come up and I can't leave till Friday now. Can you let me know as soon as possible, please? Thanks. Bye.

75.2

1 Hello, Rosa. It's Serena. Look. Can you play tennis on Saturday morning? I can't make the afternoon, I'm afraid. Bye.

2 Hi, Rosa. It's Wallace. When are the visitors arriving? I want to make sure I'm free to meet them. Thanks. I hope all is OK with you. Bye.

3 Rosa. This is Yasmin. Will you be in Cairo on Friday evening? I'd like to meet for a meal, but Thursday's no good for me. Call me on my mobile or send an email. Look forward to hearing from you. All the best.

4 Morning, Rosa. It's Jack. Where did you stay in Rome last month? I'm looking for a nice hotel for a trip in July. Can you let me know as soon as possible, please? Thanks.

5 Hi, Rosa. Millie here. Sorry to bother you, but what time does the meeting start on Monday? I've lost my diary and I can't remember if it's 2.30 or 3.30. Thanks a lot.

6 Hi, Mum. It's Bob. Have you got the phone number of the car insurance company? I've had a sort of accident in the supermarket car park – nothing serious, well not really serious. Sorry! Bye.

77.2

My name's Boris. I spend most of my money on my car. I bought it last year. It was quite expensive, so I had to get quite a big loan to buy it.

I live with my parents, so I don't pay any rent. I want to get my own flat, but I can't afford it at the moment. Apart from paying off the loan on my car, I'm saving up for a holiday.

I keep most of my money in an Internet account, because I can do things 24/7. I don't have to wait for the bank to open. The interest rates are better, too. I can do most things on the Internet – I can check my balance, I can transfer money to other accounts, and I can pay bills, too. I can't withdraw cash on the Internet, of course, so I still need a normal account at a bank. I transfer money by direct debit from my Internet account to my normal account. Then I can withdraw money at any cash machine. My employer has to pay my salary into my normal account, too. Then I transfer it.

78.2

1 She said that she had just moved to London.
2 She said that she had been in France with her husband for ten years.
3 She said that they were divorced now.
4 She said that she had come back so that she could be near her parents.
5 She said that they were getting very old.
6 She said that I still looked the same.
7 She said that she was trying to find a flat.
8 She said that she wanted to buy a house, but she couldn't afford it.
9 She said that she'd seen The Coffee Shop.
10 She said that she would call in to see me at the café sometime.

80.2

1 **Tannoy** Cashier number 1, please.
   Cashier Hello. What can I do for you today?
   Customer Could I withdraw some cash from this account, please? The cash machine isn't working.
   Cashier Yes, we're sorry about that. The engineer's coming to look at it. How much would you like to withdraw?
   Customer A hundred, please.
   Cashier OK. Just one moment. There you are. Is there anything else I can help you with?
   Customer No, thank you. Goodbye.
2 **Tannoy** Cashier number 2, please.
   Cashier Good morning. How can I help?
   Customer I'd like to apply for a loan, please.
   Cashier I see. I'm afraid I can't deal with that here. You'll need to speak to one of our advisers.
   Customer Oh, how do I do that?

   Cashier If you take a seat over there, where it says 'Customer Services', somebody will be with you shortly.
   Customer Thank you.
3 **Tannoy** Cashier number 3, please.
   Cashier Good morning. How can I help?
   Customer I'd like to transfer some money from this account to my bank in Poland, please.
   Cashier Have you got the details of your account in Poland?
   Customer Yes, here you are.
   Cashier OK. Just one moment ...
4 **Tannoy** Cashier number 4, please.
   Cashier Good morning. How can I help you?
   Customer I want to set up a direct debit to pay my gas bill, please.
   Cashier I see. Have you got the card for your account?
   Customer Yes, here you are.
   Cashier OK. Just a minute. Could you sign the form here, please.
   Customer Certainly.
   Cashier Thank you. Is there anything else I can help you with?
   Customer No, thank you. Goodbye.
5 **Tannoy** Cashier number 5, please.
   Cashier Hello. What can I do for you today?
   Customer Could you tell me what the interest rate on this account is, please?
   Cashier Certainly. Just a minute. It's 2.5%.
   Customer Thank you.

81.2

Narrator The next day at the Coffee Shop.
Ryan They did what? They broke down your front door?
Lucy Yes. I was sitting on the floor in my front room sewing my bridesmaid's dress. Suddenly Jordan, Peter and Sarah crashed through the front door.
Cindy But why didn't you answer the door or your phone?
Lucy I didn't hear it. I was listening to music with my headphones on.
Ryan I wish I'd been there to see it.
Lucy Apparently, they thought I'd had an accident.
Cindy I see. And how are things with you and Jordan now?
Lucy Oh, we're back together again. He was very sorry about it.
Ryan Do you mean about the trip to Paris?
Lucy Yes. He said that he'd got his priorities wrong and he knew now what was really important in his life.
Cindy Oh, how nice.
Ryan Where is he today? Is he filming?
Lucy No. He's at my house with Peter. They're repairing my front door!

Irregular verbs

Verb	Past simple	Past participle
be	was / were	been
beat	beat	beaten
become	became	become
begin	began	begun
bet	bet	bet
bite	bit	bitten
blow	blew	blown
break	broke	broken
bring	brought	brought
build	built	built
burn	burnt / burned	burnt / burned
buy	bought	bought
can	could / was able to	been able to
catch	caught	caught
choose	chose	chosen
come	came	come
cost	cost	cost
cut	cut	cut
dig	dug	dug
do	did	done
draw	drew	drawn
drink	drank	drunk
drive	drove	driven
eat	ate	eaten
fall	fell	fallen
feel	felt	felt
fight	fought	fought
find	found	found
fly	flew	flown
forget	forgot	forgotten
get	got	got
give	gave	given
go	went	been/gone
grow	grew	grown
have	had	had
hear	heard	heard
hide	hid	hidden
hit	hit	hit
hold	held	held
hurt	hurt	hurt
keep	kept	kept
know	knew	known
lead /liːd/	led	led
learn	learnt / learned	learnt / learned
leave	left	left

Verb	Past simple	Past participle
let	let	let
lose	lost	lost
make	made	made
mean	meant	meant
meet	met	met
pay	paid	paid
put	put	put
quit	quit	quit
read /riːd/	read /red/	read /red/
ride	rode	ridden
ring	rang	rung
run	ran	run
say	said	said
see	saw	seen
sell	sold	sold
send	sent	sent
set	set	set
shake	shook	shaken
show	showed	shown
shrink	shrank	shrunk
shut	shut	shut
sing	sang	sung
sit	sat	sat
sleep	slept	slept
smell	smelt / smelled	smelt / smelled
speak	spoke	spoken
spell	spelt / spelled	spelt / spelled
spend	spent	spent
stand	stood	stood
steal	stole	stolen
stick	stuck	stuck
sweep	swept	swept
swim	swam	swum
swing	swung	swung
take	took	taken
teach	taught	taught
tell	told	told
think	thought	thought
throw	threw	thrown
understand	understood	understood
wake	woke	woken
wear	wore	worn
win	won	won
write	wrote	written

Pronunciation chart

iː /siː/ see	**ɪ** /sɪt/ sit	**ʊ** /pʊt/ put	**uː** /tuː/ too	**ɪə** /nɪə/ near	**eɪ** /deɪ/ day	↗↖ / ↘↗ →
e /bed/ bed	**ə** /əbaʊt/ about	**ɜː** /tɜːn/ turn	**ɔː** /sɔː/ saw	**ʊə** /pjʊə/ pure	**ɔɪ** /bɔɪ/ boy	**əʊ** /gəʊ/ go
æ /kæt/ cat	**ʌ** /ʌp/ up	**ɑː** /fɑːðə/ father	**ɒ** /hɒt/ hot	**eə** /ðeə/ there	**aɪ** /maɪ/ my	**aʊ** /haʊ/ how
p /pen/ pen	**b** /bæd/ bad	**t** /tiː/ tea	**d** /dɔː/ door	**tʃ** /tʃeə/ chair	**dʒ** /dʒæm/ jam	**k** /kæn/ can
g /get/ get						
f /faɪv/ five	**v** /væn/ van	**θ** /θɪn/ thin	**ð** /ðə/ the	**s** /sɪt/ sit	**z** /zuː/ zoo	**ʃ** /ʃuː/ shoe
ʒ /juːʒəli/ usually						
m /mæn/ man	**n** /nɒt/ not	**ŋ** /sɪŋ/ sing	**h** /hæt/ hat	**l** /leg/ leg	**r** /red/ red	**w** /wet/ wet
j /jes/ yes						

chart © Adrian Underhill

OXFORD
UNIVERSITY PRESS

Great Clarendon Street, Oxford OX2 6DP

Oxford University Press is a department of the University of Oxford.
It furthers the University's objective of excellence in research, scholarship,
and education by publishing worldwide in

Oxford New York

Auckland Cape Town Dar es Salaam Hong Kong Karachi
Kuala Lumpur Madrid Melbourne Mexico City Nairobi
New Delhi Shanghai Taipei Toronto

With offices in

Argentina Austria Brazil Chile Czech Republic France Greece
Guatemala Hungary Italy Japan Poland Portugal Singapore
South Korea Switzerland Thailand Turkey Ukraine Vietnam

OXFORD and OXFORD ENGLISH are registered trade marks of
Oxford University Press in the UK and in certain other countries

© Oxford University Press 2009

The moral rights of the author have been asserted

Database right Oxford University Press (maker)

First published 2009

2013 2012 2011 2010 2009

10 9 8 7 6 5 4 3 2 1

ISBN: 978 0 19 430728 4

Printed and bound by Gráfica Maiadouro S.A. in Portugal

ACKNOWLEDGEMENTS

*The author would like to thank all the people at, or engaged by, Oxford University Press
who have contributed their knowledge, skills and ideas to producing this book.*

*The author would like to dedicate this book to his children, Mandy, Jenny, Daniel, Katy
and Donna, and to his stepchildren, Viola and Peter.*

*The author and publisher would like to thank the following for kind permission to
reproduce photographs*: akg-images p97 (20th Century Fox/Album); Alamy
pp1l (PhotoAlto), 8(4) (Oleksiy Maksymenko), 8(5) (Powered by Light/Alan
Spencer), 11br (picture), 11cr (Manor Photography), 19d (Ashley Morrison),
19f (BlueMoon Stock), 21(12) (Jim West), 21(2) (Motoring Picture Library),
21(3) (SHOUT), 21(5) (Jupiterimages/ Comstock Images), 21(6) (Manor
Photography), 24l (Nic Cleave Photography), 24r (Blend Images), 29(11)
(Jupiterimages/ Brand X), 29(6) (Nigel Cattlin), 29(9) (Aerial Archives), 30b
(Ashley Cooper), 31b (A. T. Willett), 43t (Douglas Peebles Photography), 45bl
(Image Source Black), 51(1) (JJM Stock Photography/Financial), 51(2) (Ron
Yue), 51(6) (Gallo Images), 53b (Adrian Muttitt), 53tl (Vario images GmbH
& Co.KG), 64 (PhotoAlto), 70b (cbimages), 71c (Blend Images), 71l (MBI), 75
(Blend Images), 80 (David R. Frazier Photolibrary, Inc.), 89 (Chris Lewington),
93l (Huw Jones), 95 (Rebecca Erol); Corbis UK Ltd. pp1r (Fancy/Veer), 17r
(Howard Pyle/Zefa), 19a (Moodboard), 29(1) (Reuters), 29(10) (Jim Hollander),
29(12) (Alan Evans/Epa), 29(3) (Jeremy Horner), 29(5) (Will Burgess/Reuters),
29(7) (Galen Rowell), 29(8) (Marc Serota/Reuters), 31b (Jim Reed), 45cr (Fancy/
Veer), 47 (Comstock Select), 56 (Nice One Productions), 69t (Hans Georg Roth),
70t (Steve Bowman), 71r (Michael Prince), 87 (Amanaimages); Getty Images
pp2111 (Theodore Anderson), 35 (Julian Finney), 40l (Reza Estakhrian),
69b (Commercial Eye); iStockphoto pp3l (Zhang Bo), 8(1) (Vladimir Boriso),
8(2), 11bl (Maurice van der Velden), 11cl (Kelvin Wakefield), 19c (Brian
McEntire), 21(4) (Zeljana Dubrovic), 21(8) (Luminouslens), 30t (Arkady
Chubykin), 40r (Pamela Moore), 51(3) (Skip ODonnell), 85 (Jose Tejo), 93r;
John Frank Nowikowski p51(5); Martyn F. Chillmaid pp19b; 19e; Oxford

University Press pp8(3) (Photodisc), 45cl (Ingram), 45r (Gareth Boden), 45t
(Photodisc), 56 (Photodisc); PA Photos pp21(1); 21(7); 29(2) (Nelson Salting/
Associated Press), 29(4); Photofusion Picture Library pp21(9) (Paul Bigland),
53tr (Christa Stadtler); Photolibrary Group pp3r (Klaus Tiedge/Blend), 17l
(Image Source), 32 (Allan Danahar); Rex Features pp15 (Kamal Moghrabi),
21(10); 59(1) (Everett Collection), 59(2) (Everett Collection), 59(3) (SNAP),
59(4) (c.Paramount/Everett), 59(5) (c.Dreamworks/Everett), 59(6) (Everett
Collection), 59(7) (c.Universal/Everett), 59(8) (Everett Collection), 59(9)
(c.Paramount/Everett); Tran Thu Trang p51(4) (Photographers Direct); Zooid
Pictures p77 (Ned Coomes)

Illustrations by: Ben Hasler/nbillustration: pp 7, 22, 23, 38, 48, 49, 62, 73, 83
Mark Duffin: pp 42, 43 (2-6), 67, 79 Cyrus Deboo: pp 5, 9, 49(2), 57, 65 Chris
Pavely: pp 2, 23, 37, 39 Roger Penwill: pp: 13, 17, 25, 33, 41, 61, 99 Hannah
Firmin: p 63

Story illustrations by: Klaus Trommer/storyboards.nl: pp 4, 6, 10, 12, 14, 18, 20,
26, 28, 34, 36, 44, 46, 50, 52, 54, 58, 60, 66, 68, 74, 76, 78, 81

Commissioned photographs by: Gareth Boden: pp 8 (1/2), 11 (1), 27

Locations provided by: Jamal's Tandoori Restaurant, Oxford, p 27